Amazing Minds

Amazing Minds

The Science of Nurturing Your Child's Developing Mind with Games, Activities, and More

JAN FAULL, M.ED.

with Jennifer McLean Oliver, Ph.D.

BERKLEY BOOKS, NEW YORK

THE BERKLEY PUBLISHING GROUP
Published by the Penguin Group
Penguin Group (USA) Inc.
375 Hudson Street, New York, New York 10014, USA
Penguin Group (Canada), 90 Eglinton Avenue East, Suite 700, Toronto, Ontario M4P 2Y3, Canada
(a division of Pearson Penguin Canada Inc.)
Penguin Books Ltd., 80 Strand, London WC2R 0RL, England
Penguin Group Ireland, 25 St. Stephen's Green, Dublin 2, Ireland (a division of Penguin Books Ltd.)
Penguin Group (Australia), 250 Camberwell Road, Camberwell, Victoria 3124, Australia
(a division of Pearson Australia Group Pty. Ltd.)
Penguin Books India Pvt. Ltd., 11 Community Centre, Panchsheel Park, New Delhi—110 017, India
Penguin Group (NZ), 67 Apollo Drive, Rosedale, North Shore, 0632, New Zealand
(a division of Pearson New Zealand Ltd.)
Penguin Books (South Africa) (Pty.) Ltd., 24 Sturdee Avenue, Rosebank, Johannesburg 2196,
South Africa

Penguin Books Ltd., Registered Offices: 80 Strand, London WC2R 0RL, England

While the author has made every effort to provide accurate telephone numbers and Internet addresses
at the time of publication, neither the author nor the publisher assumes any responsibility for errors,
or for changes that occur after publication. Further, publisher does not have any control over and
does not assume any responsibility for author or third-party websites or their content.

PRINTING HISTORY
Berkley trade paperback edition/August 2010

Library of Congress Cataloging-in-Publication Data

Faull, Jan.
    Amazing minds : the science of nurturing your child's developing mind with games, activities,
and more / Jan Faull ; with Jennifer McLean Oliver.
        p.   cm.
    ISBN 978-0-425-23224-8 (alk. paper)
1. Child rearing.   2. Child development.   3. Child psychology.   I. Oliver, Jennifer McLean.
II. Title.
    HQ769.F278   2010
649'.51—dc22   2010012578

PRINTED IN THE UNITED STATES OF AMERICA

10   9   8   7   6   5   4   3   2   1

*To my granddaughters, Emilia,
Flora, and Violet*

Acknowledgments

During most of my career as a parent educator I focused on parents with toddlers through teens. Then in 2000 I attended a conference where Andrew Meltzoff, Ph.D. and Patricia Kuhl, Ph.D. were keynote speakers presenting information from their book written with Alison Gopnik, Ph.D., *The Scientist in the Crib.* That presentation inspired me to delve into research on infants and toddlers, which ultimately lead to the writing of *Amazing Minds.* To those three researchers and all the others referenced in this book, I'm truly grateful. Their scientific investigations give a clear view of what babies and toddlers are seeking to know.

Then in 2005, 2007, and 2009 three miracles occurred in my life: the birth of three granddaughters, Emilia, Flora, and Violet, respectively. Having the privilege of witnessing their development, from the intimate relationship of grandmother to granddaughter, was not only a blessing but a personal validation of the research. Along with these three babies, I also wish to thank their parents Anna and Phil, and Jerry and Christy who are on the frontline every day nurturing these little girls' development. Also to Alan, my youngest, whose development is embedded in my memory because he wrote the book on funny and challenging events as he traveled from infant to toddler to fine young adult.

The support staff involved in producing a book is far reaching, so there are many people to thank: Jennifer McLean Oliver Ph.D., my research assistant; Maura Kye-Casella, my agent; Denise Slivestro, my editor at Berkley Books; and Lexi Walters, editor at Babyzone.com. Nancy Wilson taught me how to access research articles at Suzzallo Library on the UW campus and Kathy Oberg of Highline Community College read the entire manuscript, making sure it was appropriate for community college Early Childhood Education students.

Then there are groups of friends who have been with me from the conception of this book: my professional parent education colleagues, my hiking and walking groups, my neighbors from the best neighborhood in the world, my church family, my birthday and book groups and extended family. I also want to thank PEPS (Program for Early Parent Support) who gave me the opportunity to serve on their board for the last three years.

For thirty-four years I've been a parent educator, teaching classes, speaking, and writing for parenting audiences. I've learned more from the parents I've served than they have learned from me. A heartfelt thank-you to them all because they know that parenting is about big people nurturing little people so that they can be big themselves someday.

Also I want to thank Bruce and Jolene McCaw for their support of the Talaris Research Institute, where I had the opportunity to work with Andy Meltzoff and Patricia Kuhl and their research that laid the foundation for *Amazing Minds*.

Lastly, thank you to Terrill Chang, whose love bolstered me daily to tackle the ups and dows of writing this book.

Contents

Foreword

Discoveries from many scientific studies coming from laboratories around the world over the last several decades have revolutionized our ideas about how infants and toddlers think, learn, and develop, and word is starting to get out. Parents and others who care for children want to understand what scientists are discovering about early learning. They have a desire and responsibility to ensure their children receive the support needed during this formative period, and they want to know what they should do to provide it. These are the timely questions that are addressed in *Amazing Minds*.

As a scientist and co-director of the University of Washington's Institute for Learning and Brain Sciences in Seattle, I am delighted to write the foreword of this excellent book and to endorse its goal of sharing scientific discoveries and providing interpretations and usable, practical advice, based upon the science, for the many loving parents out there who are hungry for information of this kind.

As we all know, babies are born immature. They can't speak or use tools, but very quickly they acquire these skills, and so much more, as their brains rapidly grows in size and complexity. During this time of rapid development, the brain has sensitive periods, or windows of opportunity, during which time certain parts of the brain's circuitry are more malleable, more "plastic," than at other times. That plasticity is what allows for the efficient and exuberant learning when the environment provides the necessary stimulation. For example, children absorb their native language and achieve fluency by age three just by listening to people talk around them and to them, something the most advanced supercomputer cannot yet accomplish. Similarly, young children learn a second language very easily during their early development. Yet, as many of us have discovered, learning a second language becomes more effortful later in life, after we pass our sensitive period for second language learning.

As children develop, they naturally seek the type of environmental stimulation that supports their learning. In *Amazing Minds*, Jan Faull, M.Ed. with Jennifer McLean Oliver, Ph.D., help parents recognize what children are seeking to learn at different ages and how to respond. They step through the learning agenda of the child in the first few years as he develops his senses, language, memory, reasoning skills, emotions, ability to use tools, and ability to take the perspective of another person and suggest ways, based upon the science, that parents can support that learning.

Often when parents hear about windows of opportunity for learning, they worry that there is a special product that their infant must have to maximize his or her chances of getting into Harvard or Yale at eighteen. What parents need to know is that they themselves are the child's favorite plaything—that they themselves provide just the kind of stimulation that the child needs. As is described in *Amazing Minds*, the important thing is that parents share time with their children, that they are responsive and talk and play with them, with patience, and at the child's pace. Simple activities such as playing peekaboo, banging on pots and pans together, naming what your child points to, and other similar activities suggested in this book, are the kind of environmental influences that provide stimulation that supports learning.

Some parents wonder: If a little stimulation is good, perhaps more is better? Again, this book helps parents find the right balance for them and their babies. What is important is that parents respond to their child's cues. Children will naturally try to regulate the input they receive. A one-year-old will lean back and turn away as if to say, "I've had enough and I need to absorb what I've just learned." Children implicitly register how much is enough and how much is too much and overwhelming. *Amazing Minds* helps parents learn to be sensitive and responsive to their child's needs, giving their child stimulation he or she can use and enjoy. Learning should be fun!

I first knew the author, Jan Faull, through her parenting column in the *Seattle Times*, and I appreciate that she is someone who is dedicated to helping parents and is also interested in basing her messages on science. She takes parents seriously and science seriously, and seeks to bridge the gap that often exists between the two. To complete the bridge and provide a scientific complement to her own experience as a parent educator, Jan brought Jennifer McLean Oliver, Ph.D., into the project. Jennifer is a cognitive psychologist and applied mathematician whose work includes researching topics in the field of cognitive development and early learning. Her experimental research specialties are in visual perception, memory, and attention.

Jennifer worked with Jan to choose the research studies to include in the book and to provide accurate descriptions and valid interpretations, all written in a way that is interesting, meaningful, and easy for all parents to understand, regardless of their background. Based on Jan's years of experience working with children and families, as a preschool teacher, parent educator, author, and speaker, she provides her personal interpretation of that research as well and suggests practical applications, simple things that are not pricey and come naturally. Jan shows how to follow the child's lead and how talking, playing, and singing with a young child are the kinds of activities that are key to supporting early learning and are just the activities that young children find most engaging. I think that parents and others who care for children will find the book readable, fascinating, and useful.

Science is beginning to reveal a causal connection between early learning, brain development, and success in school and in society later in life. There are indications that giving our time and support to our children during the first three to five years is the wisest way we can make an investment in the future of our children and our society. *Amazing Minds* helps parents and others who care for children learn more about *how* to invest their time and how to best support their children.

Andrew N. Meltzoff, Ph.D.
Coauthor of *The Scientist in the Crib: What Early Learning Tells Us About the Mind*

Introduction

You have probably heard the term "infant stimulation." What this phrase might mean to you is that, beginning from birth, it's the adult's job, whether parent or caregiver, to provide certain objects and events for a baby to notice and respond to in order for the child's brain to develop optimally.

Some sources say holding, talking, and singing to an infant is enough stimulation; others tell parents and caregivers to read aloud, play foreign language audiotapes, and purchase objects and toys covered in black-and-white fabric. The information at either end of the spectrum focuses on the parent/caregiver role in enhancing development of the baby's brain.

No doubt the parent's role as nurturing and responsive caregivers is critical to the child's ability to survive and thrive. Some parents do what comes naturally. Many turn to grandmothers, aunts, nannies, or child development experts to show them the way. Others follow the latest trends: take infants to various music and movement classes, buy certain brain-building toys, and sit newborns in front of DVDs.

While infants arrive in the world physically helpless, fragile, and dependent on parents and caregivers, they are not passive recipients of stimulation. Their brains are already active; their senses are ready and waiting for certain environmental factors to come their way.

Perhaps it is time to turn the tables and ask, "What stimulation are babies seeking? What sights, sounds, and movements are infants drawn to notice? What is a baby trying to determine about the setting in which he lives?" That is, let all those interested turn their attention to what the baby is looking for instinctively in her surroundings, rather than what elements the parents and caregivers are supposed to provide.

Babies bring with them at birth an intellectual agenda all their own. They are hardwired to search out consistencies in their surroundings, and in doing so they satisfy their fierce curiosity about the world around them. The amazing brain of a baby expects certain experiences to occur and actively searches for them.

With the use of audio and video recordings and sophisticated baby-safe electronic equipment, scientific researchers have revealed just what babies are interested in determining in order for them to develop their minds. Now it's time for those who touch babies first and those interested in child development to gain this same understanding.

Because parents naturally have a strong need to connect with their babies, it's important for them to know just what babies are determined to discover. While every parent wants to engage with their infant, none wants to offer erroneous stimulation that may frustrate or deter the baby from using his brain in a way that's appropriate.

As a child develops month by month, she knows to hunt for

certain elements. By realizing what a child is programmed to discover in order for him to develop his brain and mind, parents will be better able to engage a child in ways more meaningful to the child and in ways more satisfactory to the parent. It all starts with a baby looking for familiar faces, smells, and voices; her willingness to copy facial movements; and her interest in noticing edges between contrasting black and white.

As an experienced parent, grandmother, parent educator, and child development and behavior specialist, I offer in this book my interpretation of the research, and suggest what it means for parents and other baby-watching adults, and how they can apply it to the children with whom they work and live. There is a tremendous amount of research that sits in books and journals on library shelves and is not accessible to most people interested in babies and toddlers. My research assistant, Jennifer, a cognitive psychologist, and I pulled some of the most interesting research studies off those library shelves and described and interpreted them in this book with the goal of helping to make some of that knowledge accessible and useful so all can better support the development of children.

Chapter 1

Senses at Work

For centuries those closest to babies have suspected and speculated about babies' senses, and researchers have proved that many of those suspicions and speculations are correct.

A newborn, of course, spends much of his time sleeping, and when he's awake, parents are busy feeding, changing, bathing, rocking, and cuddling him. They know it's their job to care for their infant because he's dependent and fragile. During those times, however, through his eyes, ears, skin, nose, and tongue, the child is soaking up messages about Mom and Dad. He's doing his best to connect, as doing so secures the likelihood that he'll not only survive but thrive. Somehow baby knows he's helpless and therefore needs to secure Mommy and Daddy's protective, responsive care.

Most parents look into their baby's eyes and wonder, "What does my baby see? Is the world just a blur to her or is she watching for something?" The responsive parent realizes that when a newborn's body is quiet and her mind alert, her eyes seem to search and then focus—which is exactly what newborns are capable of doing. Parents are also likely to realize that their baby can hear, feel touches, smell, and taste. While all the senses are at work from birth, vision is the least developed, although visual acuity improves quickly during the first months of life.

Does My Baby See Me?

The answer to that age-old question is yes, your baby sees you. You're the perfect object for him to look at. Although your newborn's vision is still developing, he is born already equipped to see the most important things to him—like the features of your smiling face as you hold him in your arms. Your face looks a little blurry to your baby at first, but her vision will improve dramatically during the next six months. She will learn better control of the muscles that focus the eyes, and as her eyes and brain develop, she will be able to see finer detail (Berk, 2009). When you're changing your baby's diapers and clothing, feeding and bathing your baby, and talking with her, you're likely about a foot away from your baby's eyes—the perfect distance for your baby to become well acquainted with your features.

The Research

As most know, babies arrive with well-developed lips and tongues ready to suck. In one study, researchers exploited this skill by electronically hooking a pacifier up to a video screen. When the babies sucked on the pacifier, they would see a picture of a human face, which they liked, and they soon made the connection that by sucking they would keep the face on the screen. When the baby lost interest and stopped sucking, the picture would go away. If the picture was of the infant's mother, the baby would suck harder and longer to keep the familiar face in his line of vision.

To test the baby's ability to recognize her mother, the researchers used a picture of the baby's actual mother as well as one of an unfamiliar person who matched the mother's appearance in hair color, eye color, complexion, and hairstyle. Even so, when the experimenters counted how often the babies sucked in order to keep Mom's picture available, compared to their sucking rate for the photo of the woman who only resembled their mother, the babies—only a day or two old at the time of the testing—would suck more to keep Mom's picture in view. When baby after baby sucked longer on the pacifier to see Mom's familiar face, researchers realized that infants could differentiate unfamiliar faces from familiar ones and would work harder to keep the familiar ones in sight (Walton, Bower, and Bower, 1992).

The Interpretation

During baby's first week, his amazing mind is ready to recognize his mother's face. Baby knows that his mother's attentive, adoring face brings loving care, and that she'll do the most to protect him and make it easy for him to survive.

Research tells us that babies hear when in the womb, so your baby has been hearing your voice for some time before he is born. Once he is born, the sound of your voice directs the child to look at your face, and then amazingly, by four hours old, he'll know your face, from those of other less familiar people (Sai, 2005).

Baby must know that one, two, or three loving caregivers will tune in and quickly read his cues for care. That's why he's not satisfied with just any face; he's most content when his senses tell him that a familiar, loving person is in close proximity. At some level, a baby knows that he is fragile and dependent and needs another person close by in order to survive. He's looking, searching, and scanning the environment to connect with a human face, and he prefers one that's familiar A baby arrives equipped to recognize a few familiar faces and the smells, touches, and voices that accompany those faces. These familiar caregivers—Mom, Dad, Nanny, Grandma, Grandpa—are the people a baby attaches to during the first six months of life.

Babies make the connection that not all people will help them out in their need for comfort, food, socialization, and stimulation, as much as their familiar parents. It must be heartening to baby when Mommy's or Daddy's face pops into his line of vision. The people he's quickly become acquainted with are right there, ready to provide what the child cannot provide for himself.

What Should Parents Do?

Should parents paste their pictures all over the walls of their child's bedroom? No, that's not necessary. Parents need to simply take note of their baby's actions, movements, and expressions, and be responsive to them.

When baby cries with hunger, feed her. When she indicates she's tired, let her sleep. When she's distressed, take her away from any confusion and rock her quietly while singing softly. When she's quiet and alert, move near her and talk. By doing so, you give the baby the opportunity to become familiar with your face. She's comforted, at ease, knowing you're there to care for her.

Bold Contrasts Between Black and White

It's not only a parents' face that babies focus on. During the first two months of life, babies' eyes scan their environment—even in the dark—seeking to find a sharp contrast between dark and light or black and white, which signals the edge of an object. Once the baby locates an edge, her eyes move all around it, examining it carefully (Bee and Boyd, 2007).

The authors of the book *The Scientist in the Crib: What Early Learning Tells Us about the Mind* (Gopnik, Meltzoff, and Kuhl, 1999) say it best: "Paying attention to edges is the best way of dividing a static picture into separate objects." That's why newborns prefer to look at patterns with edges that are clearly visible to them; strong edges provide clear definition of objects in the infant's environment.

One day you might be wearing a black-and-white bowling shirt and you'll notice your baby's eyes riveted to the stripes. Another day Grandpa might come to visit his granddaughter, and rather than making eye contact with Grandpa, she may be looking intently at his black-rimmed glasses. The strong contrast between the glasses frame and Grandpa's face catches the child's attention. She's trying to determine where the face begins and ends and where the frame begins and ends.

It might become obvious that a baby is looking for certain patterns in the environment. Just what is it that catches and holds the baby's attention? What patterns is a baby's brain programmed to focus on?

The Research

Before the 1960s, most thought newborns could perceive light, color, and movement, but assumed that visual learning and development after birth would be necessary before infants could perceive shape, pattern, and form in general. Then, in the early 1960s, researcher Robert Fantz found a way to empirically investigate whether or not infants could perceive form. He developed and used what he called a "looking chamber." In his studies, the infant lies in a crib, looking up into a box or chamber at objects attached to the ceiling of it. Watching the infant's eyes through a peephole in the chamber, an observer times how long the infant looks at an object. The observer knows when the infant is looking at an object because a reflection of that object appears in the infant's eyes, over the pupil. Researchers today still use looking time to investigate infant perception, they just have more sophisticated, high-tech versions of Fantz's original chamber.

In one experiment, Fantz presented newborns with six different pictures, one at a time, in random order, on six-inch-diameter disks. Three of the disks had black-and-white patterns—a schematic face, concentric circles, and a section of newspaper print. The other three were disks of solid color—white, fluorescent yellow, and dark red. He found that the babies looked about twice as long at the patterned disks as at the solid-colored disks, indicating not only that they perceived the patterns, but also that they preferred to look at them.

Because a newborn cannot yet focus her eyes well, the world looks pretty blurry, so low-contrast patterns are not very visible and thus do not attract her attention. On the other hand, babies' eyes gravitate toward patterns of high contrast—black-and-white stripes, checkerboards, and bull's-eyes—with distinct edges (Fantz, 1961; Fantz, 1963).

The Interpretation

When babies stare at strong contrasting edges, they're determining where objects begin and end. The bolder the edge, the easier it is to determine, hence the attraction toward the strong and obvious contrast of black-and-white stripes, checkerboards, and bull's-eyes. Infants' under-refined ability to see allows them to notice edges of strong contrast like black on white, but not edges of faint contrast like pale pink on pale yellow. Since they're programmed to recognize elements in their surroundings, they're actively searching for objects, and those with bold, clear edges are the ones they can make out.

People look for consistencies in their physical environment. When people enter a new physical space, they're automatically wondering about what's familiar, what's different, are they safe, can they maneuver? So it is with babies, and it all starts with noticing edges, which eventually leads to determining distinct demarcations: floors, walls, ceilings, and windows.

Once babies realize what's consistent about their physical world, they feel safe to satisfy their curiosity about the new and changing aspects of it. If environmental edges change too much, baby is overwhelmed, confused, and worried. If the spaces where babies live remain mostly the same, the baby is free to notice and find interest in the variety of objects around him. Humans become very sophisticated about reading edges; this skill takes time to refine, and it starts when babies are drawn toward objects with high contrast.

What Should Parents Do?

When a baby is lying contentedly on her stomach during "tummy time," she might be drawn to notice a contrasting edge. It could be the black-and-white stripes on her blanket. When you realize she's obviously concentrating on an edge, there's no need to interrupt her concentration.

Well-meaning parents might not realize what their baby's looking at, they might think their baby is staring blankly. Not realizing the child is working to notice the contrasts of the black-and-white stripes, a parent might place a toy on the blanket in front of the child. Instead, it's better to allow the child to satisfy his need to stare at the bold contrasts. The baby is not only determining where the black and white figures begin and end—dividing them into separate objects—he's actually concentrating, entertaining himself and satisfying his curiosity. He's drawn toward an element in the environment that's holding his interest. He doesn't need Mom or Dad right now; there's no need to interrupt him. By fussing, he'll let a parent know when he's had enough of stripe gazing and needs someone to move him on to something else.

Should parents invest in attire and décor that boasts stripes, bull's-eyes, and checkerboards? It's really not necessary. Most environments where babies live offer enough contrasts for the baby to determine the edges around him.

Once research determined that babies prefer objects of high contrast, it didn't take long for American marketing to respond. You've probably seen toys, blankets, and diaper bags made of bold black-and-white prints. Purchasing this line of printed objects will make a baby neither smarter nor more advanced in intellectual development, but such patterns will pique a baby's interest and give her something relevant to focus and practice on.

It's important to know and respect a baby when he's staring at an edge in his environment, and even affirm the activity by using your best form of parentese: "Oh, you're looking at Daddy's glasses. I'll stay right here so you can get a good look at them."

If you're choosing between a floor blanket with patches of black and white fabrics and one pieced together with various pastel-colored fabrics, researchers would tell you to pick the one with pieces of black and white bold prints. On the other hand, if you're choosing pajamas or a crib sheet, you might pick one with pastel colors as the bold black and white stripes might stimulate the child rather than soothe him to sleep.

Interested in Motion

Objects and people that move also capture a baby's attention. In the earliest days of life, babies will turn their heads and move their eyes to see something that moves in front of them (Kellman and Arterberry, 1998).

To a baby, a dog and the carpet the dog is lying on present one continuous image; it's difficult for her to know where the dog begins and ends and where the carpet begins and ends. When the dog rises and walks across the room, the baby is more easily able to see clearly that the dog and the carpet are separate entities.

If two objects touch while standing still or when moving together, young babies have trouble distinguishing one from another. On the other hand, if the objects are moving independently, or just one moves, they can glean information about them regarding shape, color, and texture (Berk, 2009).

The Research

Researchers had two-month-old babies watch a two-dimensional display on a computer screen, of a moving rod the center of which was hidden behind a small box. Only the two ends of the rod were visible. The rod was tilted slightly and moved back and forth from side to side, remaining tilted. Behind the box and rod was a textured background that helped the babies distinguish the box from the rod. After a while, as the babies habituated to the moving rod event, they looked at it less and less, showing diminishing interest as the display became more familiar.

Next, the researchers presented the babies with two alternating test displays. One test display showed the babies the rod moving in front of the textured background, this time without the box in front of it.

In the other test display, the box was removed as well, but this time what appeared in the space where the box had been was not the center of the rod, but the textured background. Instead of seeing one single long rod, the babies saw only the two ends of the rod that had been visible in the habituation display; they saw two short, separate rods moving in synchrony.

These babies looked longer at the disconnected rod test display, compared to the single rod. Researchers took this as evidence that the disconnected rod test display was not what the babies expected based upon what they'd seen in the habituation display. The babies had inferred that the rod was one entity and were perplexed when they were shown the rod as two separate pieces.

The moving rod, plus the textured background and the fact that the box in front of the rod was small—all aided the babies to conclude that the rod in the habituation display was one continuous object even though they could only see the two disconnected ends of it. A control group of babies who hadn't seen the habituation display showed no difference in looking time between the two test displays.

When newborns were tested, unlike the two-month-olds, they preferred looking at the single long rod test display, suggesting to researchers that babies are not born with the cognitive ability to infer what is not directly seen and to perceive object unity. However, this ability is acquired quickly—within only two months (Johnson, 1997).

The Interpretation

Think about what the visual world looks like to your baby. He notices edges, sees shapes, colors, textures, movement, but without much life experience yet, how does he know what pieces of the scene go together to form a single unified object? Motion is the primary source of information for young babies to start sorting all this out. While your baby doesn't see as well as you do, there's lots he can perceive, but he does so better when an object or a face is moving slowly in front of him. In this study, if the rod hadn't been moving behind the box and if the background hadn't been textured, the babies would likely have thought the box and the rod were one unit. Because the rod moved around slowly behind the box and because that box and the background were of distinctively different textures, the babies were able to perceive the rod as one object and the box as another.

What Should Parents Do?

When you and your spouse are paralyzed in adoration as you stand one behind the other, gazing lovingly at your baby, realize it's difficult for your baby to distinguish one of you from the other. When you move slightly toward or away from each other or from side to side, your baby can see the distinction between the two of you more easily. The best parenting rule to follow is to keep in gentle motion as you move about your baby; doing so helps her see you and differentiate you from others and from the wallpaper behind you.

Also, watch your baby track the objects that hang from his mobile. When changing your baby's diapers, notice how your baby is following your face as it moves around.

As your baby ages, her ability to track toys improves, so then you can set her on your lap and roll a ball across the floor, pull a toy or push another, at a slow speed. You can see for yourself at what speed your child can track these objects. Dangling an object from a string and moving it slowly back and forth won't hypnotize your baby, but instead allow him to use his eyes in a way that will enhance and support development. Doing so engages your baby and meets her where her learning lies.

Watching Out for Looming Objects

Let's say one day you're gently rolling a ball around the room for your baby to track. Big brother wants to get involved. He picks up the ball and instead of rolling it, he bounces it toward you and the baby. What does baby do? He blinks and flinches. You realize that while your baby is not yet able to dodge or deflect the ball, he has enough visual ability to notice that the ball is looming before him, and so he reacted to this potentially dangerous event.

The Research

In one study, researchers found that during the first month of life, even though a baby does not often blink at the approach of an object, she is more likely to blink at an approaching object than a withdrawing object. Then, over the next six weeks, the probability of blinking at the approach of an object goes from 16 percent up to 75 percent (Pettersen, Yonas, and Fisch, 1980, as referenced in Yonas and Owsley, 1987).

Next, researchers sought to understand what controlled the defensive blinking. Was it merely a primitive reflex or was it based on an actual perception of impending collision? These researchers monitored the blinking and head movements of three- to four-month-old infants in response to several kinds of optical displays. One display gave the appearance that an object was approaching at a constant speed (characteristic to this display was an explosive expansion pattern in the last few seconds before impact). Another display gave the appearance that an object was slowing as it approached. A third display only showed a rapid change of brightness such as what would occur as an object looms just before collision.

The three- to four-month-olds showed avoidance behavior, blinking, and movement of their heads backward only when there was an explosion in the expansion pattern, corresponding to an object approaching at a constant speed. One-month-olds who were tested blinked with equal frequency to both explosive and non-explosive expansion (Yonas, Pettersen, Lockman, and Eisenberg, 1980, as referenced in Yonas and Owsley, 1987).

The Interpretation

By about three months, babies have acquired some ability to perceive depth, particularly when an object looms before them. In the course of a baby's daily activities, he's carried around or set down to sleep, play, eat, or interact. In the process, people and objects naturally move and turn in front of his eyes, allowing for views from different distances and different perspectives. Around four months of age, infants have learned more about depth and can recognize that people and objects are three-dimensional (Arterberry, Craton, and Yonas, 1993).

What Should Parents Do?

If you'd like to see for yourself that your baby is equipped to notice an object looming toward her, tie a string to a soft toy. Have the baby track the toy as you swing it back and forth. Then have the toy slowly move toward your baby's face. Does your baby blink? Probably your baby will. Be careful as you engage in this activity. Your baby might feel stressed by an object constantly coming toward her. Probably it's best just to do what's natural for you and your baby. Pick her up, move her around, pass her off to another person, then set her down. As you do so your baby's eyes are adjusting to all these different positions. She's not a passive agent in these activities; she's active, interested, and aware, particularly when she's awake and alert. But do know that if an object does come looming toward her, she'll likely blink like mad in an attempt to protect her eyes.

Noticing What an Object Is

At about two months a baby's vision improves so that he is interested in not only where an object is, but also what it is. As a baby's ability to track objects improves, he seeks to identify them. Babies this age begin to scan rapidly across an entire object rather than concentrating only on edges. As a result, they spend more time looking at the internal features of an object or array of objects and are thus better able to identify individual objects. What is amazing too is the level of detail that they notice, even at this young age.

Let's say you have a modern art picture that hangs vertically in your home. You like it just fine that way. Then someone comes to visit who tells you you've hung it wrong, it's supposed to hang horizontally, so you re-hang the picture horizontally. If your baby is between three and four months, she'll notice. If you have a shelf with two teapots on it, add a third and your baby will notice that too. If you have a big picture hanging over a little picture and decide a week later that you don't like it that way and change it, so that the little picture now hangs over the big picture, your child will take notice of that change too. You'll realize that he's noticed because he alerts to the difference; his body stiffens and his eyes widen.

You may think that you're the only one with such a little smartie on your hands, but research tells us most three- and four-month-olds notice such changes (Bee and Boyd, 2007).

The Research

Researchers showed babies, ages twelve to twenty-four weeks, a series of four black-and-white, schematic, happy-face figures: circles with little points on the sides for ears, some lines at the top for hair, two eyes, a nose in the middle, and a curved line below representing a smiling mouth. The four happy faces were identical to one another except for the eyes and nose. One had circles for its eyes and nose, the second had plus signs, the third had triangles, and the fourth had diamond shapes. These pictures were presented to the babies in random order and repeatedly. At first the babies were interested in looking at the sequence of happy faces, but after a while, after seeing many of them, they looked for a shorter and shorter time at each new presentation before turning away. They lost interest, or in other words they habituated.

Next came the test phase. The researchers presented four new figures to the babies. The first two were happy faces, identical to the ones seen previously but with different eyes and nose: One had squares, the other X's. These test faces had a familiar configuration to the habituation faces, but had new features. The new happy faces didn't pique the babies' interest—they didn't look any longer at these new faces.

The next two test figures were identical to the first two test figures except that the features were mixed up with the mouth above the nose and the eyes on either side of the nose. Now the babies looked longer, that is, they dishabituated. This strange facial pattern clearly caught their attention.

These researchers also tested the babies with another set of stimuli. They showed them four pictures of patterned shapes (concentric circles, diamonds, stars, and barbells) with a small version of the shape above a large one. After a while the babies habituated to the pictures. In this situation, the researchers wanted to know if the babies turned bored from looking at repeated examples of the configuration, small over big, or if they turned bored from looking at the same concentric-patterned shapes over and over. So they showed each baby a new set of concentric-patterned shapes, this time using a mushroom shape and an X shape, with a small version over a big version. When the babies saw the different shape with the same configuration, small over big, if they could talk they might have said, "Ho hum, same old boring small thing over big thing." They didn't show renewed interest even though the shapes had changed. But when the researchers changed the configuration to big over small, the babies looked longer. It was as if the babies were saying, "Hey, here's something new!" They were alert to the change of configuration (Caron and Caron, 1981).

The Interpretation

This research shows just how much babies' vision is advancing. At three months babies take notice of different shapes and also different configurations of those shapes. They are making sense of their visual world, noticing not just individual items, but also noticing that the arrangement of items can carry meaning. The babies in this study realized that it didn't matter if the facial features were made of circles, plus signs, triangles, or diamonds; they were still in the same configuration, of a face. When the facial configurations were mixed up, however, no matter what the shape of the individual features, the babies perked up and looked perplexed, obviously noticing that the faces were awry. Because they are noticing configurations, they are alert to when those configurations are changed, like small thing over big thing changing to big over small.

What Should Parents Do?

To keep your baby's mind sharp, make little changes to your baby's environment. For instance, tie ribbons to the animals on your child's mobile. If you've had two dolls sitting on the shelf that's on the wall next to the diaper changing table, add a third. See if your baby notices. Change the pictures in the places where your child will take notice. For a week wear the same necklace, then change it. Most likely, you'll see interest written all over your baby's face.

There's no need to make drastic changes in the environment daily; that would be too much for your baby to absorb. Make subtle and simple changes occasionally, and most likely your baby will notice and appreciate seeing the new objects and the changes in patterns and quantities of things (up to about three objects).

Judging Depth When Moving

Some children learn to crawl, others scoot, but regardless how a child moves across the floor, parents turn concerned for their baby's safety once she's mobile. Every parent wonders, "How can I protect my child from falling down the stairs or off the edge of the sofa?"

By the time babies begin to crawl, their vision will be refined to the point where they can determine edges around the room, identify objects, and perceive depth better and better. Depth perception helps baby know how far she is from an object and where objects are, relative to one another. This leads to an understanding of the layout of her environment, helping her to successfully maneuver and ultimately survive. However, as we shall see, the ability to visually perceive depth is not sufficient for most babies to instill a wariness of heights. Research shows that babies need some experience being independently mobile to learn to make use of depth cues and develop a healthy caution around heights.

Furthermore, even though a baby can see the edge of a step and knows that the next one is a distance below, he can't at first successfully and skillfully maneuver going up or down the steps. Therefore, the parent's role is to let the baby practice with the parent right there for safety's sake. The rest of the time those stairways should be barricaded.

Here's an example to drive home this point. Isaac came to visit Grandma and Grandpa. He wasn't walking but was an experienced crawler, except when it came to stairs, because his home had none. Therefore he had no idea how to maneuver up and down the three steps that led from his grandparents' living room to their dining room. The first time he approached the steps, he didn't hesitate, and he fell before either Grandma or Grandpa could reach him. This one fall was all it took for him to notice the drop-off from then on, and he learned from coaching by Grandma and Grandpa to bounce down the stairs on his behind.

The Research

In 1960, researchers Gibson and Walk devised an interesting way to demonstrate that babies could perceive depth. They set crawling babies on a large, thick glass surface. Just under and flush with the surface on one side was a checkered cloth. The baby was placed on top of this side of the glass table initially. Halfway across the table, the checkered cloth dropped off to about three feet below the surface. The researchers believed that if the babies crawled across the glass surface but then stopped at the fake drop-off, it would provide evidence that they had acquired depth perception and realized the danger of potentially falling off the "cliff" ahead. If they hadn't acquired depth perception, they would continue to crawl across the glass table without ever minding the appearance of the "cliff" below.

In the original study by Gibson and Walk (1960), most of the babies stopped at the "visual cliff," even when the parents were on the other side of the glass table coaxing them across. The researchers reported that the babies' behavior clearly indicated a reliance on depth perception. Often they would look over the "cliff," then back away and look up at Mom with a concerned expression, even crying at times when they couldn't get to Mom without going over the "cliff." Some babies would pat the glass over the cliff, but despite the tactile evidence, they would refuse to cross. Other babies turned around and backed over the "cliff," or used other strategies, trying to get to Mom in a safe way (Gibson and Walk, 1960).

More recent research has shown that depth perception alone does not imply a wariness of heights. The role of experience is crucial. Joseph Campos and his colleagues tested infants on the "visual cliff" apparatus eleven and forty-one days after they had become independently mobile. After forty-one days of experience crawling around at home and elsewhere, the babies were more reluctant to crawl across the "visual cliff" to their mothers than they had been after only eleven days of experience. The researchers tested early crawlers, late crawlers, and babies who started crawling at the typical time. They found that the age at which the infants started crawling made no difference. It was only the amount of crawling experience that affected how hesitant they were to cross the "visual cliff" (Campos, Anderson, Barbu-Roth, Hubbard, Hertenstein, and Witherington, 2000).

The Interpretation

When a baby starts to crawl, she'll likely crawl right off a cliff, a sofa's edge, or a set of stairs if not protected by Mom or Dad. As she crawls and gains experience, she realizes the danger involved with her newfound mobility. Whether an early crawler or a late crawler, the child needs opportunities to practice crawling in a variety of settings before she will develop wariness from the dangers that accompany it.

What Should Parents Do?

Does this research mean that once babies begin to move or after a few weeks of crawling, parents can leave them to their own devices to maneuver around at will without concern of falling? Absolutely not!

While moving babies may see the edge of the sofa, and they are starting to develop a healthy caution of heights, they aren't yet perfectly skilled at going up or coming down from the sofa. They don't know how to turn around and slither down safely; doing so takes much practice. Therefore they need parents to watch them carefully and coach them by demonstrating what to do or gently guiding their bodies while giving verbal cues such as "turn around, that's right, good for you." In time and with practice, they learn their limits and master skills for going up to and down from various surfaces so that they won't fall and hurt themselves.

Vision Sharpens for Some Objects and Weakens for Others

While your child refines his ability to see various objects and demarcations in the environments he encounters, he also loses his ability to make fine distinctions between similar things when those things are not part of his everyday existence. At six months a Japanese child will pick out differences between different kinds of chopsticks and different kinds of forks, knives, and spoons. As the child gets a little older, about nine months, since chopsticks are a part of a Japanese child's environment, the Japanese child will continue to notice slight differences between various kinds of chopsticks but may not notice the same degree of difference between two forks.

The Research

Researchers showed six-month-old babies a picture of a human face. Once the babies habituated to it, the now-familiar face was presented again, side by side with a novel but similar-looking human face. The babies' looking time to each face was recorded. This procedure was repeated with multiple pairs of similar-looking human faces. The results showed that the babies looked longer at the novel faces of each pair, indicating that the babies could tell the difference between similar individual human faces.

Then the researchers repeated the experiment using pictures of monkey faces. Again, the babies looked longer at a novel monkey face when it was presented beside a similar-looking monkey face to which they had already habituated, indicating they could tell the difference between similar individual monkeys as well as humans.

While it's amazing that a six-month-old can notice the difference between one similar-looking human face and another, and also notice the difference between similar-looking monkey faces, there's more that's fascinating about this research study.

When the procedure was repeated with nine-month-olds, these older babies looked longer at the novel human faces, just like the six-month-olds. In contrast, there was no difference in looking time between novel and familiar monkey faces. The nine-month-olds demonstrated that they could tell the difference between similar individual human faces, but did not show the same ability to discriminate between similar monkey faces. When adults with no specialized expertise with monkey-face recognition were tested, they showed the same results as the nine-month-olds.

The Interpretation

What is happening between age six months and nine months that can account for this change? Researchers suggest that a "perceptual narrowing" occurs during this time. The babies' facial recognition ability tunes in to the type of faces most frequently observed: human faces.

If the babies had been from an environment where monkeys were a common everyday part of the culture, they likely would not have lost the capacity to distinguish similar-looking monkeys from one another. Since most babies encounter many human faces, they work at distinguishing one from another. As babies work at becoming competent in their first environment—home—it's there that they use their developing visual ability to focus on and determine what's the same and what's different in all that surrounds them.

As a side note, this early tuning of the face recognition system does not mean that a child cannot learn later in life how to discriminate monkey faces or the faces of other species of animals (Pascalis, de Haan, and Nelson, 2002).

What Should Parents Do?

If baby's environment is boring, her capacity to distinguish objects is underutilized. However, if baby is moved daily from one stimulating situation to another, she'll likely be overtaxed and will possibly be stressed. Parents should hope to strike a balance between new and different events for their child to look at and experience while providing consistent and predictable people and places for their child to become well acquainted and familiar with. In this regard, it's best to know your child. Some children can manage more changes than others. One child may be highly interested in a new person or place and another child may feel stressed.

Rather then buying your child new toys day in and day out, it's better to let him get to know a toy, and then add something new to the toy or otherwise change it slightly, thereby renewing the child's interest. Say, for instance, your child has a jack-in-the-box. After you've played with it over and over, tie a ribbon around Jack's neck. Watch your child's expression to see if she notices that something new has been added to Jack's wardrobe.

Although vision is the least developed of all the senses at birth, it improves rapidly over the first six months of life. By six months your baby's vision is almost 20/20 (Slater, 2001). If you sense by age six months or older that your child is not seeing accurately, be sure to mention it to your doctor. As we'll see next, the other senses—touch, hearing, smell, and taste—are more developed from birth.

Touch

Touch a baby, he feels it. From the day of birth, touch is so basic to the parent-child relationship that it's almost taken for granted. When parents see their baby, it's instinctive to caress and massage him and rub their cheek against their baby's. Research tells us that mothers are so sensitive to the feel of the skin on their newborn baby's hands and cheeks that by touch alone they can tell which baby is their own (Kaitz, Meirov, Landman, and Eidelman, 1993).

From birth, a child's sensitivity to touch is well developed. Babies need touch in order to thrive; it promotes early physical growth, and gentle caressing increases a baby's ability to be responsive to all that surrounds her (Berk, 2009). When loving caregivers caress an infant, the infant responds with more smiling and is more attentive to the person who is touching him (Stack and Muir, 1992). It's not only the touch of people newborns respond to; their acuity to touch is so well developed, they can distinguish one object from another with this sense.

The Research

Researchers in Paris examined newborns' sensitivity to touch in a maternity hospital. The researchers brought with them a tiny cylinder and a tiny prism. A researcher placed one of the objects in each newborn's hand in such a way that the baby couldn't see the object. With a slight press of the object to the palm of the baby's hand, the palmar-grasp reflex was triggered, and the baby would close her hand around the tiny object and make little movements with her hands and fingers, feeling it. Typically, after a little while, the baby would drop the object. If the holding time reached sixty seconds, the researcher would gently remove the object from the baby's hand. The holding time was recorded and the same object was gently pressed to the baby's palm again, repeating the procedure. What the researchers found was that the newborns' holding times decreased over the successive presentations of the object; that is, the newborns habituated to the object.

Next, the researchers placed a new object into each baby's hand, the one (cylinder or prism) that the baby hadn't held before. Now the holding time jumped up as the babies explored the new object. The newborns dishabituated to the new object, indicating an ability to detect that the two objects were different (Streri, Lhote, and Dutilleul, 2000).

The Interpretation

It's important to note that between three and four months babies lose this ability to spontaneously grasp an object, but in the meantime the palmar reflex helps them explore their world. Once the reflex drops out of sight, babies begin to develop the ability to grasp objects deliberately on their own rather than by means of a reflex, and once they grasp an object it goes directly into their mouth for further exploration.

Look at a cloth napkin, a wooden dowel, a plastic rattle, and a rubber ball. Can you imagine how they feel? Of course you can, because when you were a baby you explored objects thoroughly with your hands and your mouth. Although this phase of an infant's determination to touch and taste objects is one where parents need to be on guard for safety's sake, it's an important time of lifelong learning regarding how objects feel and taste.

What Should Parents Do?

Give your child a plethora of objects to grasp and hold. He's learning about his world through feel. Don't hold back; offer a smorgasbord of objects made of different textures and shapes, including hard things and soft things. Since each object your baby reaches for and picks up immediately goes into her mouth so that she can explore it with her lips and tongue, the parent's job is to make sure anything a child can put in her mouth is safe, so that the baby can't swallow and choke on it. You'll be gratified to know that this phase of exploring objects with the mouth doesn't last forever; in fact, it peaks at about age seven months and then gradually tapers off. Next your baby's interest and abilities shift into intricate touching and looking at objects, using only the hands and eyes to explore them (Ruff, Saltarelli, Capozzoli, and Dubiner, 1992).

Taste

Obviously, as babies touch objects and put them into their mouths, not only is the sense of touch working, but taste as well. In fact from birth an infant's sense of taste is well developed. How do we know? From watching babies' facial expressions. If a mother eats Brussels sprouts, her breast milk might taste a tad bitter. She'll see a slight look of disgust on her infant's face when he takes his first sip of Brussels sprouts–laced breast milk. If the mother introduces formula or soymilk, if she watches her child's face, she'll realize by his expression that he's recognized a difference from one milk's flavor to the next.

The Research

Researchers prepared solutions of sucrose, citric acid, and quinine sulfate. Adults tasting these solutions perceived them as definite and clear examples of sweet, sour, and bitter, respectively, and the tasting induced correspondent facial expressions.

The researchers put tiny amounts of these solutions on the tongues of newborns within the first hours of life, prior to their first bottle or breast-feeding. When tasting the solutions, the newborns displayed facial expressions similar to those of the adults. When tasting the sweet flavor, the babies' expressions resembled a smile, followed by a typical licking of the upper lip and a burst of eager, loud, joyful sucks. When tasting the sour flavor, the babies pursed their lips, wrinkled their noses, and blinked their eyes. The response to the bitter taste was quick and dramatic. The babies opened their mouths in a distinct archlike fashion, showed a flat tongue, and spit or retched. This difference in response indicates that babies can distinguish these three basic tastes (Steiner, 1979).

Even though babies prefer sweet tastes to bitter or sour ones, they can acquire a taste for substances that they first rejected. Researchers gave babies allergic to cow's milk formula, a soy- or other vegetable-based substitute, which is typically very strong and bitter-tasting. In time, they not only accepted the substitute but soon preferred it to the sweeter, dairy-based formula that they once loved. The babies became accustomed to the new, although stronger-tasting, formula, particularly when they made the connection that it would satisfy their hunger (Harris, 1997, as referenced in Berk, 2009).

The Interpretation

Nature equips babies with the ability to taste as a means of survival. The food they need for growth is sweet breast milk, which they welcome. Toxic substances that could harm the baby often taste bitter, so baby reflexively rejects anything that tastes bitter.

What Should Parents Do?

Once your baby starts eating solid foods, you'll see a disgusted face when he tries for the first time, say, broccoli or other bitter-tasting vegetables. In time he'll become accustomed to the taste, but it takes a while for babies to warm up to tastes that they're naturally inclined to reject. So don't get discouraged when you hear "yucky" emerge from your child's mouth when first tasting peas. On the other hand, sweet-tasting foods are always welcomed by youngsters; they need no time to learn to love them, as they have loved sweets from the first taste of mother's milk.

Smell

Put a banana under your baby's nose, notice the look on her face. You'll likely see a relaxed, pleasant expression. If your baby smelled a rotten egg, she'd likely frown at its odor. The baby's expression tells you that she knows one smell from another and has a preference. Depending on your pediatrician's advice, you won't introduce solid foods to your baby until age six months or older, so until then your child won't have the opportunity to taste or smell as wide a variety of foods. Nevertheless, if there's a distinct odor, baby responds with pleasure or repulsion (Steiner, 1979).

Although newborns respond differently to bananas and rotten eggs, what babies are truly programmed to smell is the scent of their mother and of breast milk (Cernoch and Porter, 1985; Marlier and Schaal, 2005). Their ability to locate the source of food enables them to survive.

The Research

Research scientists proved a newborn's ability to detect familiar smells with an experiment that started by placing twelve- to eighteen-day-old breast-fed babies in a bassinet, lying face upward, when they were quiet and alert. To one side of the baby was hung a gauze pad redolent with the smell of the baby's mother. She had been asked to wear the pad taped to her armpit during the previous night. On the other side was a pad exuding the smell of a non-lactating woman, obtained in the same manner. After one minute, the pads were removed, followed by a two-minute break. Next, the pads were replaced for another minute, with their positions reversed. The amount of time that the infants were oriented to each of the pads was recorded.

The researchers found that the newborns spent significantly longer oriented toward the pad containing the smell of their mothers than toward the other pad. When the experiment was repeated, but this time the stranger was a lactating woman, the results were the same. These results indicate that breast-feeding infants do not just respond to a scent associated with lactation, they recognize the characteristic signature of scents produced by their mother (Cernoch and Porter, 1985).

The Interpretation

The research tells us that babies arrive not only able to detect various smells in their environment, but also that they know the difference between their mother's scent and a less familiar person's scent, and that, of course, they prefer their mother. When smelling her, they relax because they know that nutrients and nurturing are close at hand. Just because a baby prefers her mother's smell doesn't mean that she can't detect and be comforted by the scent of Dad, Grandma, Nanny, and big sister. After all, these people as well as Mommy are interested in baby's survival. If a baby is bottle-fed, clearly she will be highly interested in the smells of those people administering the bottle. But if Mom is breast-feeding exclusively and baby is hungry, it's Mommy's smell even before feeding that will stop the hunger cries. Once Baby smells her, he knows that food is on its way, and his survival is secure.

What Should Parents Do?

Hold baby closely so that she can soak up your smell and become familiar with it and you. This goes for all of baby's caregivers. Since babies must be carried, it's a natural process that happens for baby's sake. He smells loving people and he feels safe and secure.

Let's say one day Grandma is holding her granddaughter. The baby seems content as Grandma carries her around while rocking her back and forth. Then she passes the baby off to Mommy. Baby starts to fuss. What is this about? Baby smells her mom, probably was getting hungry, and so her mom's scent triggers hunger pains and cries.

Hearing

Newborns don't hear efficiently; however, they do hear a wide variety of sounds, even before birth, and their hearing improves greatly over the first few months after they are born (Saffran, Werker, and Werner, 2006).

When a newborn baby is lying on her back, if you come close to her head and talk to her, she'll turn in the direction of your voice. If you move yourself to her other side, she'll turn her head again toward the sound of your voice. From this simple activity, you're aware that from birth a baby can hear and will slowly orient to the general direction from which a sound emanates.

This early orienting response, which occurs during the first month of life, is thought to be a fleeting newborn reflex because Baby tends to stop doing it for a few months. Then at about four months, a more mature orienting response emerges: baby will orient to sounds again, and now does so more quickly. This more mature ability to localize sound sources improves, becoming more precise, during the first several years (Litovsky and Ashmead, 1997).

The Research

Shortly after delivery of their babies, new mothers were recorded reading a Dr. Seuss book while their newborns were out of the room. Within twenty-four hours of making a recording of each mother's voice, the researchers coaxed the mother's baby into a quiet alert state, put little earphones on him, and placed a non-nutritive nipple into his mouth. The nipple was connected to the recording and programming equipment, and the newborn soon discovered that when he sucked on the nipple, a voice sounded in his ears.

The newborns were monitored for five minutes. As is typical, they sucked on the nipple in bursts alternating with pauses. Next, for half the newborns, the researchers programmed the equipment to play the recording of their mother's voice during each sucking burst when the pauses between sucking bursts were relatively long, and to play a recording of another woman's voice when the pauses were relatively short. They programmed the reverse response requirements for the other half of the newborns.

Amazingly, eight out of ten newborns, with at most twelve hours of contact with their mothers since birth, figured out that they could control which voice they heard and adjusted their pause length between sucking to hear the voice they preferred, that of their own mother.

Four of these eight were tested twenty-four hours later, but with the reverse response requirements. That is, if before, a long pause produced mom's voice and a short pause produced another woman's voice, this time the reverse was true. Again, these tiny babies adjusted their sucking patterns, working to gain access to their mother's voice (DeCasper and Fifer, 1980).

The Interpretation

From birth, babies are equipped to detect their mother's voice. When they hear her, voice they know they're more likely to survive, so they relax. They heard her voice in utero, so once they are born they're drawn to her familiar sound and connect it with her face. If Dad were the primary caregiver or if a baby was adopted right after birth, it wouldn't take baby long to prefer Dad or her adoptive parents over others. Babies tune in to the familiar person who will do the most to secure their survival.

What Should Parents Do?

Should parents and caregivers do anything about a child's ability to discriminate between their voices and those of strangers? Sure. They should talk to their baby. It's important for caregivers to vary the sounds they use to speak and sing to the baby. Know that a baby has high interest in hearing Mommy and Daddy's voices and will attend to whatever they say or sing, and that, when he hears their voices, baby feels emotionally safe and will pay attention to the words and language they use.

A baby's skill at differentiating familiar from unfamiliar voices, which starts in utero, allows him to know that familiar people are around to care for him. He relaxes and is comforted knowing his parents or other intimate caregivers are nearby and ready to attend to his needs.

You may be amazed to know that your baby arrives with her senses already at work. Knowing this information, many might inadvertently overstimulate babies because it's fascinating to speculate just how much that brain might be willing to learn and because parents want to make sure they are giving their child every opportunity to succeed in life. Not to panic. The consistent care and responsive attention parents and caregivers naturally provide is just what a newborn is seeking. It's all he really needs. Once your baby's connected with familiar voices, touches, tastes, faces, and smells, he's free to satisfy his curiosity further without worrying who will take care of him. He knows he can rely on certain predictable people. Also when a baby feels safe and secure, she isn't stressed, and therefore, there's a better chance for her brain to develop optimally.

Since research has confirmed what attentive parents have always known—that babies see, hear, taste, feel, and smell—how should parents respond? It's tempting to take this information and make more of it than what the baby requires for optimal intellectual development.

Should parents take their babies to face, smell, touch, taste, and sound recognition classes? Should they place tape recorders around so babies can hear Mommy's and Daddy's voices nonstop? Since babies' senses are at work, should parents purchase a vast array of toys, books, and dolls for them to see, smell, and listen to? Should parents parade lots of family members and friends in and out of their home so the baby can recognize lots of different smells, faces, tastes, touches, and sounds?

The answer: probably not. More is not necessarily better. All of that might be too much stimulation for a baby. Babies, like most adults, can only take in so much. While a sterile, boring environment isn't appropriate, parents need to be cautious not to bombard their child with too many objects and people. There's no need; overstimulation serves no purpose. In fact, it might cause the baby undo stress that can interfere with healthy brain development. The newborn is seeking to connect with a few consistent caregivers; beyond that number, additional caregivers do not necessarily provide greater benefit to the child.

The newborn's brain is most likely stimulated appropriately in the natural atmosphere of his home. There's no point to clattering loud toy after loud toy in front of a baby's face with the hope of building a better brain. A parent's or familiar caregiver's loving face alone holds a lot of interest for a child.

Mom and Dad's faces reassure the child that she's emotionally and physically safe with either nearby. Additionally, the parent's face stimulates the child's mind and piques the child's interest. Because the caregiver can easily vary his or her facial expressions, the child never seems to tire of the movements of a recognizable face. The face smiles; the mouth makes numerous movements when talking; lips open and shut; eyes blink; the tongue can protrude and retract; the voice makes interesting noises that fascinate the baby. When parents and caregivers imitate the baby's sounds and movements, baby is flattered; consequently more such interactions follow.

While the parent's face is performing so many interesting actions, the baby gets to know his mom or dad. He likes the entertainment the face provides and the comfort it brings to his little life. No toy can duplicate it. As parents engage with their baby in this manner, baby feels loved, protected, and stimulated, and his brain has what it needs to develop. What the baby arrives needing to find is a person to help him survive and thrive; parents' ability to care for their baby addresses that need; the parent's face, voice, and smell assures the child he'll receive the care he needs.

Another skill that comes intuitively to many parents is the ability to read a baby's cues to engage and disengage. Watch an infant's eyes, and you'll know if she's interested in examining your face; when she is, that's your cue to talk, move your eyes and eyebrows, and make silly little sounds. Once she's had enough stimulation, she'll disengage; if you then continue to interact, she'll most likely turn fussy. That's your cue to hold her, rock her, or move her to a quiet spot away from stimulating sights and sounds.

REFERENCES

Arterberry, M. E., L. G. Craton, and A. Yonas. 1993. Infant's sensitivity to motion-carried information for depth and object properties. In C. E. Granrud, ed. *Visual Perception and Cognition in Infancy*. Hillsdale, NJ: Erlbaum.

Bee, H., and D. Boyd. 2007. *The Developing Child*. Boston, MA: Pearson Education, Inc.

Berk, L. 2009. *Child Development*. Boston, MA: Pearson Education, Inc.

Campos, J. J., D. I. Anderson, M. A. Barbu-Roth, E. M. Hubbard, M. J. Hertenstein, and D. Witherington. 2000. Travel broadens the mind. *Infancy* 1: 149–219.

Caron, A. J., and R. F. Caron. 1981. Processing of relational information as an index of infant risk. In S. Friedman and M. Sigman, eds. *Preterm Birth and Psychological Development*. Orlando, FL: Academic Press.

Cernoch, J. M., and R. H. Porter. 1985. Recognition of maternal axillary odors by infants. *Child Development* 56: 1593–98.

DeCasper, A. J., and W. P. Fifer. 1980. Of human bonding: Newborns prefer their mothers' voice. *Science* 208: 1174–76.

Fantz, R. L. 1961. The origin of form perception. *Scientific American* 204: 66–72.

Fantz, R. L. 1963. Pattern vision in newborn infants. *Science* 140: 296–97.

Gibson, E., and R. Walk. 1960. The "visual cliff." *Scientific American* 202: 64–71.

Gopnik, A., A. N. Meltzoff, and P. K. Kuhl. 1999. *The Scientist in the Crib: What Early Learning Tells Us About the Mind*. New York: Morrow Press then HarperCollins.

Harris, G. 1997. Development of taste perception and appetite regulation. In G. Bremner, A. Slater, and G. Butterworth, eds. *Infant Development: Recent Advances*. East Sussex, UK: Erlbaum.

Johnson, S. P. 1997. Young infants' perception of object unity: Implications for development of attentional and cognitive skills. *Current Directions in Psychological Science* 6: 5–11.

Kaitz, M., H. Meirov, I. Landman, and A. I. Eidelman. 1993. Infant recognition by tactile cues. *Infant Behavior and Development* 16: 333–41.

Kellman, P. J., and M. E. Arterberry. 1998. *The Cradle of Knowledge: Development of Perception in Infancy*. Cambridge, MA: MIT Press.

Litovsky, R.Y., and D. H. Ashmead. 1997. Development of binaural and spatial hearing in infants and children. In R. H. Gilkey and T. R. Anderson, eds. *Binaural and spatial hearing in real and virtual environments*. Mahwah, NJ: Erlbaum.

Marlier, L., and B. Schaal. 2005. Human newborns prefer human milk: Conspecific milk odor is attractive without postnatal exposure. *Child Development* 76:155-68.

Pascalis, O., M. de Haan, and C. A. Nelson. 2002. Is face processing species-specific during the first year of life? *Science* 296: 1321–23.

Pettersen, L., A. Yonas, and R. O. Fisch. 1980. The development of blinking in response to impending collision in preterm, full term, and postterm infants. *Infant Behavior and Development* 3: 155–65.

Ruff, H. A., L. M. Saltarelli, M. Capozzoli, and K. Dubiner. 1992. The differentiation of activity in infants' exploration of objects. *Developmental Psychology* 28: 851–61.

Saffran, J. R., J. F. Werker, and L. A. Werner. 2006. The infant's auditory world: Hearing, speech and the beginnings of language. In D. Kuhn and R. Siegler, eds. *Handbook of Child Psychology: Vol. 2: Cognition, Perception, and Language, 6th ed*. Hoboken, NJ: Wiley.

Sai, F. Z. 2005. The Role of the mother's voice in developing mother's face preference: Evidence for intermodal perception at birth. *Infant and Child Development* 14: 29–50.

Slater, A. 2001. Visual perception. In G. Bremner and A. Fogel, eds. *Blackwell Handbook of Infant Development*. Malden, MA: Blackwell.

Stack, D. M., and D. W. Muir. 1992. Adult tactile stimulation during face-to-face interactions modulates five-month-olds' affect and attention. *Child Development* 63: 1509–25.

Steiner, J. E. 1979. Human facial expression in response to taste and smell stimulation. In H. W. Reese and L. P. Lipsitt, eds. *Advances in Child Development and Behavior, Vol. 13.* New York: Academic Press.

Streri, A., M. Lhote, and S. Dutilleul. 2000. Haptic perception in newborns. *Developmental Science* 3: 319–27.

Walton, G. E., N. J. A. Bower, and T. G. R. Bower. 1992. Recognition of familiar faces by newborns. *Infant Behavior and Development* 15: 265–69.

Yonas, A., and C. Owsley. 1987. Development of visual space perception. In P. Salapatek and L. Cohen, eds. *Handbook of Infant Perception Volume 2: From Perception to Cognition.* Orlando, FL: Academic Press.

Yonas, A., L. Pettersen, J. Lockman, and P. Eisenberg. 1980. The perception of impending collision in 3-month-old infants. Paper presented at the International Conference on Infant Studies, New Haven, CT.

Chapter 2

Infants' Interest in Language

A mom remembers the first time she talked to her daughter. She didn't say in an adult monotone voice, "Hi, Anna. How are you doing?" No, indeed. Even though she had never seen or talked to a one-day-old newborn in her life, she somehow just knew to use a high-pitched, slow, clear, and expressive voice, and when she did, she realized that her infant was particularly attentive.

Parents naturally talk to their babies, and when they do, they realize that they're speaking in a way that's saved only for the youngest of children. Some parents may have used this manner of speaking to an infant niece or a friend's baby. Even older siblings know to change their voice in a way that keeps their baby brother's or sister's attention (Shatz and Gelman, 1973). When they do, they're speaking motherese or siblingese.

What's motherese, fatherese, parentese, siblingese, or caregiverese? It's the way parents and other caregivers naturally talk to babies and what they bring—beyond loving, attentive care—to the baby-caregiver connection. Many refer to this form of speaking as infant-directed speech because it doesn't depend on who is speaking it—people of all ages and cultures talk to babies in a similar way. It occurs when parents intuitively coordinate their responses with their baby's, knowing just how and when to talk, smile, and coo. When speaking parentese, caregivers raise their eyebrows, open their eyes wide, and talk in a high pitch with over-accentuated wording; intonation is melodic and singsongy, speech is slow, with long pauses, and short repetitive sentences (Stern, Spieker, Barnett, and MacKain, 1983, and Fernald and Simon, 1984). No one teaches people to speak this way, nor do they consciously set out to learn it, although learning has likely taken place. After all, most adults were spoken to in this fashion as babies and have probably observed people speaking parentese, especially during childhood. Although one might forget the technique, once one is faced with a baby, the method resurfaces quickly.

Before babies actually say words for themselves, they travel through a prelinguistic phase. At about one to two months, they coo by making lots of repetitive vowel sounds, such as *oohh*, *ahhh*, and *uuuuuu*. At about six or seven months they have developed enough muscle control to babble, which involves stringing together consonant-vowel sounds (Bee and Boyd, 2007).

Around three months of age, when babies begin cooing, and then a few months later, when babbling occurs, a lovely dance takes place between the loving parent or caregiver and the child, during which the adult speaks to the baby in parentese and baby takes his turn to coo or babble back. It's the beginning of a give-and-take conversation that validates the child, proves interest, develops a human connection, and affirms the child's existence.

As Mom or Dad engages in this communicative dance with baby day after day, the dance becomes more refined. They get better at it. It's similar to what happens when two people first meet and talk, or take a turn on the dance floor for the first time; it's a little awkward for each partner. Then as they get to know each other, they learn to read each other's cues and know each other's moves, so when they meet again to talk or dance, they're able to pick up quickly where they last left off.

In this regard, will babies engage with anyone in a cooing or babbling conversation? Watch babies with their parents and then with a person they don't know very well; the difference in the interactions will answer this question.

One woman recognized vividly the difference between a nine-month-old's response to her and to the baby's mother. A mom brought her baby to the office one day to show her off to her fellow employees. The mom needed a bathroom break, so she asked one of her coworkers to watch the baby for a moment so she could step out. The coworker was eager to interact with the baby and made her best effort to speak parentese to the baby, who was sitting in her portable car seat. The woman cooed, babbled, and smiled. The baby tentatively cooed, babbled, and smiled at the woman, almost as if being polite to this unfamiliar person. Then Mom returned. Immediately the baby and Mom took to the communicative dance floor without hesitation. What unfolded was a loving, well-rehearsed verbal exchange that both obviously knew well and enjoyed. This scene makes the point that while most adults can pull out their parentese skills when engaging with a baby, babies don't just coo and babble profusely or skillfully to anyone in offices or grocery stores. They perform best with the familiar loving partners with whom they've established a secure bond. Speaking parentese to a child isn't just noise; babies are drawn to the sounds of parents' voices when parents are speaking this way, and prefer them to other sounds in the environment.

Even though your baby will most likely wait until after his first birthday to speak actual words, there's even more going on in baby's brain and mind that's laying the foundation for verbal communication. Research tells us that at one month a baby can pick up the subtle difference between the sounds of *pa* and *ba* when spoken by the same person and by two months can even do a more challenging task of recognizing a vowel as the same when spoken by people whose voices sound far different such as Mommy, Daddy, or little brother. Between birth and about six months a child can detect the sounds used in languages everywhere, even if he's never heard them in his own home, but somewhere between about six and twelve months, baby focuses in on the speech sounds used in his immediate environment. He becomes less sensitive to sounds unique to foreign languages and more skilled at recognizing those sounds necessary to master his ability to communicate in his native tongue.

Not only is your baby interested in hearing your voice and watching the movements of your mouth, particularly when you're talking in parentese, but also be aware that a baby responds differently and is amazingly attentive when sung to in a way saved only for him— using a high pitch, a slow tempo, and emotional expressiveness.

Baby Prefers Speech

Though there are many sounds in the environment that babies can hear, researchers have determined that babies are programmed to tune specifically into language. It's as if they're hardwired to learn to speak; language catches their attention. Babies arrive equipped to communicate, so they are able to detect language and like it over and above other sounds in their environment.

The Research

Researchers investigated whether young infants demonstrated a preference for listening to speech as opposed to acoustically similar non-speech sounds. This research setting was equipped with a computer monitor on which a red flashing light was presented to attract the children's attention and a hidden speaker was placed on top of the monitor. Once the baby noticed the light and then fixated on the screen, the testing began. A black-and-white checkerboard was displayed on the monitor at the same time as one set of experimental sounds was played (either speech or non-speech). The baby would look at the screen but then eventually look away and the sound would cease. When the infant looked back at the monitor, a checkerboard was displayed again, along with the presentation of another sound (either speech or non-speech). This procedure was repeated ten times. On half of the times the speech sound was played and the other half of the times the non-speech sound was played, in a random order. The infants looked at the screen longer, and thus listened longer, when real speech played as opposed to when non-speech sounds played, even though the non-speech sounds were carefully constructed to emulate many of the physical characteristics of speech (Vouloumanos and Werker, 2004).

The Interpretation

Children are drawn to listen for the sounds of language. At two-and-one-half months, they are so tuned to language that they can discriminate between the real thing, which they prefer, and sounds that are similar but not the real thing. Their ability to make such discriminations prepares them for speaking, which is only months away. It's as if babies are on a quest to learn language. It's key to the human condition.

What Should Parents Do?

Notice your baby when people speak. Is he listening? Is he paying attention? Most likely he is, particularly if he's in a quiet alert state. Some parents don't talk to their baby. They think that since the baby doesn't talk, there's no point in it. Let it be known, there is a point in talking to your baby no matter how young. Babies are primed for language, so you do your best by your baby to provide language for her to hear. It stands to reason that you'll jump-start your child's ability to learn language by providing a language-rich environment from day one.

Infants Prefer Parentese

Your child is drawn to your voice when you're using infant-directed speech, and prefers it to other forms of speech. She's working to detect the differences in the sounds that come out of your mouth, and it's easier for her when you speak in parentese. Adult-to-adult speech doesn't interest baby as much as adult-to-infant speech. Parentese distinguishes linguistic boundaries, making them clear, thus familiarizing babies with the language or languages they will eventually speak themselves. The higher pitch and the pitch patterns used in parentese expand sounds, making them more dramatic and obvious, which grabs baby's attention.

The Research

Four-month-olds were given a choice between listening to recordings of four women talking to another adult or recordings of the same four women talking to their four-month-old infant in parentese. When the babies heard the women speaking parentese, they were more likely to turn their heads in the direction of the speaking sounds (Fernald, 1985).

Then the researchers isolated the various features fundamental to parentese—the patterns of pitch, amplitude, and rhythm—to investigate which aspects determine babies' preference. The researchers took the speech samples of the previous study and used computer techniques to filter out the words, keeping the amplitude (loudness) constant and leaving only the pitch and rhythm. The researchers noticed that, to their ears, the motherese-based samples sounded like highly distinctive musical glissandi—sounds which are performed by sliding rapidly through notes on a scale using a musical instrument or singing voice—whereas the normal adult speech–based samples sounded like low, continuous murmurs. The babies showed a reliable preference for the sounds derived from infant-directed speech with its overall higher pitch and wider range and exaggerated modulation of pitch, compared to adult-directed speech.

When the researchers processed the speech samples, keeping the pitch constant and leaving only the amplitude and rhythm features, the babies did not show a preference for the sounds derived from infant-directed speech versus adult-directed speech. Nor did babies have a preference for the different rhythm patterns of the sounds from the two speech samples when pitch and amplitude were held constant (Fernald and Kuhl, 1987).

The Interpretation

This research proves what sensitive and aware parents from all cultures (as we'll see in the next research section) have always known: babies prefer child-directed speech, parentese. Most parents figure this out all on their own, as do siblings and grandparents.

What Should Parents Do?

This research tells parents to use a higher pitch when speaking to their babies and to vary it by making their higher pitched voice go up and down. Even though moms naturally have a higher pitch to their voice, dads need not worry. Dad can use his own higher pitch and modulate it up and down, and baby will listen just as well as she listens to Mom.

Parentese in Many Languages

As we've seen, in the 1980s, researchers analyzed infant-directed speech in English and found that it was marked by higher pitch, slower tempo and expanded intonation contours compared to adult-directed speech. The same was found to be true in German (Fernald and Simon, 1984). Researchers were curious to know if adults all over the world speak to their babies in the same way. An important test of this hypothesis was to examine a tonal language like Mandarin Chinese or Thai, in which a change in the pitch height and intonation contour of a word may alter its meaning. For example, the word *ma* in Mandarin can mean "hemp," "scold," "horse," or "mother" and the word *glai* in Thai can mean "near" or "far" depending on the pitch height and contour.

The Research

Researchers recorded Mandarin-speaking mothers as they spoke to their two-month-old infants and as they spoke to a friend on the telephone. When the recordings were computer analyzed, a similar pattern emerged as what was found with English and German speakers. The Chinese mothers spoke to their babies with a higher pitch, slower tempo and expanded intonation contour compared to their speech with an adult (Grieser and Kuhl, 1988). A more recent study confirmed these findings and further analyzed the acoustical features of Mandarin infant-directed speech to determine whether or not the observed changes in intonation relative to adult-directed speech affect the meaning of the spoken words. It was found that meaning is indeed preserved. As Mandarin speakers raise the pitch and expand the pitch range of tones in words addressed to babies, they maintain the relative order of pitch height and range that determine the meaning associated with those tones. In fact, while preserving the meaning certain features of the tones are exaggerated, potentially making them easier for their babies to learn (Liu, Tsao, and Kuhl, 2007).

The Interpretation

From this research we have evidence that parents the world over find a way of speaking to their babies that they pay attention to and that makes language easier for them to understand and learn. Every language studied thus far, from American English to Zulu, has its own version of parentese or infant-directed speech. While babies arrive equipped to tune in to language, parents seem equipped to support their language learning by using this special speaking style. With babies, it is not so important what you say to them, but how you say it.

What Should Parents Do?

Speak to your child using your best form of parentese no matter what language or languages you speak. Your baby is drawn to infant-directed-speech and will only benefit from hearing you speak in this special manner saved only for him.

Is Everyone Equipped to
Speak Parentese?

Parents marvel at themselves when speaking parentese. Some parents ask, "Where did I learn to speak this way?" Somehow, moms and dads just know to talk to their baby using a high pitch, while raising their eyebrows and opening their eyes wide, and talking with over-accentuated wording. Does anyone who encounters a baby automatically shift into parentese? It seems that grandparents and siblings do. What about others?

The Research

In a speech in Bellevue, Washington, in 2000, Andrew Meltzoff, co-director of the Institute for Learning and Brain Science at the University of Washington, described a rather humorous research study to determine if only adoring parents speak parentese or if it's a skill embedded in the psyche of even the most unlikely mother figures.

Researchers put the University of Washington's football team, the Huskies, one at a time, in a research laboratory with a baby. No one told the football players why they were there or what they were supposed to do.

The Husky was to simply be there with the contented baby. After a while in the laboratory, the babies would fuss for food, comfort, or socialization. At first, each Husky was reluctant to approach the baby; most would look around the laboratory hoping that a parent or caregiver would rescue him by attending to the baby. When no one came to his rescue, lo and behold, Husky after Husky made his best effort to speak to the baby using parentese, which involved slowed speech, exaggerated vowel sounds, and a high pitch.

The Interpretation

Does this experiment prove that all humans come equipped with the ability to connect naturally with babies? Probably not, but what it does explain is that even the seeming antithesis of mother figures (macho football players) appear to have the intuitive skill to attend and respond to an infant with a special way of talking. It's a magical connection that enables caregivers to connect with the youngest children (Meltzoff, 2000).

What Should Parents Do?

Speak in parentese to your baby and encourage others to do so as well. Don't hold back. Go ahead and show off for others. All will marvel at how tuned in your baby is to you and this form of communication, and you'll likely inspire others to try parentese out for themselves.

Detecting Differences in Speech Sounds

Your baby likes it when you speak parentese to him but what exactly is he hearing? You know he pays attention to your voice and likes to watch your lips move, but does he notice the different sounds that come out of your mouth? It seems he does.

The Research

Researchers had one-month-old babies suck on a nipple that produced a phonetic sound such as *pa*, which the babies noticed. The babies made the connection that by sucking on the nipple they were able to hear the sound *pa* in their ear, which apparently pleased them as some made up to eighty sucks a minute to keep it coming. After a while, however, the children in the research study lost interest in hearing the same old *pa* sound. Babies, like all of us, turn bored from listening to familiar sounds or from witnessing similar events over and over again. Live by a freeway and pretty soon you don't hear it anymore.

Once the babies appeared bored, then the researchers played another speech sound, possibly *ba*. The one-month-old babies then perked up, alerted to the new sound, and started sucking again on their pacifiers to keep the *ba* sound in their ear at least until they turned bored again. Using this method, researchers found that newborns are sensitive to even slight differences in speech sounds from languages all over the world. When it comes to sounds in foreign languages, they are more sensitive than adults to perceiving differences, even though the researchers discovered a few pairs of speech sounds that newborns do not discriminate by means of their pacifier-sucking patterns (Jusczyk, 1997, Berk, 2009).

The Interpretation

Babies arrive able to detect the subtleties of speech sounds such as *pa* and *ba*. There are many phonetic speech sounds, and your baby can likely hear the differences between them all. That's how tuned in your newborn is when it comes to hearing the specifics of language. She is actually equipped to hear the phonetic speech sounds in all languages.

What Should Parents Do?

Since you know that a baby's ears and mind are working to distinguish the sounds in the native language of his own home, there's no need to be embarrassed when others are present; shed your inhibitions and talk in parentese when your baby is quiet and alert. It stands to reason that this simple interaction between parent and child is the beginning of language learning for a baby.

Realize also that you don't need to overdo it by insisting that everyone in baby's earshot speak parentese to one another all the time. That's absurd. While baby tunes in when people speak to him in parentese, he's just fine when the people surrounding him speak to one another in their own natural flowing language.

If you're so inclined, when your baby is quiet and alert, use different phonetic speech sounds when interacting with her. Say "pa, pa, pa." Once your baby turns bored, switch to "ba, ba, ba." See if she perks up. Use "da, bo, fe" and the like. Since baby is equipped to notice these different sounds, she'll likely find such sounds amusing and engaging. Such interactions are appropriate and meaningful to your baby; they meet her where her abilities lie.

Speech Sounds Spoken by Men or Women

Here's something else rather amazing about a baby's ability to recognize speech sounds. While babies can pick up the subtle difference between *ba* and *pa* at one month old, by two to three months, they can also categorize vowel sounds whether spoken by either male or female adults.

The Research

Researchers had two-, three-, and six-month-old babies listen to sounds through a little earphone while seated on their mother's lap. There were three phases to the experimental procedure—a shaping phase, a training phase, and a categorization phase.

In the shaping phase, the babies heard a male voice saying a sequence of /a/ (*ahhh*) and /i/ (*eee*) sounds sometimes with rising pitch, sometimes falling pitch. When a baby responded to a change in vowel, immediately a mechanical toy in a Plexiglas box was illuminated and moved for a few seconds, which the baby enjoyed. If a vowel change occurred and a baby didn't respond, after a pause, he'd get to see the toy in the box. The main purpose of this shaping phase was to make it clear to the baby that the reward of seeing the interesting toy was linked to the vowel change. The secondary purpose was for baby to begin to learn that his response was in some way linked to the reward as well. The types of responses that babies gave included a head turn toward the box, a decrease in overall movement, a tensing of the body as if interested or curious about the sound, or a widening of the eyes as if saying, "Boy, that's different!"

In the training phase, the procedure and stimuli were the same except that the baby would only get to see the toy if he actually responded to a vowel change. If a vowel change occurred and the baby didn't respond, he was not rewarded by seeing the toy. The purpose of this training phase was for the baby to learn that both a change of vowel *and* a response from him were now necessary to get the reward. The babies quickly learned to respond only to a vowel change and to ignore a change in pitch contour, demonstrating a first level of categorization ability: They recognized that an /a/ is an /a/ and an /i/ is an /i/, no matter how it is spoken.

Next came the categorization phase. The procedure was the same as in the training phase. What was new was that the vowel sounds were spoken alternately by a male and a female voice. Would the babies recognize a vowel as the same whether it is spoken by a male or a female? The answer is yes! Eighty percent of the babies did not respond the first time they heard the same vowel spoken by both the male and female voices. They had learned through training that the reward only came when they responded to a vowel change. The fact that they didn't respond indicates they recognized the vowel was the same though spoken by different voices. Throughout the categorization test, the babies, even the two-month-olds, tended to respond only to a change in vowel, ignoring as irrelevant who was speaking (male or female) or how it was spoken (rising or falling pitch) (Marean, Werner, and Kuhl, 1992).

The Interpretation

Of course older children and adults can categorize speech sounds whether spoken by an adult male, adult female, or child. They know a word is the same whether spoken by an older person, by someone with a speech impediment, or by a person whose second language is English. There are prototypical sounds in language that only need to be salient enough for people to detect their uniqueness. Babies, who are programmed to detect slight differences in speech sounds, can also categorize those sounds no matter who is speaking them, which is pretty amazing. This skill drives home the point that prior to ever uttering a word for themselves, babies are not only able pick up the nuances between speech sounds, but they're able to do so no matter who is doing the talking.

What Should Parents Do?

Have all sorts of people speak to your baby. As your baby hears the speech sounds in her immediate environment, she becomes better and better at tuning into those sounds and then eventually will make those sounds for herself. Your baby will tune in to the sound of *pa* no matter who says it. The speech sounds not available to her drop from her repertoire. The natural home atmosphere provides for baby exactly what she needs, people talking to her in infant-directed speech and people talking to one another. Just know that babies are not passive to the speech sounds around them. They hear them all and use them all as they employ their innate ability to hear, speak, and comprehend the language of their own home.

Recognizing Native Speech Sounds

Language development researchers know that babies are born ready to learn any language. Then between six and twelve months of age babies begin to specialize their language skills as they pay attention to the utterances, intonation, and diction of the language or languages used in their own home. Babies mimic the sounds they hear in their environment, thus strengthening the ability to make the sounds they'll need when they actually learn to talk.

Since researchers determined first that babies up to about age six months can perceive and discriminate many if not all the speech sounds in all languages around the world, including languages they've never heard, how did researchers discover that babies' discrimination ability improves for some sounds and declines for others between six and twelve months?

The Research

Esteemed language researcher Patricia Kuhl and her colleagues conducted a study in which they had Japanese babies in Tokyo and American babies in Seattle listen to the sounds *ra* and *la*. The six- to eight-month-old babies from both cultures could distinguish between the two sounds equally well. But the ten- to twelve-month-olds in the two countries showed a marked difference in their abilities. The older American infants were more sensitive to the difference between *ra* and *la* than the younger infants, whereas the older Japanese infants were less sensitive. Why? Because the Japanese language doesn't make a distinction between *ra* and *la*, and English clearly does (Kuhl, Stevens, Hayashi, Deguchi, Kiritani, and Iverson, 2006).

When babies were only one month old, they were willing to suck on a nipple to hear sounds they liked, and nipple-sucking rate could indicate that they noticed changes in sounds. By seven months the researchers had to come up with different ways to keep babies' attention and to determine just what sounds they could distinguish and categorize.

In research laboratories in Tokyo and Seattle, six- to eight-month-old babies sat on their mother's lap while a person to the right of the babies manipulated a variety of interesting toys, which were selected to grab the babies' attention. Then to the left of the babies there was a loudspeaker, which repeated a single background speech sound, *ra* for half the babies, *la* for the other half. The babies were trained to turn toward the loudspeaker whenever the background speech sound changed to the opposing sound, and were reinforced for turning with something special—a box next to the loudspeaker would light up, illuminating an animated toy, maybe a bear dancing or a monkey beating a drum. While the babies were drawn to watch the bear and monkey perform, once the light went off and the bear stopped dancing or the monkey stopped drumming, the babies turned back to watch the person to the right manipulate the toys.

Both the Japanese and the American six- to eight-month-old infants turned their heads appropriately 65 percent of the time. Clearly they could discriminate the *ra* and *la* sounds as their performance was better than chance (50 percent). The ten - to twelve-month-old American infants did even better, up to 74 percent. But the ten- to twelve-month-old Japanese infants' performance went down to 60 percent. They were still able to discriminate the sounds, but not as well as the younger infants.

This pattern of performance for the Japanese babies occurred because their language doesn't make such a distinction between the two sounds; at one year old the babies' speech categories resemble those of the adults in their culture. Therefore, as Japanese children advance in age, it's more and more difficult for them to distinguish between *ra* and *la*. Children the world over come to hear clearly the speech sounds spoken by those who surround them and become less sensitive to the speech sounds they don't hear frequently.

The Interpretation

This research isn't just about how Japanese native speakers lose the ability to differentiate between the sound of *rake* and *lake*, it's about all babies tuning in to the nuances unique to the language spoken around them. Between six and twelve months, babies start to screen out speech sounds not used in their immediate environment, thereby losing some sensitivity to the speech sounds of foreign languages. By tuning into the sounds used in their own home, they increase their responsiveness to them, and at the same time, they stop attending to sounds that are not needed for mastering their own language.

Therefore, if a Japanese-American couple wants their child to be able to perceive and pronounce all the speech sounds present in both Japanese and English, it's best to give the baby the opportunity to hear both languages from birth.

What Should Parents Do?

Let's say your first language is English and your spouse's is Japanese. The two of you have decided that you'll speak English to your baby and your spouse will speak Japanese to the baby. Then you wonder, "Will my child be confused and language development delayed if we expose him to these two languages simultaneously from birth?" You may also ask yourself, "What happens when I speak Japanese to my spouse when my baby's listening?" You know you want your baby to be fluent in both languages, but you're perplexed; how do you go about raising a child who is bilingual?

If one parent speaks Japanese and the other speaks English and the parents hope to raise a bilingual baby, they need to start speaking in parentese to the baby in both languages from the very beginning so that the baby will retain and improve his sensitivity to the sounds of both languages. Doing so underlines once again that language learning starts from birth, not when a child utters her first word.

Additionally, language learning occurs in a social context where people speak to one another and to the baby. If you speak both languages, the child will not be confused. He'll sort it all out in good time. He'll learn to speak Japanese to one set of grandparents and English to the other.

What if both parents are native speakers of, say, Mandarin Chinese but live in the United States? If they speak Mandarin exclusively, how will their children learn English? They'll learn it from being immersed in the culture where English is the dominate language. They'll only learn Mandarin from Mom and Dad. If the Mandarin-speaking parents want their children to learn Mandarin as fluently as a native, they need to speak it most of the time when home, but, of course, when out and about in the community the child will be exposed to English. In this way the children will learn Mandarin at home and English at school and in the outside world.

Let's say a two-and-a-half-year-old child enters child care having only heard Mandarin his entire life. Not only that, he's actually speaking Mandarin as effectively as two-and-a-half-year-old children in China do. Upon entering a child-care center, he might experience some frustration as he attempts to communicate. But parents do not need to worry too much. Toddlers are resilient, and the Mandarin-speaking child will quickly learn to communicate by using gestures and will soon understand and begin to use the dominant language at the child-care center.

Teaching Your Child a Non-Native Language

If you and your spouse speak English only and you'd like your child to learn Mandarin Chinese, you might think that buying and playing audiotapes of Mandarin spoken in parentese and DVDs of people speaking Mandarin will serve the purpose of maintaining and increasing your child's sensitivity to the speech sounds unique to the language. Research tells us this won't be the case.

The Research

Patricia Kuhl and her research team had nine-month-old American babies from homes where only English was spoken participate in the study. Some of the babies played with native adult speakers of Mandarin and listened to stories read by them for twelve twenty-five-minute sessions over the course of four weeks. Another group spent the same amount of time in front of a TV playing DVDs, filmed from the baby's perspective, of the same speakers reading and talking to them. A third group just heard the audio but didn't see the visual of the DVD. At the end of the sessions, only the children in the live playtime situation with real live people speaking Mandarin demonstrated a high level of sensitivity to speech sound contrasts unique to Mandarin; in fact it was almost equal to that of a native. The DVD and audio presentations had no effect on the infants' sensitivity to Mandarin speech sounds. Learning language takes place in a social context; this fact is true whether there's one language involved or more (Kuhl, Tsao, and Lui 2003).

The Interpretation

The research drives home the point that babies not only need to hear the sounds of a language and see lip movements to develop sensitivity to the sounds unique to it, but they also need to interact with a person speaking those sounds. Speaking to your baby in parentese, playing with your baby while speaking about what you're doing, and speaking to others in the language or languages of the home is all part of language learning when seeking to raise a bilingual child.

What Should Parents Do?

If you want your baby to speak Mandarin Chinese as a native and neither you nor your spouse speak it, you could hire a native Chinese nanny who will speak to your baby in Mandarin, or when she's older you could enroll your baby in play groups where the babies and caregivers speak Mandarin, or later you could enroll your child in a Mandarin immersion school so that she can retain, use, and learn the grammar and vocabulary of that language.

All of this research underlines the point that even though most children don't communicate with spoken words during the first year, their ability to hear your words and watch your lips mouthing the sounds you make contribute to verbal communication, which is just around the developmental corner.

Second Language Learning

If parents would like their children to be fluent in a second language, the younger the child is exposed to the language, the better. While it's unclear how second language learning is affected by age, one study shed some light on the issue.

The Research

Researchers tested the English grammar of Chinese- and Korean-born adults who immigrated to the United States at varying ages. Those who came to the U.S. between the ages of three and seven years scored as well as native speakers. As the age of arrival in the United States increased, however, grammar scores declined (Johnson and Newport, 1989).

The research did not indicate a sharp drop-off in a child's ability to learn a second language competently, but rather that there was a continuous, gradual decrease as a person ages.

The Interpretation

If a person is between three and seven years when coming to the United States not knowing English, she will most likely end up speaking and using grammar as if a native speaker. The older the person is when she begins to learn a non-native language, the harder it is for her to learn the nuances of grammar.

What Should Parents Do?

If you want your child to learn the grammar of a second language like a native, exposure from birth or at least between ages three and seven is the best approach. Waiting until high school is far past the optimal period for second-language learning.

Baby Responds Differently to Music

Another aspect of baby's listening and responding skills involves music. When parents sing to their babies rather than talk to them, even if it's in parentese, babies respond differently. With baby in arms, parents in all cultures sing; it's a universal phenomenon.

When a baby hears singing, he almost always stops crying or kicking and really listens. A parent may wonder if her baby will be a gifted musician or if her child's interest in music is similar to all babies'.

The Research

In a laboratory experiment, researchers asked mothers to come in with their five-and-a-half to six-and-a-half-month-old babies. They asked each mother to talk to her baby in the way she normally did at home but to refrain from singing. Next, they asked each mother to sing songs that she usually sang to her baby at home. The mothers sang in the way that mothers typically do to their babies, with a distinctive singing style, which involves high pitch, slow tempo, and emotional expressiveness, and they spoke to them using motherese. The researchers made video recordings of these mothers singing and speaking.

A week later, each baby watched and listened to the recordings of his mother while trained observers noted his physical movements and visual fixations. The results revealed that infants looked longer at and exhibited more periods of fixation with minimal body movement for the singing, indicating there was more sustained attention to maternal singing than to maternal speech (Nakata and Trehub, 2004).

The Interpretation

Clearly infants are highly attentive to both maternal speech and singing, but they seem more engaged by singing. Parentese may be more effective in recruiting attention and may be more arousing, hence baby may look away more to keep from becoming over-aroused or he may look away to lead the mother's gaze, whereas singing is more effective at sustaining attention and is less arousing. It's the rhyme, rhythm, and repetition involved in music that babies seem to love.

What Should Parents Do?

Since your baby loves music and you're naturally inclined to sing to your baby, there's no need to exercise restraint. Go ahead and sing to your baby several times a day, in playful interactions but also as you prepare him for sleeping, bathing, feeding, and diaper changing.

Understand, however, that babies don't pay the same amount of attention when you sing using your regular adult singing voice;

they like it when you sing using high pitch, slow tempo, and emotional expressiveness.

You don't need researchers to tell you of the calming and relaxing consequences of singing. Mothers and other sensitive caregivers seem to know instinctively just when to take a baby to a quiet corner and sing softly while rocking baby back and forth. Doing so pulls the child's attention inward and thereby coordinates the child's senses, reducing and sustaining the child's arousal level. In this regard, singing seems to be more effective than speech at soothing an upset infant.

Parents do best by their children when they speak to them, whether it's parentese to babies or in adult-directed speech to their older children, in a way that's authentic, respectful, and kind, while communicating love and admiration for who their child is.

It's important for parents and those intimately connected to children to not forget the affirming communication dance that occurred between them and their child when they spoke parentese. As a child grows, there will be days when she comes to tell you about something that happened and might say, "My doll's sleeping," or "My teacher's cat had kittens," or "I hate algebra and I'm never going back to that class again." It's important in such situations to remember the initial exchanges between you and the infant when you spoke parentese and the child cooed and babbled.

The beautiful exchange in which you affirmed the child—waited your turn, nodded as she spoke, met her response with a similar one—solidified your relationship, engaged the child, and opened her up to further exchanges.

This communicative connection is necessary not only when children are babies. When your child is a preschooler and says,

"My doll's sleeping," your interested response should be something like "Your doll's sleeping? We better whisper." When your school-aged child bounds through the door with "My teacher's cat had kittens," rather than saying, "Don't think you're getting one," instead say, "Your teacher's cat had kittens? How many did she have?" Later, if your child asks for one of the kittens, then offer your yes or no response. If your son in middle school comes home saying, "I hate algebra and I'm never going back to that class," resist saying, "Of course you're going back to algebra class. You need algebra to get into college." While this is true, your child will end the conversation and you'll not find out what happened that day in algebra class. So instead say, "You hate algebra and you're never going back to that class again? It sounds like something terrible happened in class today." This response affirms and engages the child, and opens up the child to explain the situation that occurred in algebra class.

When you're speaking parentese, such communications come naturally. An age-appropriate version will serve you well all the years you connect with your child in similar conversations.

REFERENCES

Bee, H., and D. Boyd. 2007. *The Developing Child*. Boston, MA: Allyn and Bacon.

Berk, L. 2009. *Child Development*. Boston, MA: Pearson Education, Inc.

Grieser, D. L., and P. K. Kuhl. 1988. Maternal speech to infants in a tonal language: Support for universal prosodic features in motherese. *Developmental Psychology* 24: 14–20.

Fernald, A. 1985. Four-month-old infants prefer to listen to motherese. *Infant Behavior and Development* 8: 181–95.

Fernald, A., and P. K. Kuhl. 1987. Acoustic determinants of infant preference for motherese speech. *Infant Behavior and Development* 10: 279–93.

Fernald, A., and T. Simon. 1984. Expanded intonation contours in mothers' speech to newborns. *Developmental Psychology* 10: 104–13.

Johnson, J. S., and E. L. Newport. 1989. Critical period effects in second language learning: The influence of maturational state on the acquisition of English as a second language. *Cognitive Psychology* 21: 60–99.

Jusczyk, P. W. 1997. *The Discovery of Spoken Language*. Cambridge, MA: MIT Press.

Kuhl, P. K., E. Stevens, A. Hayashi, T. Deguchi, S. Kiritani, and P. Iverson. 2006. Infants show a facilitation effect for native language phonetic perception between 6 and 12 months. *Developmental Science* 9: 2. Fast-track Report, F13–F21.

Kuhl, P. K., F. M. Tsao, and H. M. Lui. 2003. Foreign-language experience in infancy: Effects of short-term exposure and social interaction on phonetic learning. *Proceedings of the National Academy of Sciences* 100: 9096–9101.

Liu, H. M., and F. M. Tsao, and P. K. Kuhl. 2007. Acoustic analysis of lexical tone in Mandarin infant-directed speech. *Developmental Psychology* 43: 912-7.

Marean, G. C., L. A. Werner, and P. K. Kuhl. 1992. Vowel categorization by very young infants. *Developmental Psychology* 2: 396–405.

Meltzoff, A. N. 2000. Presentation at the Nursing Child Assessment Satellite Training (NCAST) Conference. Bellevue, WA.

Nakata, T., and C. Trehub. 2004. Infants' responsiveness to maternal speech and singing. *Infant Behavior and Development* 27: 455–64.

Shatz, M., and R. Gelman. 1973. The development of communication skills: Modifications in the speech of young children as a function of listener. *Monographs of the Society for Research in Child Development* 38: 5 (serial no. 152).

Stern, D. N., S. Spieker, R. K. Barnett, and K. MacKain. 1983. The prosody of maternal speech: Infant age and context related changes. *Journal of Child Language* 10: 1–15.

Vouloumanos, A., and J. K. Werker. 2004. Tuned to the signal: the privileged status of speech for young infants. *Developmental Science* 7: 270–76.

Chapter 3

Combining Senses

You now know that from birth your baby's senses are at work. There's more, however, in regard to your baby's senses that are important to know. Senses don't work in isolation from one another; they work together in a synchronized fashion. The world provides input to more than one sensory system at the same time.

As you're reading this chapter, you're seeing the words on the page, you're feeling the book in your hands, you're smelling your cup of herbal tea and then tasting its luscious flavor. You're also hearing various sounds around you: the cat purring, the refrigerator humming, and you might be listening for your baby to wake. All of these senses mesh with what you know to be true and predictable about the environment that surrounds you.

If, however, you thought you had read the word "chamomile" printed on the tea bag and then when brewing and sipping your cup of tea you smelled and then tasted green tea, you would realize something was awry. Either the bag was wrongly labeled, you read it incorrectly, or possibly you grabbed the wrong bag once your kettle had started boiling. From this perplexing situation, your curiosity would be piqued, so you would do a little investigating until you determined that what you thought to be true fit with what you smelled and tasted. Lo and behold, you realize that you grabbed the wrong tea bag.

A baby, like you, is not only using his senses but begins early on to combine them, one with another. He knows his mother's face, smell, touch, taste, and sound, and he begins to know that his mommy's appearance and voice go with her scent. If she came into her baby's room to change a diaper while talking in parentese but smelled like a cow, baby would likely be perplexed and wonder why. Baby expects his familiar mommy to smell, look, feel, taste, and sound like the person he already knows her to be.

When your baby smells your scent, hears your voice, feels your skin, sees your face, and tastes your breast milk in your familiar combination, she feels content and unstressed. This familiarity brings the assurance that she'll receive the same predictable loving care and along with it her survival.

Babies are seeking to combine not only the use of their five senses, but the sensation of movement as well. If Grandma is singing a soft, slow lullaby while rocking quickly back and forth in the rocking chair, the rhythm of the song and the movement of the rocking chair aren't coordinated. Baby senses this discontinuity and will likely be disturbed. She'd like Grandma to slow down and rock the chair to the beat of the lullaby.

Babies, because they are working to use their senses in a coordinated fashion, are more easily irritated when unharmonious sensory stimulation bombards them. For instance, if Mom walks into the room and begins speaking in a strange voice, baby might get frightened. Baby feels content when Mom sounds the way he expects her to or when a caregiver sings a song while moving to the tempo of the song. You're not really that different. You may feel disoriented watching a dubbed foreign film; you're watching the actor's mouth move, but the words you hear don't match the mouth movement. Or if you're at a party watching people dance, you'll be drawn to watch the dancers who move in time to the music, not the ones who are out of step with it.

Babies are also disturbed by too much sensory input, and sensory overload might make your child cranky. Think about it: while you're driving home from work after a trying day, your own senses might be discombobulated from the traffic noise you hear combined with the movement of your automobile and the sound of the radio blaring. You may well be annoyed, but even so, you're far better equipped than a baby to handle the various kinds of sensory stimulation that come your way.

Early on babies are able to link multiple sensory sensations. Newborns can match the feel of an object that's been in their mouth with how it looks, therefore they, like all of us, use the feel of something to identify how it looks. Additionally, as babies learn about the world that surrounds them, they can do so better when they're presented with more than one form of sensory stimulation. Babies as young as three months can detect a change in an object's movement when they see it move and hear the sound it makes with that movement.

For instance, if you waltzed across the room in view and earshot of your child, and then skipped across the room, your baby would pick up on the difference between the rhythms of your two types of movements. If you were outside, and your baby could only see you through a window first waltzing and then skipping, but not hear the sound of your feet moving, she would be more challenged to pick up the difference in the rhythm of waltzing versus skipping. More than one mode of sensory stimulation, such as sight combined with sound, makes a rhythm more apparent.

There's even more to what babies are learning about the sounds around them. At five months babies know if an object or person is moving toward them or away from them; if the sound of a person moving away from a baby was gradually amplified, she would wonder why.

Senses work in combination with one another, and it all starts in the early months of a baby's life.

Combining Senses—Touch with Sight

It makes perfect sense that babies combine the use of their senses as they learn about their environment. Even though newborns will grab on to an object like a finger and make little movements with their hands to feel what they've grasped, they don't have the coordination to fully explore an object with their hands until they're a bit older. But since sucking is a well-developed skill from birth, researchers wondered if babies could detect the different textures of things they suck on and match what something feels like with its visual appearance.

The Research

As young infants will not explore objects with their hands, researchers offered one-month-olds an object to explore with their mouths. They brought the object to and from the infant's mouth with a cupped hand so that the infant couldn't see what it looked like. The objects used were essentially pacifiers, but one had a small, smooth, silicone sphere in place of the nipple, and the other had a sphere with nubs on it in place of the nipple.

After the baby sucked on either the bumpy or smooth pacifier for ninety seconds, the pacifier was removed and two objects were presented to the baby visually in a looking chamber. The visual objects were identical in shape to the bumpy and the smooth pacifiers (although larger and painted bright orange, presumably for greater visibility). Baby after baby would move his eyes toward and look longer at the visual shape that matched the shape of the pacifier that he had felt in his mouth. The babies made a connection between the feel of the pacifier that had been in their mouth with what they then saw (Meltzoff and Borton, 1979). More recently, in a similar experiment, infants as young as thirteen hours old were making such matches (Kaye and Bower, 1994).

The Interpretation

From this research we know that babies at one month old can match the feeling of something they suck on in their mouths with a picture of that object. It stands to reason that babies are using more than one sense to help figure out events in the world around them.

At some point, when a baby hears Mom's voice, he'll expect to see her. If a mother has always breast-fed and then introduces breast milk through a store-bought nipple, baby will wonder why the taste of the milk isn't accompanied by the feel of Mother's nipple. When he hears a dog barking, he won't be surprised to see Rover bound into view. If, however, he heard his mother's voice and Dad walked into the room, the child would be taken aback. Or imagine how odd it must seem for a baby the first time he hears his mother's voice coming out of the telephone. It sounds like Mom, but it certainly doesn't look like her!

While babies are able to complete some rather straightforward sensory tasks of matching what they feel with what they then see, or what they hear with what they see, too much sensory stimulation is difficult for most babies to sort out. Think of your home. On any given day, the TV news is on in the background, then the dog starts to bark, while the spaghetti sauce is cooking on the stove. Now the phone rings. Suddenly, baby turns fussy. She's not hungry; you just fed her. She's not tired; she just awoke from a nap. What could it be?

It's too much sensory stimulation; she can't take the bombardment of sensory messages.

What Should Parents Do?

In the ordinary setting of a home a baby will naturally use more than one sense to sort out the various events that occur in a day. If you need to pump your breast milk and offer it to your baby in a bottle, do so. Just know that your baby recognizes the difference. It will take her a while to adjust to the new nipple.

When a baby is upset, most parents just instinctively know to take their baby to a quiet spot and rock him gently while singing softly in sync to the rocking motion. Soon baby is content and calm once again.

Sensitive parents will also know how to manage overstimulation. It's common for parents to say, "We can only manage one outing a day. Any more and my baby seems stressed and can't settle down. It's as if he's annoyed and agitated." Most parents are able to sense just how much sensory stimulation their child can manage and do their best to protect their baby from more.

Combining Two Senses Is Useful

While parents need to monitor a baby's sensory stimulation, it's also important to realize that as babies are learning about various events in their environment, they do so better when they receive information from more than one sensory input.

The Research

To each of a group of three-month-old babies, researchers presented an audiovisual recording of a toy hammer striking a wooden surface in a distinct complex rhythm. The infants gradually habituated to the rhythm over several presentations of the recording, looking longer at first, then less and less, to each presentation. Next, the same rhythm was presented, but this time at a different tempo (faster for some of the babies, slower for the others). For most of the babies, their looking time increased significantly with the change of tempo, that is, they dishabituated. This indicated that the babies noticed the change. They had learned enough about the complex rhythm during the habituation phase to notice that there was a difference between a slower version and a faster version of it.

Did the fact that the babies both heard and saw the hammer tapping out the complex rhythm facilitate their learning about it? Yes it did. In a follow-up experiment, the researchers presented three-month-olds with only the visual or only the audio portions of the recordings. In this case, the infants showed no evidence of being able to discriminate between the slower and faster versions of the rhythm (Bahrick, Flom, and Lickliter, 2003).

The Interpretation

To babies under six months, much sensory input is unfamiliar and confusing, so by hearing and seeing an event, a baby is better able to make sense of it. Infants are not just able to combine their senses, but also rely on the combination to detect changes in their environment.

What Should Parents Do?

In your home, when the spaghetti sauce in bubbling on the stove, take your child over to it so that he can see the bubbles, hear them, and smell the sauce. By doing so, you allow your child to focus in on the sauce and combine what he hears, smells, and sees into one synchronous event.

If you have a windup toy monkey that beats a drum, have your child see and hear it pound on the drum. When a dog's barking out in the backyard, take your child to the window to watch it. If you have a piano, and Grandpa comes to play, have the child watch as well as listen. Doing so will make the experience more meaningful to your baby.

Synchronizing Movement with Sound

In the environment objects move and make sounds that mesh. A ball bounces across the floor; its bouncy movement meshes with its *boing* sound. You realize this is the way an object's movement and sound work together, and so does your baby.

The next piece of research drives home the point about a baby's ability to watch and listen to an object that's moving and then match its rhythmic movements with the appropriate sound.

The Research

In several delightfully clever experiments in the 1970s, researcher Elizabeth Spelke showed that four-month-old infants connect sound patterns with movement. In one experiment, she showed babies two films sequentially, one showing a woman playing peekaboo repeatedly—hiding her face with her hands, uncovering her face, and then saying, "Hello, baby, peekaboo," to the camera—and the other showing a hand holding a wooden baton striking a wood block and a tambourine repeatedly and rhythmically.

Next, the infants watched the two films simultaneously, but heard only one of the soundtracks being presented from a speaker located between the two visual displays. In this situation, babies showed a preference for looking at the film that matched the soundtrack they were hearing. When they heard the woman saying, "Hello, baby, peekaboo," most of the babies looked longer at the peekaboo film, but when they heard the block and tambourine sounds, most looked longer at the film featuring the baton striking the block and tambourine.

These results indicated that infants can coordinate sights and sounds. Furthermore, upon perceiving a sound, the infant will seek visual information about the source of the sound. Spelke suggested that this exploratory strategy of seeking information from other sensory modalities upon receiving information from one is an effective way to discover information about objects and events. She also suggested that it may be the basis for the ability to perceive unified objects and events amid a flow of multisensory stimulation in the environment (Spelke, 1976).

The Interpretation

We adults know that when we sense something through one modality, we tend to seek additional information from another. If we see an interesting object, we might reach out to touch it; if we hear a sudden noise, we will look around for the source. This is how we explore and learn things we need to know. Babies do the same.

Given a choice, babies will seek sensory situations that are synchronized, and babies like it when you help them out. Therefore, it's not surprising that as Grandma gently bounces her grandbaby on her knee while softly reciting a nursery rhyme, baby quickly turns content. She seems to love that the up-and-down rhythmic movement matches the rhyme's sound, whether it's "Hey Diddle Diddle, the Cat and the Fiddle," "Jack and Jill Went Up the Hill" or "Humpty Dumpty." It's harmonious sensory events that the child seeks herself, and if she's unable to find them, she would like you to find that harmony for her.

What Should Parents Do?

To entertain your baby, set her in an infant seat and put on some dance music. Now dance in time to the music. This activity will delight, calm, and entertain baby while helping him on the road to integrating the use of his senses in a baby appropriate manner.

When you're experiencing one of those over-the-top sensory events that turns baby cranky (a five-year-old's birthday party, the mall on the day after Thanksgiving, or a Fourth of July fireworks show, for instance), take him out of the mix and hum quietly while waltzing baby around the room. The soothing sound of your voice and the rhythm of your movement will work magic to bring baby to contentment once again.

Babies Read Lips

Another synchronization that occurs quite naturally between parents and their babies involves parents speaking to their child in parentese. Since baby is combining sound with movement, he soon knows that the movement of your mouth goes with the sounds that come out of it. If you were a ventriloquist and one day spoke to your child without moving your mouth, your baby would be perplexed. It just wouldn't seem right to him to hear your words but not see your mouth move along with the words that he is hearing.

The Research

Research couple Patricia Kuhl and Andrew Meltzoff showed four-and-a-half-month-olds two silent films for ten seconds each. One was of a face repeatedly mouthing the vowel sound *eee*, the other was of a face repeatedly mouthing the vowel sound *ahhh*. After this familiarization phase, both faces were presented side by side, along with an audiotape of the sound *eee* or *ahhh* played in synchrony with the lip movements of the faces. The babies spent more time looking at the face with the lips making the matching sound. These results along with results from other control experiments led researchers to conclude that infants can indeed detect auditory-visual correspondences for speech (Kuhl and Meltzoff, 1982).

The Interpretation

Not only can infants detect which lip movements go with which vowel sounds, they likely find it more satisfying to their senses to watch lips that move in sync with the sounds they are hearing. Think of watching an overseas news feed when the lips of the newscaster aren't quite matched with the sound of the person's voice. It's annoying. It's natural to want to see lips and hear words working simultaneously together in a coordinated fashion. This need to synchronize words with lips is probably why viewers would rather watch a foreign film with subtitles than one that has been dubbed in their native language.

As discussed in the last chapter, babies learn language in a social context, with people speaking to them and to one another. They not only need to hear the speech sounds of their native language, but also they need to be able to match those sounds with the movements of the speaker's mouth. Audiotapes or DVDs simply don't provide adequate opportunities for babies to see lips move along with the words they're hearing and don't provide the engaging interactive social element either. It's the combination of speech sounds spoken in parentese coupled with lips moving in a naturally coordinated fashion that children seek as they begin to detect the speech sounds that make up the language that they will soon learn to speak. This information is true when learning a second language as well as when learning a first.

What Should Parents Do?

When you talk to your baby using parentese, know that your baby is paying attention not only to your voice, but also to your lips. Therefore face-to-face interactions do more for your baby than talking to her from across the room. Since she's meshing sounds with movement, give her opportunities to see your lips, affording your child the opportunity to match your voice with your lip movements.

Detecting Increasing and Decreasing Sounds

As a car comes closer to you, the sound of the engine increases. As the car moves down the road, you hear the sound of its engine less and less. Your baby notices this too. As your baby hears the sound of a battery-powered toy car's wheels increase in volume, he not only sees it coming nearer to him but also detects its location by hearing the change in volume that indicates that it's coming closer.

The Research

Another illustration of babies' ability to mesh sights and sounds of movement comes from Jeffery Pickens. He showed five-month-old babies two silent films side by side; one showed a toy train approaching, the other showed the train moving away. Then out of a loudspeaker, he played an engine sound, either a sound getting gradually louder corresponding to an approaching sound source, or a sound getting gradually fainter corresponding to a retreating sound source. The babies looked longer at the film that matched the sound they heard. This research demonstrated babies' sensitivity to the relationship between the sights and sounds of an object in motion (Pickens, 1994).

The Interpretation

Realize that when you walk toward your baby and then walk away, she picks up on the difference of the sounds depending on how close or far away she is from you. She also anticipates how close a moving object—the dog, a battery-powered car, a windup toy—is getting to her by its increasing volume. Babies are better equipped to manage and predict events in their environment when they can use two senses—hearing and seeing—to detect approaching objects.

What Should Parents Do?

Since you know that your baby is interested in approaching objects and the accompanying louder sounds they make and is equally aware of retreating objects and the accompanying softer sounds they make, play games that involve approaching and retreating objects, and that includes you. For fun, stomp as you walk down the hall to your baby. When your baby is having a little tummy time, zoom a car from behind the sofa toward your baby and then have it move back again behind the sofa. This simple game catches your baby's attention as he's perfectly equipped to detect approaching and retreating objects not only by sight but by noise level as well.

Matching Objects with Arbitrary Sounds

So far you can see the apparent ability of a baby to match the sights and sounds intrinsic to movement. The train's engine sounds louder as it approaches. As a dog barks, the opening and shutting of the dog's mouth meshes with the sound the baby hears. The sounds you make with your mouth correspond to the movements of your lips. But what about the arbitrary relationships between objects and sounds that adults recognize? We've learned that the sound of a siren goes with the sight of a police car, and that a certain ring tone is produced by our telephone. Moreover, we know thousands of other arbitrary associations between sounds and objects because we recognize the sound of the name of an object when spoken. When is a baby able to connect the sound of a word with a person, animal, or thing?

The Research

In a study with seven-month-olds, researchers created audio-visual displays which paired the /a/ (*ahhh*) sound with one object and the /i/ (*eee*) sound with another object. The objects used in the study were a plastic crab and a porcupine, or a plastic lamb chop and a wooden star. The children watching the displays could not see the face of the female actor who uttered an /a/ or /i/ sound in infant-directed-speech, they could only see her hand along with an object. The /a/ or /i/ sound was uttered twenty-six times per minute at irregular, unpredictable intervals. The pairing of sounds to objects was made in one of three ways, defining three different conditions in the experiment: moving-synchronous, moving-asynchronous, and still. Three groups of infants participated, one group for each condition.

In the moving-synchronous condition, the hand in the audio-visual display moved an object forward and back or laterally, as if showing it to the infant, in synchrony with the sound that corresponded to that object. For example, if the /a/ sound was being paired with the toy crab, each of the twenty-six times the infant heard /a/, she simultaneously saw a hand move the crab forward and back. Next she'd be presented with a pairing of the /i/ sound with the toy porcupine in the same moving-synchronous manner.

In the moving-asynchronous condition, the hand moved the object at random times, not synchronized with the sound. For example, if the /a/ sound was being paired with the toy crab, the infant would hear an erratic series of /a/ sounds and see a hand move the toy crab forward and back multiple times, but the sight and sound would be out of sync. Next the /i/ sound and the toy porcupine would be paired in the same asynchronous manner.

In the still condition, the object remained still in the video, accompanied by the erratic series of sounds. For example, if the /a/ sound was being paired with the toy crab, the infant would hear a series of /a/ sounds and see a static image of the toy crab. Next, she'd hear a series of /i/ sounds while seeing a static image of the toy porcupine.

Infants in each condition watched alternating /a/ and /i/ videos until their looking time dropped to a low-criterion level, that is, they habituated, or became very familiar, with the stimuli.

After a ten-minute rest, each infant was given a test. A sequence of sounds (either the /a/ series or the /i/ series) was presented from a speaker for a few seconds and then the two visual displays that the child saw during the habituation phase were presented simultaneously, one on each side of the speaker. For example, an infant would hear a sequence of /a/ sounds and see on one side the visual-only display of the toy crab that had previously been paired with the /a/ sound (the matching display in this example) and on the other side the visual-only display of the toy porcupine that had previously been paired with the /i/ sound (the non-matching display). This test was repeated twelve times, half with the /a/ and half with the /i/ sound.

The researchers expected that, if the infants had learned and remembered the sound-object pairing from the habituation phase, once they heard one of the sounds in the test phase, they would visually search for the object that had been paired with that sound. For each infant and each of the twelve test trials, the researchers recorded which way the infant looked upon first hearing the sound, to the matching display or the non-matching one. The results showed that only the infants in the moving-synchronous condition showed evidence that they had learned and remembered the sound-object pairings. Their first looks were to the matching display more often than to the non-matching display.

In a second experiment, the seven-month-olds who had habituated to sound-object pairings in a moving-synchronous display remembered the pairing four days later. This longer-term memory is especially impressive given that they had received only a few minutes of exposure to the pairings during habituation (Gogate and Bahrick, 2001).

The Interpretation

This research shows that when an object is moved in a synchronized fashion with an arbitrary sound of one syllable, seven-month-old children learn and remember that a particular speech sound goes with a particular object. This temporal synchrony provides the baby with information to his eyes and ears simultaneously, which helps him make the connection that the sound he hears refers to the thing he sees.

What Should Parents Do?

As long as parents move objects in front of their babies while matching the movement in parentese with a one-syllable word—something most parents will instinctively do—their babies are fully capable of remembering that /a/ goes with crab or "ball" goes with a sphere-shaped object that bounces across the floor going *boing, boing, boing.*

Parents Use Several Senses When Speaking

As you're now aware, babies are better able to learn about objects when they are using more than one sense to do so. Baby hears water coming from the faucet, but he'll understand what's happening more easily when he can see the water, hear it, and touch it, and in time he'll be able to pair it with the word "water." Parents seem to sense this need and will typically adjust their interactions to provide multimodal sensory experiences from which the baby benefits.

The Research

Researchers asked mothers to teach their babies the words for two objects and two actions using any means they normally would to communicate with their child. The researchers chose nonsense words to ensure that they would be novel to the babies. These words were "chi" and "gow" as the names for two puppets, and "pru" and "flo" as the names for two actions. Out of sight of the babies, the researcher defined the action words to the mothers by demonstrating "pru" as a leaping action with a toy bear and "flo" as a shaking action with a toy shark.

The mothers didn't simply hold up the toy and say, "This is a chi, it flos." They were much more animated. The mothers would say the new words in parentese, in sync with moving the object, using a moving-synchronous method for teaching their babies the new words. For example, the mothers may have said, "The chi is pruing" as she had the toy bear leaping about the play space. Without being instructed to do so, they linked the name with the object or action by combining visual and auditory information and often in temporal synchrony, providing their child with the best opportunity to learn the new words (as we saw in the previous research section).

Sometimes in addition to moving the object in synchrony with saying the name in parentese, the mothers would also touch the object to the child, thus adding a third source of coordinated sensory information. For instance, one mother of an eight-month-old said "flo" four times in a series and simultaneously shook the toy shark from side to side in full view of her infant and also against her infant's leg.

"Multimodal motherese" is the term the researchers coined to refer to this way in which the mothers naturally engage their babies through more than one sensory modality to facilitate learning. In this experiment, 99.99 percent of the mothers' utterances of the new words were multimodal.

The vast majority of the times the mothers in the study with the youngest babies (five- to eight-month-olds) said one of the new words, she did so in temporal synchrony with object motion. The mothers of nine- to seventeen-month-olds linked the name with motion just over half of the time. And for the mothers with twenty-one- to thirty-month-olds, the percentage of time dropped down to about a third. As babies get older, they are more able to detect word-referent relations, so temporal synchrony becomes less important, and mothers tailor their communication accordingly. Also, the older the baby, the more likely the mothers in this study would be to name the object or action while the child held or manipulated the object, showing more evidence that mothers adjust their communication based on their child's level of development (Gogate, Bahrick, and Watson, 2000).

The Interpretation

This multimodal form of motherese is likely a natural behavior that has evolved in order to teach infants words that refer to objects and the actions they perform. This technique exemplifies parents' ability to adjust their interactions with their babies in such a way as to provide just enough support to their babies to advance development.

It's not just with teaching words that parents are able to adjust their level of involvement, but with other activities as well.

What Should Parents Do?

Let's say your sixteen-month-old child likes viewing the pictures on your iPhone, but soon he's determined to page through the pictures on his own. At first you hold his finger, moving it across the screen to view the pictures. Quickly, he catches on to the technique and can complete the task for himself. He's delighted that he's competent to manage the task and view a series of pictures of himself and others.

This method of providing just enough support to advance a child's development is referred to as the zone of proximal development (Vygotsky, 1978). This zone refers to the gap between what children can accomplish on their own and what they're trying to accomplish. In the last experiment, the children were trying to learn a new word-referent relationship so at first parents communicated multimodally (using sight, sound, movement, and sometimes touch), but then as the children didn't need such experiences to pick up on the meaning of new words, parents backed off with their involvement. Sensitive parents and others, such as siblings, slightly older peers, and teachers, provide just enough assistance so that the less skilled child can eventually accomplish independently what she can now accomplish only with assistance from others. This assistance allows the child to go beyond her current level of competence to the next step in accomplishing a task. The parent senses what the child is trying to do by knowing the child's skill level and reading her signals; the parent then gives just the right amount of support to reach the goal.

Physical Reasoning Starts with Sensory Experiences

Young children are active learners engaging with their environment to become competent in it. They use their senses together to understand about objects and in doi...

physical phenomena that surroun...

A physicist understands tech...

ious situations depending on th...

a baby is not a technician in this reg...

for physical consistencies in the enviro...

dict what's safe and what's alarming. For ...

how vacuums work. After they become famil...

(some children are afraid of vacuums at first), they ...

ested in what the vacuum will suck up. In time, they re...

vacuums suck up little things but not big things. So if a sma...

was being sucked up by a vacuum cleaner, the child wouldn...

think a thing about it, but if a big ball somehow was malleable

enough to get sucked up by a vacuum cleaner, the child would

wonder why.

The Research

In a set of experiments, researchers investigated the ability of five-month-olds to coordinate tactile and visual information and then make use of that information to interpret physical events—in this case, a ball going through a tunnel.

First, each infant was acquainted with a tunnel and the testing situation. The experimenter lifted and moved the cardboard tunnel for the baby, showing her that it was rigid, open at both ends, and unobstructed.

Next, each infant was shown a ball that appeared to the infants to go through the tunnel. Two screens hid the ends of the tunnel; the ball disappeared behind the screen on one side and emerged at the appropriate later time from behind the screen at the other end. Some infants were shown a ball that was small enough to fit

92 Amazing Mi...

through th...
looking ...
was too ...
anywa...
seco...
ind...
p...

tunnel easily. The infants looked at the event, and their
me was recorded. For another group of infants, the ball
big to fit through the tunnel, but it appeared to go through
y (due to experimenter sleight of hand). The infants in this
d group looked significantly longer at this "impossible" event,
icating that it wasn't what they had expected to happen. The
ysical reasoning of the five-month-olds was developed enough
so that they knew such a big ball couldn't pass through the small
tunnel. Then in a second experiment, with a new group of babies,
the researchers allowed the babies to touch a ball without seeing
it, before watching the ball appear to pass through a tunnel as in
the first experiment. One ball was compressible, the other rigid,
both of the same size, matching the size of the ball the babies
would see pass through a tunnel. Two tunnels were used, one larger
than the size of the balls, one smaller.

The looking time of the infants who watched the ball go
through the large tunnel was the same whether they had touched
the compressible or the rigid ball prior to viewing the event. They
knew that either ball could fit through the tunnel.

In contrast, when the infants watched the too-big ball "go
through" the small tunnel, those who had previously touched the
rigid ball looked much longer at the event than those who had
previously touched the compressible ball. The infants who touched
the compressible ball apparently realized its pliability and that it
could squish up and go through the tunnel, so they were not surprised by the pass-through event. But the infants who touched the
rigid ball realized it couldn't be made to fit through the tunnel and
were surprised to see it appear to pass through. These results suggest that what infants learn about objects through touch has a
profound effect on how they interpret physical events (Schweinle
and Wilcox, 2004).

The Interpretation

This experiment drives home the point that by adding the sensation of touch, the babies are better able to make determinations about their physical world. It stands to reason that as babies incorporate their senses, they process information more efficiently, learn faster, and show better memory. As babies' capacity for using several senses at the same time develops, they're better equipped to actively understand the orderliness of the predictable physical world in which they live.

What Should Parents Do?

Get out some shoe boxes. Put soft and hard toys in the boxes as your child watches. Allow your child to touch the various compressible and rigid toys. Your child will be intrigued that you can squeeze more soft toys into the boxes than hard toys. As your child learns to sit and his dexterity improves, he'll manage putting toys in and out of these boxes; he'll be engaged in this activity all on this own.

As your child continues to develop, allow your infant and later your toddler time to see, touch, smell, taste, and listen to the sounds of various objects. By doing so he'll store in his memory the taste, texture, sound, sight, and scent of everything in his environment, such as his beloved blanket and teddy bear and his favorite ball, box, and book.

When your baby is mouthing baby-safe objects, know that this experience is a sensory activity that will be stored up in his memory. Therefore, when it's time to change your baby's diaper and you see him mouthing a squishy toy giraffe, allow him to take the giraffe along to the changing table. By doing so, you're respecting his involvement in this sensory learning activity.

There are some children who seem to have more difficulty than others in sorting out sensory stimulation. If when you take your child to any new environment, she consistently can't adjust to the sensations she experiences, talk to your child's doctor about her behavior; the doctor might suggest therapy to help integrate her senses.

Also be aware that it's not only babies whose senses get overloaded. This same situation can happen with older children. When you realize an older child's senses are overloaded, eliminate unnecessary sensory stimulation and allow your child to play with water at the sink or bring out play dough; these activities permit the child to combine his senses while focusing on one simple sensory task, which provides a calming effect. Unstructured physical activities such as bicycle riding, running, and swinging also help to synchronize a child's disconnected and overstimulated senses.

If going to school, soccer practice, then piano lessons, and finally homework ends with your child in tears, you may need to make some changes in her extracurricular activities.

If going to the circus with its three rings of activity and the various vendors calling out to audience members, to buy cotton candy, toy monkeys, and the like is too much for a child to manage, the family might need to leave early and head for home.

Also, remember the research by Jeffrey Pickens that involved the two trains, one moving forward and the other moving away, that was then accompanied by the train's sound either getting louder or fainter. The children at five months matched the movement of the train with the appropriate sound of coming or going. This skill of recognizing sound patterns will serve your child well as he strikes out into the world and learns how bicycles, cars, and trains and their respective noises become louder as they approach

and fainter as they move away from him. In time, when this awareness is combined with vision, he'll learn to move his body accordingly for safety's sake.

When your child is about three years old, a fun game to make
or purchase is a "feel box." This is nothing more than a box filled
with familiar items—a key, a ball, a button—which a child can
pick up and hold without seeing them, and then guess what's she's
holding.

Now you know that babies are working to refine their ability
to use senses together. It's work that the baby is attempting to accomplish, but the work isn't easy. Therefore, when attempting to
rock your baby to sleep, resist talking on your cell phone, because
the movement of the chair and your conversation will conflict.
Your baby won't be able to settle down. When you stop your conversation, and then sing softly while rocking your child in time to
the music, your baby will be content as his senses of sound and
movement mesh rather than clash. The moment will pass more
pleasantly for you and your baby once you adjust yourself to the
baby's need to have what he hears coordinate with the movement
of the rocking chair.

Think of a grandpa making silly popping sounds with his
mouth while moving his head back and forth in time to the sounds.
Some might say it's an okay activity for Grandpa, but isn't it better
for the child's intellectual development to provide a DVD for baby
to view?

The research in this chapter shows that Grandpa knows best.
His activity addresses the child's need to combine sensory stimulation. Grandpa knows what baby likes, and now you know why:
this simple activity helps baby combine what she sees with what
she hears; a skill everyone seeks to master.

Lastly, keep in mind the zone of proximal development discussed earlier in this chapter. Recall that this term refers to the gap

between what a child can do on his own and what a parent, teacher, coach, or mentor must guide the child to do. Caregivers fill in this gap by offering just enough support so that the child can eventually become competent on his own. Most parents have a sense for a child's need for help balanced with the child's desire to succeed in accomplishing various tasks all on her own. This sense serves children well. You'll use it often, but most apparently when your child learns to ride a bicycle. You'll hold onto the back of the bike and run along behind until you sense your child has found his balance, at which time you'll let go. He'll fall once or twice until, with practice, he can manage to ride on his own, and once he does, he'll never forget. Learning to cut with a knife, pound a nail with a hammer, use the remote control on the TV, use a computer, read, and swim all require parents to step into this zone of proximal development in order for the child to gain competency with as much support and as little frustration as possible.

REFERENCES:

Bahrick, L. E., R. Flom, and R. Lickliter. 2003. Intersensory redundancy facilitates discrimination of tempo in 3-month-old infants. *Developmental Psychobiology* 41: 352–63.

Gogate, L. J., and L. E. Bahrick. 2001. Intersensory redundancy and seven-month-old infants' memory for arbitrary syllable-object relations. *Infancy* 2: 219–31.

Gogate, L. J., L. E. Bahrick, and J. D. Watson. 2000. A study of multi-modal motherese: The role of temporary synchrony between verbal labels and gestures. *Child Development* 71: 878–94.

Kaye, K. L., and T. G. R. Bower. 1994. Learning and intermodal transfer of information in newborns. *Psychological Science* 5: 286–88.

Kuhl, P. K., and A. N. Meltzoff. 1982. The bimodal perception of speech in infancy. *Science* 218: 1138–41.

Meltzoff, A. N., and R. W. Borton. 1979. Intermodal matching by human neonates. *Nature* 282: 403–4.

Pickens, J. 1994. Perception of auditory-visual distance relations by 5-month-old infants. *Developmental Psychology* 30: 537–44.

Schweinle, A., and T. Wilcox. 2004. Intermodal perception and physical reasoning in young infants. *Infant Behavior and Development* 27: 246–65.

Spelke, E. S. 1976. Infants' intermodal perception of events. *Cognitive Psychology* 8: 553–60.

Vygotsky, L. S. 1978. *Mind in Society.* Cambridge, MA: Harvard University Press.

Chapter 4

Imitating and Remembering

As you now realize, babies arrive equipped with various abilities. In addition to using their already working senses, and working to combine them, a child arrives equipped to imitate a few mouth movements that parents display.

Baby See, Baby Do

From birth, babies are interested in imitating mouth movements and able to do it. They can't copy people clapping their hands, but they can copy certain actions a parent or other caregiver makes with his or her mouth. Babies are born with well-developed lips and tongues. So if a person sticks her tongue out at a baby a few times then pauses and waits, the newborn will likely stick his tongue back at that person. Since babies can imitate such behaviors with the mouth and tongue, playing imitation games is a fun and appropriate way to use a baby's innate ability while engaging with him. Sticking out the tongue is an action that a baby can copy; it's an appropriate—although somewhat silly-looking—way to interact with an infant.

The Research

Infant researcher Andrew Meltzoff set out to prove babies' ability to imitate. He visited neonates in the hospital right after birth. When a baby was in the quiet alert state, Dr. Meltzoff would stick out his tongue and later open his mouth. Within seventy-two hours after birth, most babies would respond on cue by copying his mouth movements. The youngest on record was forty-two minutes old (Meltzoff and Moore, 1977; Meltzoff and Moore, 1983).

Now, if Dr. Meltzoff had snapped his fingers at the baby, that would have been an impossible skill for a newborn to imitate. But babies are able to thrust their tongues out of their mouths and open and protrude their lips, and will do so in response to seeing another human being do the same thing. Imitating behaviors of the mouth and other areas of the face are the first actions that babies enjoy and are able to duplicate.

The Interpretation

How can it happen that tiny babies have the ability to copy behavior? How did each baby in the research experiment know that she was like Dr. Meltzoff and could do what he could do? It's another wonder of life. Although the infants cannot see their own faces, they perceive them. Somehow they know that their faces can do what the person in front of them can do.

At some level, babies must know that in order to survive they'll need to learn to manage themselves in a variety of environments. It's going to take a long time before they can read a how-to manual for getting along in the world, so they come equipped to watch the important people who surround them and to learn by imitating what they do. There are other ways children learn, but imitation is particularly quick and efficient.

What Should Parents Do?

Since you likely want to engage with a baby, when a baby sends the message that he wants to socialize, you can do so by slowly thrusting your tongue out of your mouth. Then it's important to wait and give the child a little time to respond. Don't be surprised if the baby does exactly what you did. Next, open your lips slowly. Give the baby time to notice and respond. Later, purse your lips. Again, be sure to give the baby response time. It's a fun game that baby truly enjoys.

By doing this, you're engaging with the baby in a way that meets the child's skill level and interest. Later, the baby will copy you as you blink your eyes, shake or nod your head. It's the perfect parent-child exchange that babies seek, and it's gratifying to both participants.

Deferred Imitation

As you and your baby interact during the first year of her life, you'll likely play imitation games. When you do, you'll most likely do so in real time. You bang the table with your hand; your six-month-old copies you. You put a blanket over your head to play peekaboo; your nine-month-old does the same. While changing your baby's diaper, you may purse your lips and then blow out some air, making a "raspberry," and lo and behold your child mimics your actions.

Then one day let's say you decide to hang a picture. As you go about the task, your fourteen-month-old watches you intently. To your knowledge your child has never seen you or anyone else take a nail and pound it with a hammer and then place a picture on the nail. The next day your baby picks up the hammer that you left on the coffee table and proceeds to bang it against the wall.

Although you're alarmed and instantly take the hammer from your child's hand, you're also amazed that he remembered what you did yesterday with the hammer and that he's trying this skill out for himself. He remembered and copied your actions. This is called deferred imitation. While this one isolated event amazes you, there's likely much more that your baby has learned and remembered by watching you and others.

The Research

In one research project with two parts, an experimenter demonstrated particular actions on three objects to nine-month-old babies who were sitting on their mothers' lap. The first object was an L-shaped construction: a wooden rectangle lying flat on the table, connected by a hinge to another wooden rectangle oriented vertically. The experimenter would push at the vertical piece so that it would fold down on top of the other piece. The second object was a small box that had a button on it. The experimenter would push the button, which would trigger a beeping sound. The third object was a plastic egg, filled with metal nuts. The experimenter would shake the egg creating an interesting noise.

After the experimenter demonstrated each object, he gave the babies the opportunity to try each one. Half of the babies copied two or three of the actions they had just seen the experimenter do with each of the objects. The other babies copied one or none of the actions. Clearly, babies at nine months are starting to learn how to imitate simple actions. Then in the second study, with a new group of babies, the experimenter did exactly the same thing, demonstrated the same actions with the same objects, but this time after the demonstrations, the babies went home. They were not given an opportunity to use the objects for themselves. Then the next day, the babies returned to the laboratory. Now, without seeing the experimenter use the objects again, they had the opportunity to use the objects for themselves. Would they remember what they had seen the experimenter do with the objects the day before and imitate him? The answer was yes. In fact, the results were the same as in the first study: half of the babies copied two or three of the actions, the others copied one or none. The delay did not interfere with the babies' abilities to perform the actions (Meltzoff, 1988a).

It's important to know that there were control groups in both studies. In each study, another group of babies had the opportunity to try out these same three objects without seeing them demonstrated first by an experimenter. While the babies in the control groups performed some of the target acts spontaneously, the babies who had seen them demonstrated performed significantly more of those acts. Over both studies, 20 percent of the babies in the demonstration groups performed all three actions, 0 percent of the control group babies performed all three. The researchers concluded that there was evidence that nine-month-olds can learn simple actions just by watching them, and imitate those actions even after a twenty-four-hour delay.

With a new group of children a few months older, researchers conducted another similar experiment. This time, however, the researchers demonstrated particular actions with five unique objects for twelve-month-olds. In this study, not only were the children presented with more objects, but this time for some babies the demonstrations occurred in an unusual looking tent, for others at home, and for others in a plain lab room. For all the babies there was a delay between viewing the demonstration and then having a chance to manipulate the objects themselves in the plain lab room. As opposed to the previous study, the delay ranged from one day to four weeks. In all the groups, the babies who saw the object demonstrations—no matter how long a delay—produced more of those target acts than babies who did not see the demonstrations. Even the children whose demonstrations occurred away from the lab were able to retain much of what they saw and replicate it in the lab later (Klein and Meltzoff, 1999).

In the next experiment, with an entirely different set of fourteen-month-old children, experimenters demonstrated five actions that were potentially somewhat familiar to the children. The experimenter pulled an object with a string, flattened a wooden hinged L-object, pushed a button on a box causing it to beep, rattled a plastic egg with metal nuts inside, and jiggled a string causing a bear at the other end of it to dance. Then the experimenter demonstrated a completely novel act. He leaned over from the waist and touched his forehead to a plastic panel on top of a box causing it to light up.

After the children watched these demonstrations, they went home for a week. Then they returned to the laboratory and were presented with the six objects. How many actions would they remember and which ones? Would they remember the more familiar toy pulling, object flattening, button pushing, egg rattling, and bear dancing displays or the completely novel act of the experimenter's head touching a panel resulting in the panel lighting up?

The results of this study were also quite revealing. Whereas only 12 percent of the babies in the control group performed three or more of the target acts spontaneously, 92 percent of the children who witnessed the target acts performed three or more of them. As for the novel act, 67 percent of the babies who had witnessed the demonstration repeated it, but none of the babies in the control groups performed the unusual act spontaneously.

The researchers noted that the babies who imitated the targeted actions did so directly and confidently. They seemed equally or more engaged in producing the novel act (forehead pressing on the panel that lighted up). When they watched the researcher produce the act during the demonstration, they appeared to be quizzical and frowning, but when they had the opportunity to try the panel out for themselves, they smiled triumphantly upon making a successful performance (Meltzoff, 1988b).

The Interpretation

From these three research projects there is much to behold about babies' ability to imitate and remember. Babies are drawn to watch the people around them. A baby's job is to become competent in his first environment which, of course, is his home. Therefore he watches his parents use various objects around the house: the vacuum cleaner, the toaster, and the sink's faucet, to name only a few. While at first the child may not have the skill to use such objects as his parents do, once he gains the skills, he's eager to try out using various objects for himself. He wants to mimic what Mom and Dad do with these objects and use them for himself as he attempts to master his environment.

While the child probably does remember most of the objects that his parents use, it's the unique object he's most fascinated with and eager to try out for himself. Use a toaster that your child has seen you use day after day, he's likely bored with it. Pull out the orange juice squeezer that you use only on special occasions, and he'll be highly engaged as you demonstrate its use. Given a choice, your child will be intrigued by the seldom used orange juice squeezer over the daily used toaster even though it might be more of a challenge to understand because it's less familiar.

If you go to a foreign country, when you come home you don't tell of the traditions, mores, and customs that are similar to yours; you're drawn to describe the unique events of the culture you visited. These you noticed and remembered as you attempted to be successful in this new environment. So it is with your child. He becomes readily accustomed to the daily events, but a new event he watches closely until it becomes old hat.

What Should Parents Do?

While you may not want your child using the toaster independently for fear of burned fingers, or pushing a lever to squeeze the juice from an orange for fear of squeezed fingers, be aware of your child's drive to be competent using various objects and tools around the house. So ask and challenge yourself, "What can I allow my child to do as she seeks independence and competency?" Your relationship with your child will be better if your child sees you as a conduit to gaining mastery over each environment she encounters.

Also, take it upon yourself to test your child's powers of memory and mimicry. Let's say your mother owns a chest that has a unique method by which it opens: you need to move one lever with your left hand while turning a knob with your right. Demonstrate the device to your nine- to twelve-month-old each time you visit Grandma's. You might keep a few interesting objects and toys in the chest. Each time you visit, notice your child's interest in the chest and how it opens. If you do so, sometime between the ages of nine and twelve months you'll probably witness firsthand the power of your child's cognitive ability with regards to memory and mimicry—particularly relating to this novel opening device.

Another way to test your child's power of memory and mimicry is to set out your mobile phone and notice what your child does with it. Prior to age two, she's not pretending to talk to anyone, she's remembering and copying your actions and believes she's doing exactly what you've been doing with it. She's highly interested in using this device that she's seen you use intently with high priority and skill.

Imitating Peers

Children seek to be competent in each environment they enter. One way they accomplish skills is to mimic Mom and Dad, brothers and sisters, and other important people such as grandparents and caregivers. There's another group of people your children will watch and learn from: peers. Now, some may think that the pressure to imitate peers won't surface until a child enters elementary, middle, or high school. Researchers found that imitating peers occurs far sooner.

The Research

Fourteen-month-old toddlers came to a research laboratory where experimenters taught them how to use four unique and interesting toys in specific ways. Then the researchers took the toddlers to child-care centers where they demonstrated these specific actions with the toys to similar-aged peers. The onlookers were highly interested in the skilled toddlers' demonstration but were not allowed to try out the objects for themselves. Two days later an experimenter visited the homes of the onlookers, made the toys available to them, and watched as the children who had only witnessed an accomplished peer play with the toys now had an opportunity to interact with the toys themselves. Would they remember and copy what they had seen a peer do two days prior? Yes, they performed significantly more of the specific actions demonstrated by their "expert" peer than a control group of toddlers who had not witnessed the demonstration. Not only can fourteen-month-old children copy their peers, but they can remember what they learn in one environment and demonstrate it in another (Hanna and Meltzoff, 1993).

The Interpretation

Now you realize that your child will be learning from peers from a young age. Children will try out all sorts of behaviors that they see peers exhibit, whether it be cutting with child-safe plastic scissors or grabbing those scissors from another rather than waiting for a turn.

What Should Parents Do?

All the years you raise your children, they'll encounter positive and negative peer influences. Some you can screen, some you can't. It is your parenting job to seek environments where your children will have the most opportunity to gain positive influences from kind, productive, and responsible peers.

You can also use peer tutoring to your advantage. Let's say your child is reluctant to use the toilet. Bring a willing friend to your home to demonstrate her skill on the toilet. If your child can observe an accomplished peer use the toilet, your child might be inspired to imitate that behavior, ultimately leading to toileting success.

On the other hand, you may have never seen your mild-mannered toddler push another child to attain a toy. Then at a family holiday gathering your child sees a cousin with an attractive toy. Your child walks over, pushes the cousin, and grabs the toy right out of his hands. You're aghast! Where did he learn this aggressive behavior? It may have been from peers at his child-care center. There are both pros and cons to peer involvement even from a very young age.

Imitating Actions from the TV Screen

What about screens? Parents know that children often stop playing and glance at or become riveted to the visually changing mosaic of colors on a video screen. Once parents realize that their child is attracted to the images on the screen of a TV or computer, they may also wonder when they can expect to see children mimic behavior they've viewed there.

The Research

Researchers wondered if toddlers would imitate what they had seen on the two-dimensional TV screen in the world of real three-dimensional objects. They brought fourteen- and twenty-four-month-old children into the laboratory to watch a video recording of a person pulling apart a dumbbell-shaped object constructed out of wooden blocks connected with hollow tubes. Then with little delay, some of the toddlers in the study were given the object to see if they would copy the adult's action. The others went home and returned after twenty-four hours for their opportunity to play with the unusual object. The results showed significant imitation at both ages and in both the immediate-imitation condition and the deferred-imitation condition. This research indicates that the toddlers understood and remembered the actions they saw on TV and applied them to their real three-dimensional world.

The Interpretation

The actions that the toddlers viewed on TV were simple and purposely performed by an actor in a slow and deliberate manner. Therefore, they were unlike most TV programs, which are fast-moving and action-packed. Nevertheless, the research makes the point that fourteen-month-old children are able to mimic some two-dimensional actions from a screen (Meltzoff, 1988b).

What Should Parents Do?

Parents need to be fully aware that what young children see on a video screen can be a powerful influence. If a video screen is part of your child's environment, make sure that what the child views is positive and age-appropriate, not negative and violent, and that parents view with their children so they will be their child's filter for any perplexing or questionable experiences. It's important for parents to keep in mind also that the American Academy of Pediatrics recommends to pediatricians that when advising parents they "discourage television viewing for children younger than two years, and encourage more interactive activities that will promote proper brain development, such as talking, playing, singing and reading together" (American Academy of Pediatrics Committee on Public Education, 2001).

Mimicry Builds Relationships

Beyond learning how to complete various tasks using objects and tools, imitation seems to provide young children with a deeper understanding of self and others. Children, like all of us, know when they're being imitated and like it. It's the highest form of flattery.

Let's say you're baking bread. Your sister-in-law, who is visiting you, watches you and says, "Would you please show me how to do that?" You're flattered. She's interested in what you're doing and wants to copy you. You give her some of the dough, and she mimics your action as you knead the bread. Not only does her imitative behavior flatter you and your skill at bread baking, but because she's interested in what you're doing and how you're doing it, the activity builds your relationship with her.

There seems to be something else going on as well. By seeing her imitate your bread kneading actions, you learn about yourself: why you're doing what you're doing; how you came to learn this skill; and how you can more precisely describe your actions so that your sister-in-law can best learn the skill for herself.

Since we know that children are great imitators from birth, we also know that it's an efficient way for them to learn just about anything, from eating with a spoon to tying their shoes. It's also important that parents and caregivers return the favor and copy what children do, because when you do, children learn about themselves and find pleasure when another mimics them, and hence a more reciprocal relationship develops.

The Research

In a laboratory setting, researchers brought in fourteen-month-old children one at a time and gave each of them a toy to play with. Across the table from the toddler sat two adults: one who mimicked exactly what the child did with the toy and the other who displayed other childlike actions with the toy, which may have included shaking, sliding, pounding, poking, mouthing, or touching the toy to the head, shoulder, or neck. The research question was whether the children would respond to the experimenter who was imitating him. Would the children be aware of their own actions and recognize them being imitated by another? Would the children focus on the person imitating them or would they be interested in watching and imitating some of the actions of the experimenters who were manipulating the same toy but doing their own baby-like things with it?

As it turns out, the babies in the research study watched the experimenter who mimicked their own actions with the toy more than they watched the other experimenter. They seemed to notice and suspect they were being imitated and set out to "test" their suspicions by adjusting their own behaviors and checking to see if the experimenter was doing the same. Not only did the children watch and test the mimicker more than the other adult, but they smiled at that experimenter more too, obviously pleased with the person who was mimicking their behavior (Meltzoff, 1990).

The Interpretation

Why did the children smile at the person imitating them? The children were likely pleased with themselves because they were worthy of an adult's imitative behavior. If the children could talk, they might have said, "I'm doing this and so is he. Seeing my actions by another validates me and my actions." When an adult imitates a child, it communicates to the child that an adult is interested in him and admires him enough to copy him.

There's something else that seems to be special about reproducing a child's actions that parents and caregivers can learn from. Recall from the research that the children in the study focused on and smiled at the experimenter who copied the child's actions with the toy. Therefore when you copy a child's behaviors, realize that the child likes it, and therefore will probably like the person mimicking him. Since mimicry, not mockery, elicits smiles, thereby engaging the child and bringing about happiness, you're creating a positive interaction between you and the child; it's a positive way to solidify and strengthen your relationship.

What Should Parents Do?

When your child puts her hands together playing patty-cake, copying it reinforces the action, and you'll likely see more of this positive activity. Then, when your child needs attention, she'll likely do a little patty-caking in hopes of bringing about the same behavior from you. Mimicking a child's positive behavior reinforces it and teaches positive ways of gaining attention. Not only that, but it simultaneously builds your relationship.

Let's say Grandma and Grandpa are coming to visit for a couple of weeks. They live in Florida, you Seattle. It's been several months since their last visit. You're worried. Your child is wary of unfamiliar people, and it's clear that he likes you and his daddy best. How can you help your parents develop a relationship with your son in such a short amount of time?

The answer is easy, have Grandma and Grandpa take turns copying his behavior. Here's what to do: go into a room with toys—could be a bedroom, playroom, or family room. You talk to one of your parents while the other goes into the play area with your son. Coach your mom and dad prior to the play session, encouraging them to watch closely what the child does and to do as he does. When he scoots a car across the room, the attending grandparent is to do the same. When the child puts one block on top of the other, the grandparent does the same. The child runs across the floor, the grandparent does the same. If Grandpa or Grandma doesn't actually run, he or she can watch the child and say, "Look at you, you're running across the floor." Describing children's behavior is almost as affirming as copying it. Watch the child: he'll be pleased and will smile at the mimicker, who is building a relationship with him. Later, have the other grandparent take a turn being the copycat.

Also encourage the grandparents to reflect the child's speech. If your child says *ba* for ball, they can either say *ba* or they can say, "Yes, that's the ball." Or "Look at the ball roll across the floor."

Continue these copycatting sessions for a few days, then if you and your spouse decide to have a day away while Grandma and Grandpa babysit, you won't need to worry; your child and the grandparents will have built a rapport that all started because your parents mimicked their grandchild's behavior.

Reflecting a child's speech and copying a child's actions affirm her existence; it's actually the highest form of flattery. No child can resist its pleasure. It's the perfect place to start when working to build a loving and liking relationship with any child, no matter the age.

Parents and others closely connected to a child need to watch their behavior. Children are eager to learn by copying what others do. A child doesn't know the difference between behaviors that people wish him to copy and behaviors that they would like the child to overlook. Modeling is the most powerful teacher, overriding other forms of learning. The "do as I say" approach doesn't work with kids. Kids do as the important people in their lives do, and it starts within the first seventy-two hours after birth. The message is clear: watch what you do, because you'll likely see it repeated in children who are observing you.

By the time a child becomes a toddler you'll see him imitating all sorts of actions; everything from brushing his teeth, to pretending to shave, to combing his hair, to using a tissue to wipe his nose.

It's also important to be aware that children not only imitate parents' actions, but their language as well. One young mom learned the hard way in this example. On the Saturday before Easter, she dolled up her two-and-a-half-year-old daughter in her Easter dress, hat, and basket. It was a bright, sunny day as they headed to a neighborhood Easter egg hunt with cousins, grandparents, aunts, and uncles. As the two-and-a-half-year-old exited the family van, with consternation in her voice, she reprimanded herself by saying, "Oh sh—, I forgot my sunglasses." Her horrified mother blushed with embarrassment and family members chuckled. Ultimately, the mother terminated her swearing ways as she realized that her daughter wasn't only copying her as she combed her hair, cooked dinner, read the newspaper, and said "please" and "thank you."

Keep in mind too that from at least about fourteen months, possibly younger, you'll likely witness behaviors exhibited by your children that they learned from peers, some of which you'll deem inappropriate. When you do, speak up. Say something to the effect of "In Jesse's family it's okay to throw a ball in the house, but in our family it isn't" or "Jesse's mom let's her chew gum, but doing so is not okay with me."

Then there's television. You know now that children from at least age fourteen months mimic behavior they see on TV; therefore it's important to monitor screen viewing closely. Do your best to keep your children from viewing programs where actors display behaviors that you wouldn't want your children to perform for themselves in real life. This is an enormous job for parents today, when TV, video, computer, and cell phone screens invade most aspects of daily lives. Develop clear rules for their usage, for when and where their interruptions are okay. Establish these rules when your children are young, then adjust them as children travel the developmental years, but convey the message that screens are a privilege, not an entitlement, and that parents establish rules regarding their availability. It's far easier to set consistent rules from the beginning than to realize that screen use is out of control in your home and seek to change established patterns later on. Parents will also need to have open discussions appropriate to the child's age and ability, explaining why it's important to limit screen time, including exposure to video games and their addictive effect.

If a parent is highly dependent on his cell phone and uses it intensely and with high priority for his business and personal life, he'll likely see his young toddler copy this behavior. If the parent wants his child to imitate other behavior such as helping others, praying, or reading, he needs to exhibit these activities with the same eagerness with which he uses his cell phone.

There is a lot to keep in mind with respect to children's ability to imitate, but most importantly, realize that children are great imitators and it's an efficient way for them to learn just about anything. Make sure that what they imitate is positive and productive, not negative and damaging.

REFERENCES

American Academy of Pediatrics Committee on Public Education. 2001. Children, adolescents, and television. *Pediatrics* 107: 423-6.

Hanna, E., and A. N. Meltzoff. 1993. Peer imitation by toddlers in laboratory, home, and day-care contexts: Implications for social learning and memory. *Developmental Psychology* 29: 701–10.

Klein, P. J., and A. N. Meltzoff. 1999. Long-term memory, forgetting, and deferred imitation in 12-month-old infants. *Developmental Science* 2: 102–13.

Meltzoff, A. N. 1988a. Infant imitation and memory: Nine-month-olds in immediate and deferred tests. *Child Development* 59: 217–25.

Meltzoff, A. N. 1988b. Infant imitation after a 1-week delay: Long-term memory for novel acts and multiple stimuli. *Developmental Psychology* 24: 470–76.

Meltzoff, A. N. 1988c. Imitation of televised models by infants. *Child Development 59*: 1221–29.

Meltzoff, A. N. 1990. Foundations for developing a concept of self: The role of imitation in relating self to other and the value of social mirroring, social modeling, and self practice in infancy. In: Cicchetti, D., and M. Beeghly, eds. *The Self in Transition: Infancy to Childhood.* Chicago, IL: University of Chicago Press.

Meltzoff, A. N., and M. K. Moore. 1977. Imitation of facial and manual gestures by human neonates. *Science* 198: 75–8.

Meltzoff, A. N., and M. K. Moore. 1983. Newborn infants imitate adult facial gestures. *Child Development 54*: 702–9.

Chapter 5

Physical Reasoning

As you now realize, your baby is learning to use and combine her senses, she loves hearing your voice when speaking in parentese, and she's interested in imitating your facial expressions. Your baby is also learning about the physical world around her and how she impacts it. One day your baby might be lying on her back in her crib wiggling her arms and legs, exercising. When doing so, she might notice that her mobile attached to the side of the crib moves. This she likes because she's aware that she can make things happen. Not only that, when she's crying because she's hungry, she realizes that when mommy enters the room, picks her up, sits down in the rocker, and lifts her blouse to allow her to nurse, this sequence of events indicates that nourishment is on the way.

And there is more about the physical world that a baby is aware of and it's pretty amazing. In the first year babies understand that objects such as toy cars, wagons, and tricycles cannot move themselves but need to be propelled into motion. They also realize that people all on their own move themselves.

On top of watching for events to confirm their understanding about people propelling themselves and objects needing to be propelled, babies are also interested in stable and unstable objects. Set a vase full of flowers on the edge of a table and your baby will likely show concern. Keeping in mind a baby's interest in physical phenomena, notice her interest in balls as they roll around a room, bounce down steps, and shoot down a ramp. The physical world involves properties that a child seeks to understand. He's actually a little physicist trying to understand gravity, propulsion, and balance.

Cause-and-Effect Learning

If a baby lies in her crib looking at a mobile overhead that is attached to the crib, then wiggles and, by doing so, causes her mobile to dance about overhead, this situation is nothing less than exciting to her. The baby at some level feels powerful and in control of her environment, as if saying, "I can make things happen!"

The Research

As you know, when your baby is lying on her back and in a state that's quiet and alert, she'll exercise by raising her legs and kicking. Researchers used three-month-old babies' natural inclination to do so in this research study. They observed each baby in his crib at home. First, they installed a mobile over the crib, then after laying the baby in the crib, they counted the number of kicks the baby made in three minutes, determining a baseline kick rate. Next they tied one end of a ribbon to an ankle and the other end to the mobile hanging overhead. Quickly the babies learned that by kicking their legs, they could make the mobile jiggle, a spectacle they seemed to like. The learning was evident by the fact that in three to six minutes the babies doubled or tripled their kicking speed.

The researchers realized that the babies had learned the skill, so they wanted to find out how well these three-month-old children would remember it over time. They untied the ribbon after nine minutes and the babies continued to kick at a fast rate, indicating a strong immediate memory of their ability to make the mobile move, but how strong would that memory be after a day, a week, or even longer?

At the end of the first session, the researchers removed the mobile. They returned with it twenty-four hours later and installed it again over the infants in their cribs. Upon seeing the mobile again, the infants didn't just kick at their baseline rate, they started kicking at the double or triple rate that they had learned on the previous day that really got the mobile to dance about overhead. This told the researchers that the babies still had a strong memory of what they had learned twenty-four hours earlier. After this memory test, the researchers again tied the ribbon connecting ankle to mobile, giving the infants the opportunity to practice moving the mobile for nine minutes. These first two sessions were referred to as "training" sessions.

The researchers waited for two weeks to do the next memory test. For some of the infants they provided a little reminder one day before the test. The reminder consisted of the experimenter jiggling the mobile above the infants for three minutes (the infants did not have the opportunity to control the mobile). When the infants who had received the reminder saw the mobile the next day, they started kicking just as fast as they had two weeks before, indicating their memory was at full strength.

In contrast, the infants who had *not* gotten the reminder did *not* kick fast when they saw the mobile; they showed no evidence of remembering what they had learned about how to get the mobile to jiggle two weeks before. Once the ribbon was tied, these babies took three to six minutes to double or triple their kick rates, learning to get that mobile to dance, just as if they had never done it before.

In another version of the experiment, the researchers repeated the same procedures, except that all the babies received a reminder and a distinctive context was provided for the training and reminder sessions: the researchers draped the end and sides of the crib with a distinctive-patterned, brightly colored broadcloth liner. One day after the reminder session, the babies' memories were tested, just as before. For some of the babies, the distinctive crib liner was present during the test session. These babies started kicking fast right away, as fast as they had just after training, exhibiting perfect memory retention. For other babies, the distinctive crib liner was not present during the test session. These babies, even though they had received the reminder, when tested in a different context, exhibited poor memory retention. Their kick rates were less than half of what they had been just after training. These findings indicate that a consistent distinctive context will help babies remember specific details of an event (Rovee-Collier, 1993; Hayne and Rovee-Collier, 1995).

The Interpretation

It's apparent that babies are interested in how they can affect occurrences in their environment, leading them eventually to manage at least parts of it competently all on their own. It was the strong desire of the infants to be able to control the mobile that allowed the researchers in these studies to tap into the workings of their memory systems. Put a mechanical toy aquarium on the side of your baby's crib, in time he'll know to pound the large button to trigger the music to play and the plastic fish to swim around in the fluid inside the case. Later you'll stack a few blocks and your child will delight in knocking them over. Such activities he'll do again and again in a variety of different ways to make sure that the blocks topple over every time when given a nudge.

If you and your baby visit Grandma's house at three months, and the next visit is weeks later, you may notice that after a little reminder, your baby will remember a fun activity unique to Grandma's house. Maybe Grandma will show him a little rattle she keeps at her house for his visits and then put it in his hand. He may quickly start to shake it, making it rattle, as he learned to do on the previous visit.

In time your child will want to copy you as you proficiently use the remote control on your TV. Push a button, there's a car commercial. Push another, there's a football game or an animated cartoon. It's all about cause-and-effect learning, "When I do this, that happens."

At first when babies learn a skill, as with the babies learning to kick to make the mobile move, they only retain the memory of how to do so when the environment is exactly the same. The context of the learning situation seems to trigger their memory. Eventually babies won't need these contextual cues to remember how to perform a skill they've just learned; they'll display the skill no matter the setting.

What Should Parents Do?

Let's say your baby falls asleep easily in her own crib at home. But now you're taking your baby to Grandma's house for the day. She'll be napping in Grandma's portable crib. Therefore, don't be surprised if she has trouble falling asleep; she'll need to do so in a crib that's far different from her familiar one at home. She'll learn to do so; it just might take a few trips to Grandma's before she can fall asleep as quickly as she does in her own room and crib. It will likely help your baby fall asleep at Grandma's if you bring along familiar items that are part of the naptime routine at home such as a favorite stuffed animal or blanket. If you always nurse while singing a naptime song to your baby before laying her down, doing the same at Grandma's will help as well, as we'll see next.

Counting Events in a Sequence

Part of your baby's interest in becoming competent in his own environment involves being able to predict when events occur. You follow a clock, but your baby can't, so he notices that one event follows another, and having events occur in a sequence helps him remember.

The Research

Researchers showed five-month-old babies a sequence of four pictures in a repeating, predictable pattern: three on the left then one on the right. The tempo of the left-side picture presentation varied (slow, average, or fast), but the pattern was always left, left, left, right, throughout the duration of the test. In the fast tempo presentation, the pictures were presented for half a second, with a half-second pause in between pictures; in the average tempo presentation, the time unit was one second, and in the slow presentation it was one-and-a-half seconds. The pictures were randomly selected from a set of five animated images (smiling face, turning head, running puppy, rotating wheel, and jumping stick figure). So a baby might have seen on the left a smiley face, followed by a running puppy, then a jumping stick figure, and then, on the right, a rotating wheel. Next the baby would see additional sequences of four pictures in the left, left, left, right pattern. Because the five-month-old babies were interested in seeing the pictures, they would look to the left and to the right to see all of the pictures.

In time, after they had seen the left, left, left, right pattern repeated, they would move their eyes in anticipation and expectation of seeing a picture on the right after watching three pictures on the left. Because the timing and tempo of the left-side picture presentation varied, it was only the number of pictures on the left that predicted when the picture on the right would appear next. Apparently, the babies learned to recognize when three pictures had appeared on the left, and that they should look to the right to see the fourth (Canfield and Smith, 1996).

The Interpretation

Were the babies counting the pictures on the left: "one ... two ... three"? Not really. They were able to keep track of events in a repeating sequence. It was an established sequence of events that your baby can follow.

Not only are babies able to follow a sequence of events, but doing so helps them to remember specific events in the sequence. For instance, let's say your bedtime routine consists of putting on pajamas, brushing teeth, and reading a story. If you consistently follow this routine in this order, your child will likely remember to always brush his teeth.

What Should Parents Do?

Create routines for your children and follow them consistently. Have morning routines, getting-out-the-door routines, putting-toys-away routines, and bedtime routines. If you can make up a cleanup or going-to-bed song, it will trigger the routine. Once you start singing the song, your child will shift into the routine auto-matically. Such routines make life predictable for you and your children. Teeth brushing is simply more challenging if you insist on it sporadically. If you do it consistently as part of the morning and bedtime routines, soon it becomes automatic.

Acting in a Sequence

We've seen that babies can recognize a visual sequence as early as five months, but what about acting out sequential events? By ten months old, when they imitate actions in the same order in which those actions were demonstrated, they remember more of them.

The Research

Researchers showed ten- and eleven-month-old babies a series of objects and demonstrated a target action with each of them. The first target action was making noise by moving a spatula back and forth within a small half barrel. The second was shaking a metal can containing dry grains of rice. The third was making a sound by pressing a large red button on the surface of a drum with a drum-stick. The fourth was removing a linen hat that was attached with Velcro to a stuffed pig.

Then after a thirty-minute delay the babies were given the op-portunity to use the objects for themselves. Some of the babies were given each item to use in exactly the same sequence as they had been demonstrated (barrel, can, drum, pig), the others were given the objects in a different order. The researchers observed how many of the target actions the babies completed.

As these target actions might be produced spontaneously by a baby, the researchers also had a control group of babies to find out as a basis of comparison how often that occurs. Without demonstrating the target actions, they gave the objects to the babies and observed how many of the actions these babies completed. The average number of actions completed was between one and two.

The babies who were given the objects to use in the same order as they had seen them demonstrated completed more target actions than the babies in the control group. These results confirmed those of similar experiments by Meltzoff and colleagues highlighted in Chapter 4, indicating once again that babies can learn simple actions just by watching them done and can imitate those actions later.

In contrast, the babies who received the objects in an order different from the order demonstrated did not seem to remember the target actions so well. These babies completed about the same number of target actions as the control group.

The Interpretation

Taken all together, these results indicate that the babies' memories were based not just on the individual objects and actions; their memories were also based upon the sequential relationship of the events. Therefore, receiving the objects in the same order as they had been demonstrated helped the babies remember the target actions on those objects (Knopf, Kraus, and Kressley-Mba, 2006).

What Should Parents Do?

Establish routines. Before bed, put your baby in a clean diaper, followed by jammies. Brush your baby's tooth or teeth. Then read a story, sing a song, or say a prayer. Turn on the same soothing lullaby. Soon your baby will expect each event to follow the other, which prepares her for sleep. Once you've established a routine, your child will notice if you try to leave out any part of it and likely remind you by protesting loudly.

Also know that established routines are hard to break, so be careful not to allow any negative elements to seep into them. If you scold your child each night before bed in an attempt to get him to lie down and fall asleep quickly, this scolding segment soon becomes part of the sequence of events in the bedtime routine. Therefore do your parenting best to make routines positive and pleasant, without any negative elements slipping in, as they are hard to eliminate once established.

As you now realize, your baby is aware of how she can cause events to occur, plus she's noticing routines, both yours and hers. Not only that, she realizes the difference between how animate and inanimate objects move and her role in causing objects to move.

Animate and Inanimate Objects Moving

Babies are great observers; they're very interested as objects and people move about the room. From watching, they come to know that there are different rules that apply to the movement of animate versus inanimate objects. For example, people and animals can move themselves; inanimate objects, such as chairs, boxes, and dolls, cannot.

The Research

Researchers had five- and seven-month-old babies watch a video of a hand picking up a doll repeatedly. The babies were interested at first, but after a while they turned bored (habituated). Half of the infants were then shown a similar video of a hand picking up the doll, but this time it was a different hand or a different direction of movement or there was some other visible change. The infants did not recover interest in looking at the videos with these changes. The other group of infants were shown a video similar to the first with the only change being the introduction of a small gap between the hand and the doll. The hand reached out as before to pick up the doll and then the hand moved away in tandem with the doll, but with no contact between the hand and the doll. The doll appeared to move on its own. With this situation, the babies perked up and took notice. This event violated what they expected to be true from their experience of watching objects move about a room. The babies knew that dolls aren't able to move on their own and so they were perplexed when they did so (Leslie, 1994).

The Interpretation

This ability to detect that a doll cannot move on its own but needs a hand to move it is fairly amazing. Somehow, from only watching, the baby realizes that the person's hand is self-propelled, but the doll must be carried. Babies are beginning to understand the difference between animate and inanimate objects, and one thing they recognize is that different causal principles apply when each type of object moves. They expect people and animals, not inanimate objects, to move independently and spontaneously.

If a child sees a wagon on the sidewalk, he's unconcerned because he knows it can't move on its own. If, however, he sees a dog sitting on the sidewalk, he'll be cautious because he knows that the dog can pick himself up at any time and move around all on his own. Children have an amazing capacity to categorize, even from the first months of life (more about that in another chapter). By categorizing the four-legged, furry creature as animate and the four-wheeled, metal-framed object as inanimate, and knowing the characteristics corresponding to each category, a child becomes more competent to manage in the world in which he lives.

What Should Parents Do?

Allow your child to experience the world of animate and inanimate objects. Most likely your home environment naturally provides all you need, which is people and animals moving around on their own and objects such as vehicles, vacuums, toys, and balls being propelled into motion by pushes and pulls, or by use of a gasoline engine, battery-powered electric motor, or windup mechanism. Also it's important to respect your child's interest in moving objects and offer her time and opportunity to determine how they're moving. If your child is watching leaves fall from a tree and it's time for dinner, postpone eating for a minute or so until your child is finished watching the leaves fall. When you realize that your baby is engaged in this observation activity, put words to it, "The leaves are falling from the trees. The wind is blowing them about. In the fall leaves drop from deciduous trees." While your child doesn't understand every word now, she'll come to understand them.

Knowing What Causes the Action

Babies notice that inanimate objects can't stop from bumping into one another but people can. Two balls moving toward each other will collide and then ricochet off each other, but two people moving in the same way will sense each other's presence and move on their own in another direction to avoid a collision. Babies seem to realize that some objects—people, birds, and bugs— have an internal force that moves them around and they do so autonomously, and these objects they put into the animate category. Other objects—cars, balls, and wagons—move by an external force or operator, and these they put into the inanimate category.

The Research

In a research study, eight-month-olds watched a video showing a head-on view of a freestanding wall about six feet tall and four feet wide. A person-sized, boxlike object on wheels was partially hidden behind the wall on the right side. From the left, a man with hands held in front of his chest, palms forward, walked behind the wall and disappeared from view. Then the boxlike object on wheels began to move to the right, out from the behind the wall. The babies were shown the video repeatedly until their looking time at each presentation dropped to a low level criterion—that is, they habituated.

The researchers wanted to know what the babies inferred to be the cause of the box's motion. To find the answer, they showed the babies a similar video, but this time there was no wall. One group of babies saw the man with hands held in front of his chest, palms forward, walk toward the box and stop without contacting it; then the box started moving on its own. Another group of babies saw the man walk toward the box, contact it with the palms of his hands (as if pushing), and then the box started moving. The babies looked longer at the spontaneously moving box than they did at the person pushing the box, providing evidence that the babies were surprised to see the box move itself. They expected the cause of the box's motion to be the person pushing it.

The experiment was repeated with another group of eight-month-olds, but with one difference. This time, a second man (who was facing the first man and walked backward to the right when in motion) replaced the box in the videos. This time the babies looked equally long to both test videos, indicating that they knew that the second man could start moving with or without contact from the first. The researchers suggested that the babies who saw the second man move without contact from the first may have appreciated the possibility that he did so in order to avoid a collision and saw nothing surprising about that (Kosugi and Fujita, 2002).

The Interpretation

Babies expect that people and other animate objects move around on their own, dictating their own movements. They've determined that people and animals are made up of biological material that allows them to move around, avoiding collisions, because they are in control of their movements. Objects, on the other hand, operate under a set of rules that are dictated by external physical forces such as boxes being pushed, balls rolling down ramps, and unstable objects falling off tables, counters, and sofas.

Therefore, if Mom and Dad one day bumped into each other as they walked across the kitchen, as people sometimes do, their baby would be surprised and might think it was funny and laugh his delightful baby laugh. If you're in a shopping mall and see two people oblivious to each other collide, you'll likely be surprised too. We expect that people can avoid such incidents. But we're never surprised when we see non-living moving objects bump, crash, and ricochet off each other.

What Should Parents Do?

Parents need to do nothing more than provide babies with opportunities to see people move themselves and people move objects.

After much observation and experience, your child will "get it" all on her own that animate objects are made of biological material and so can move themselves, and that inanimate objects need to be propelled by a motor, by a push, or by the force of gravity. Also know that since babies are drawn to understand how objects move, when you're wanting to play with your child, move yourself around in front of your baby in a variety of ways and also move pull toys, push toys, balls, and the like. Your baby will be highly engaged as you do so.

Your baby is learning facts in preparation for when he starts to crawl. Knowing the difference between internal and external forces that operate in the physical world equips the child to manage himself safely when crawling, walking, and running.

By the time your child plays outside on the playground or on the sidewalk, she'll have learned to adjust her body, taking into consideration the various objects—whether animate or inanimate—that she encounters. She'll know that she and another child can move out of each other's way but a fire hydrant, for example, cannot.

Robots Perplex Babies: Are They Animate or Inanimate?

Having established that babies expect biological beings, but not inanimate objects, to be able to move about autonomously, researchers wondered what babies would think about a robot. Robots, after all, are programmed to move about on their own. Think of R2D2 or C3P0 from *Star Wars*. You might have wondered, "Is he really a robot or is he part human?" If you're confused, it's easy to see how babies might be confused too by robots who move about spontaneously like humans.

The Research

Researchers bought a two-foot-tall, radio-controlled robot from Radio Shack. They dressed the robot in a white T-shirt in order to cover up the controls and a speaker. The head of the robot had facial features such as eyes and a mouth. The body was a single unit with arms on either side and clamplike hands. It was mounted on a base and propelled by wheels located underneath the base.

The researchers examined the reactions of nine- and twelve-month-olds to the robot in three different conditions: stationary, self-propelled motion, and commanded motion. For the stationary condition, the baby was exposed to the robot in a still state. A recording of the robot's motor noise was played during this exposure so the sound would be the same for each condition. For the self-propelled motion condition, the baby was brought into the testing room and the robot moved about autonomously. For the commanded motion condition, the robot appeared to move according to commands given by the child's mother. As instructed by the researchers, she would say, "Robot, go there," while pointing to a location in the room, and the robot would move to that location.

The results indicated that both the nine- and twelve-month-olds found the moving robot to be incongruous. Compared to their reactions to the stationary robot, when the robot moved spontaneously or by command, the babies responded with more attention (puzzled looks, frowns) and more negative emotion (crying, clinging to their mothers, fussing, fretting). They seemed to recognize that the robot was an inanimate object and didn't expect it to be able to move itself (Poulin-DuBois, Lepage, and Ferland, 1996).

The Interpretation

At this early age, the moving robot is a little scary, but also fascinating. This fascination with objects that blur the animate/inanimate distinction continues for years, even into adulthood for many. Babies are testing their theories and are interested in where those theories fail. In this case, the theory that only animates can move themselves fails to account for the self-propelled robot. Eventually they will revise their theory to account for such anomalies as they begin to understand how people can make objects move in a variety of ways, even from a distance using remote-controlled motors.

What Should Parents Do?

Introduce motorized toys including those with remote controls. Your baby will be fascinated at first, maybe even perplexed. What makes that doggie wiggle and car go backward and forward? Soon your child will get the gist of remote controls and battery-powered motors. After all, he sees you daily use your remote control to turn on the television. Although your child won't understand the science behind these devices—in fact, he'll probably think that batteries and remote controls are a form of magic—nevertheless he'll realize that they're needed to get the toy dog to bark or the toy car to move. If one day you go to the house of a neighbor who owns a battery-powered robotlike vacuum cleaner, watch your child's face. He'll likely be perplexed as he tries to determine if this object is animate, or inanimate.

Stable and Unstable Objects

As children notice that people move themselves and that objects need to be propelled into motion, they also come to learn that certain physical laws are at work in the environment.

Let's say you own a big floppy purse. In a rush one day as you enter the house, you set it on the edge of the table. Your baby is crawling around under the table and notices it sitting half-on and half-off the table. Because she's programmed to survive, baby takes notice of the situation and might even be a little worried that your purse will topple to the floor and possibly hit her. She's learned enough about the world around her and the rules that govern physical objects to know about gravity and when objects are in a stable or an unstable situation. Your floppy purse sitting on the edge of the table poses an uncertain situation; she's wary of the purse falling to the floor.

The Research

Researchers showed five-and-a-half- and six-and-a-half-month-olds a block with a happy face drawn on it, which sat squarely on top of a platform. The finger of a gloved hand pushed the happy-face block along the top of the platform from left to right, sometimes going a short distance and stopping in the middle of the platform (event 1) and sometimes going a longer distance and stopping at the end of the platform (event 2). In both cases the happy-face block was fully supported by the platform. These events were shown repeatedly until the babies habituated to seeing them.

Next, the babies watched test events that were identical to the habituation events except that the platform was shorter, so that when the block was pushed the short distance (event 1), it remained fully supported by the platform, but when the block was pushed the longer distance (event 2), most of the block was pushed off the edge, leaving only 15 percent of its bottom surface in contact with the platform. In this second event, the *impossible* one, the happy-face block should have fallen off the platform, but it did not.

The five-and-a-half-month-old babies looked equally long at the possible and the impossible test events, as though they judged that the block was stable in both events. In contrast, the six-and-a-half-month-olds looked longer at the impossible event, suggesting that they realized that the block was unstable when only a small portion of it was supported by the platform and were surprised that it didn't fall.

Through experience, babies learn about the laws of the physical universe, making and refining theories. The results of this study, along with others, suggest that five-and-a-half-month-olds know that the bottom of the block must have contact with the platform for stability, but they don't yet realize that the amount of contact is important. By six-and-a-half months, babies have refined their understanding to the point of knowing that 15 percent of the block on the platform is not enough to ensure stability, but 70 percent is (Baillargeon, 1995).

The Interpretation

Babies observe their environments, looking for predictable physical phenomena. When they see an event that's unusual in regard to the laws of gravity or physics, they'll pay close attention to it. Therefore when a baby is aware of a precarious physical situation such as a floppy purse sitting on the edge of a table, you'll likely see concern written all over the baby's face.

What Should Parents Do?

Get out some blocks and build with them as your baby watches.
Build a pyramid. Then build a tower. Your baby might notice that
one is more stable than the other. Your baby will also want to play
the game "Stack and Tumble." You stack the blocks; your baby
knocks them over. How many blocks high will your tower reach
before your child quickly knocks it over?

Once your child's eye-hand coordination improves, he'll build
and topple block structures all on his own.

Moving Objects Displacing
Stationary Ones

Your baby is learning lots about how objects and people move. He's
learned that people can avoid colliding with each other, but when
one object rolls into another, not only do they collide but the one
bumped moves ahead. So if a ball rolls into another as in the game
of pool, the hit ball moves ahead, possibly falling into a pocket.

The Research

Researchers set up a series of experiments in which there were possible and impossible events; in each, a moving object displaced a
stationary one. To begin, researchers set a medium-sized cylinder
rolling down a ramp. It then bumped a toy bug on wheels at the
bottom of the ramp, causing it to roll ahead to the midpoint of a
track. After watching this event repeatedly, the six-and-a-half-
month-olds soon habituated to it—that is, they became disinter-
ested, as if they understood it.

Now, after watching such an event, an adult would predict that if a larger cylinder made of the same material were rolled down the ramp, it would hit the bug and cause it to roll a longer distance than the medium-sized cylinder did. An adult would also predict that a smaller cylinder would cause the bug to roll a shorter distance. The researchers wondered if these six-and-a-half-month-olds would be able to make the same predictions.

The researchers showed the infants two test events: a possible one and an impossible one. The possible event was just like the habituation event except that a much *larger* cylinder was used and the toy bug rolled *farther*; it rolled all the way to the end of the track, stopping when it hit a wall. For the impossible event, the researchers set up a "false device," which would defy physics: it was the same as the habituation event except a much *smaller* cylinder was used and the toy bug rolled *farther* (to the end of the track, stopping when it hit a wall). The six-and-a-half-month-olds looked longer at the impossible event, providing evidence that they knew it was impossible and didn't match their adultlike predictions of what should happen (Baillargeon, 1995).

The Interpretation

These results indicate that the six-and-a-half-month-old infants were aware that the size of the cylinder should affect the distance that the bug was displaced, and they used their observations of the medium-sized cylinder in the habituation event to calibrate their predictions about the larger and smaller cylinders in the test events.

What Should Parents Do?

Locate a few different-sized balls and your largest cutting board. This you'll use for a ramp that goes from the sofa to the floor. If you own a toddler-sized indoor slide, use that instead. Now collect a few wheeled toys of various shapes, weights, and sizes from around the house and line them up at the bottom of the cutting board and slide them into position for the various balls to hit as each zooms down the ramp.

As you send the various balls down the ramp, watch your budding physicist as she calculates the various factors that come into play. Your baby will take note of how fast different objects go down the ramp and how much one object displaces an object that it bumps into. She'll be interested in the fact that a larger ball will move a toy at the bottom of the ramp farther than a smaller ball. Your baby can't express his interest in words, but you'll see interest written all over his face. Once your baby is mobile, he'll set up various situations where he alone will discover how various objects descend a ramp, at what speed, and the effect of the collision.

One day a grandma purchased a small indoor slide for her eighteen-month-old granddaughter. The child loved climbing up and going down the slide. All of a sudden she eyed her stacking cups. She carried the cups with her to the top step of the slide and sent each one down it, watching carefully as they tumbled down the ramp. Was this some sort of random haphazard activity? Most likely not. This child was gathering information about how the larger versus the smaller cups tumbled down the ramp and at what speed. Plus, she watched as they bumped into one another at the bottom of the slide. This activity was productive and intentional. Children set up such situations all on their own, discovering laws that govern physical causality.

Your Child as Scientist

Let's say that by either imitating you or through exploratory play, your fifteen-month-old has learned to press down the knob on a toy top, making it spin around. Then one day you're at a garage sale with your toddler who eyes a toy top for sale. He toddles over, retrieves it, and even though this one is fashioned differently than his own at home, he immediately knows what to do to get it to spin around. Your child summed up the similarities of the two objects and transferred his knowledge of one to the other.

The Research

Research scientists collected together several objects, selected to be novel, easy to manipulate, and interesting to a baby, and to possess some unique property that wouldn't be obvious to the child. They chose a castanet that closed and clacked, a cube that compressed, a cylinder that slid apart while making a sound, a horn that honked, a doll whose head separated from its abdomen, and a can that wailed when tilted and shaken. These objects were referred to as *plus* objects. Another set of the same objects, referred to as *minus* objects, were altered so as to have a similar appearance (same shape but different color or pattern), but the non-obvious property was eliminated. For example, there would be the can that wailed when tilted and shaken (a plus can) and then a can of a different color but same shape that was silent when tilted and shaken (a minus can).

The researchers invited parents to bring their nine- to sixteen-month-olds into the laboratory, one at a time. Each child was offered one of the plus objects to explore for thirty seconds. Parents were interviewed to make sure that the child had not seen the object or one similar to it before. The child typically discovered through exploratory play that a certain target action on the object would reveal the non-obvious property. Next, the researchers gave the child a second object, similar to the first, but of a different color or pattern and missing the non-obvious property (a minus object).

The children who had discovered that a certain target action revealed the non-obvious property on the first object quickly inferred that the new object would respond to the target action in the same way. When they tried the target action and the object didn't respond as expected, they persisted in performing the target action, making several attempts to get the second object to work the same way as the previous similar object. For example, if a baby first explored a can and discovered it would wail when tilted and shaken (a plus can), when she was given another can that looked similar (a minus can), she quickly started tilting and shaking it, and did so repeatedly. This quick and persistent performance of the target action was demonstrated even with some of the nine-month-old children in the study.

Why did they quickly and persistently perform the target action? Because they were deliberately trying to make the second object work like the first did. The children generalized that objects of the same shape, though of a different color or pattern, should perform similar functions. They transferred what they knew about the first object and applied that knowledge to the second. The new object violated their expectation based upon their past, though brief, experience.

The researchers knew that the babies' behavior with the second object was based upon inference from their experience with the first object, because they compared that behavior to the behavior of a control group of babies. The babies in the control group were not given a plus object at all. They were given a minus object followed by another minus object. These babies occasionally produced the target action spontaneously on the second object, for example a baby might happen to shake and tilt a minus can. In sharp contrast, the babies in the experimental group who had received the plus object first produced the target action more quickly and frequently, deliberately attempting to get the second object to do what the first had done (Baldwin, Markman, and Melartin, 1993).

The Interpretation

Here's how to understand a child's determination to apply information gained from one object to another similar object. Let's say you buy a new electric coffeepot. It's similar to the ones you've owned in the past. You don't read the instruction book from cover to cover; you don't need to as you can generalize information about your previously owned coffeepot and apply it to the new one you just purchased.

If, in fact, you discover that this one does not work exactly the same, you might try again and again, like the babies in the research study, to get the new coffeepot to work as the others you've previously owned did.

Using this natural inclination to make generalizations about one object and transfer that information from one object to another makes living in the world more efficient. Think about how time-consuming it would be if we had to learn anew how to use each car, vacuum cleaner, and lawn mower we encounter. Because we can imitate others and make generalizations and transfer information from one object to another, learning about the physical world is much more efficient, and it all starts when children are babies.

What Should Parents Do?

Provide opportunities for your child to experiment with objects and materials—water at the sink, play dough at the table, or sand in the sandbox outside. Allow him to learn how various appliances turn on and off. Let him observe how water drains from the sink, goes through a funnel, or gets sucked up in a turkey baster.

From experience and from making observations, your child will realize that when a cup is tipped over, the liquids inside will spill out onto his high-chair tray and onto the floor. Keep in mind that she's a little scientist or physicist conducting experiments around the house to determine how things work, operate, and respond.

Many of the seemingly naughty activities that children involve themselves in really aren't so naughty at all; they're actually scientific experiments that children are conducting in the various environments they enter. If you'd rather not have your child spilling water or juice from the high chair to the floor, provide time in the bathtub or in the backyard when he can engage in exploratory play that will involve experiments that confirm or disaffirm the various hypotheses he's created in his mind about the physical world around him.

In only a few short months your child will be fascinated by your TV's remote control. She'll watch you and then be determined to understand the cause and effect of your actions by trying the remote control out for herself. She'll want to push the buttons to see what happens. Call it cause-and-effect learning. Then there are light switches and the buttons in elevators. Your child will insist on pushing those buttons himself and will likely turn frustrated or disappointed if you get to a switch or an elevator button before he does. He'll be interested in using your cell phone and computer and playing video games. How you teach him to use these and control their use in the home and elsewhere will be a challenge.

If you live in a two-story home, you might see your toddler line up balls at the top of the steps and then hurl them down the stairs, ricocheting off the walls and bouncing from step to step. Is this a destructive, malicious activity? Hardly. She's learning the laws of physics. Hopefully the balls will be soft enough not to cause any damage to your newly painted walls or the chandelier that lights the stairwell.

There are all sorts of experiments that children conduct. Some involve the cause and effect of keys. A child might think, "What will happen if I take the car key, insert it into the ignition, and turn it?" Some children will actually try such experiments—much to their parents' horror. Parents need to remember that a child's determination to understand how the physical environment works overrides his interest in pleasing his parents. Therefore, keep keys out of children's reach. Watch them constantly for safety's sake. But if you see your child doing something out of the ordinary such as rolling a riding toy down a slide, while you might want to make sure the vehicle doesn't hit anyone standing at the bottom of the slide, it's okay to go ahead and allow the experiment. Your child is only wondering how fast it will go.

REFERENCES

Baillargeon, R. 1995. Physical reasoning in infancy. In M.S. Gazzaniga, ed. *The Cognitive Neurosciences.* Cambridge, MA: The MIT Press.

Baldwin, D. A., E. M. Markman, and R. L. Melartin. 1993. Infants' ability to draw inferences about nonobvious object properties: Evidence from exploratory play. *Child Development* 64: 711–28.

Canfield, R. L., and E. G. Smith. 1996. Number-based expectations and sequential enumeration by 5-month-old infants. *Developmental Psychology* 32: 269–79.

Hayne, H., and C. Rovee-Collier. 1995. The organization of reactivated memory in infancy. *Child Development* 66: 893–906

Knopf, M., U. Kraus, and R. A. Kressley-Mba. 2006. Relational information processing of novel unrelated information actions by infants. *Infant Behavior and Development* 29: 44–53.

Kosugi, D., and K. Fujita. 2002. How do 8-month-old infants recognize causality in object motion and that in human action? *Japanese Psychological Research* 44: 66–78.

Leslie, A. M. 1994. ToMM, ToBy, and agency: Core architecture and domain specificity. In L. A. Hirshfeld and S. Gelman, eds. *Mapping the Mind: Domain Specificity in Cognition and Culture*. Cambridge, England: Cambridge University Press.

Poulin-Dubois, D., A. Lepage, and D. Ferland. 1996. Infants' concept of animacy. *Cognitive Development* 11: 19–36.

Rovee-Collier, C. K. 1993. The capacity for long-term memory in infancy. *Current Directions in Psychological Science* 2: 130–35.

Chapter 6

Emerging Emotions

Children develop in four important ways: socially, intellectually, physically, and emotionally. You've already learned a bit about three aspects of development. When you and your baby coo back and forth in a communicative exchange, you realize you've brought a person into the world who is driven to interact socially while building relationships with you and other familiar people.

Considering intellectual development, by now you realize you have a brilliant baby on your hands. You realize that this fragile body needs your protection, but you also know with certainty that she's not just a little blob sitting around gazing randomly at objects and people. No indeed, she has an intellectual agenda all her own that she's determined to realize. The first week she recognized familiar people from unfamiliar people, later she sought out information about moving objects and what happens when one bumps into another, and she's aware that people move themselves and that people move objects.

With regards to physical development, you've either witnessed—or will soon—your baby's refined fine motor skills, which allow him to precisely pick up objects using his finger and thumb, and his large motor skills, which coordinate in order for him to move his body across the room, first on hands and knees and, in time, by walking.

The fourth aspect of development that's emerging along with the first three is emotional development. Don't let this aspect of development go unnoticed. Babies express emotions, plus they recognize and respond to the emotions of others.

The most important thing for parents and caregivers to realize is that babies are very sensitive to the emotional environment around them. They are affected by the emotions of others, especially by those of their caregivers. It is helpful if parents keep an eye on their own emotions, not allowing themselves to get carried away by anger or hostility, and getting help for anxiety or depression if needed. A peaceful emotional climate is the best environment for baby to learn and explore.

It is also important for parents and caregivers to recognize, respond to, and value children's emotions. When they do so, children will learn to manage their emotions with age. Emotions are tricky because if they're allowed to go unrecognized and therefore unmanaged they get in the way of intellectual pursuits. A sad, mad, distressed, frightened person can't build a block tower at sixteen months or complete an algebra homework assignment at sixteen years.

Expressing Emotions

Some developmental theorists suggest that the emotional life of a baby in the first few months consists of two basic states: contentment and distress. They suggest that additional emotions arise out of these first two states as baby develops. Joy comes out of contentment at around three months. Out of distress, anger appears at around four months and then fear at six months.

In contrast, other theorists believe that babies are born with the capacity to experience a number of basic emotions, including joy, sadness, interest, and surprise. This belief is based on the theory that certain basic emotions are universal, with corresponding facial expressions that are also universal, and that infants can be observed from birth making these facial expressions. They reason that if a baby's face reflects one of the universal emotional expressions, the baby is likely experiencing that emotion (Cole, Cole, and Lightfoot, 2005).

However they arise, babies do have emotions, and they make it fairly easy for parents to guess what babies are feeling. Unlike adults, babies and young children have not learned to hide their emotions. Since babies don't talk, competent baby-watching adults easily read their facial expressions, sounds, and body language and respond to children's emotions.

The Research

Researchers collected together videotaped samples of one- to nine-month-old babies' facial responses in various situations. These situations included a mother attempting to elicit a smile from her baby, a doctor administering a vaccination to a baby, and a variety of others. Judges trained to reliably identify expressions of emotion based upon theoretical criteria selected from those samples clear and prominently portrayed expressions of the fundamental emotions. Then they enlisted college students, as untrained neutral adult judges, to watch the selected samples of babies' facial reactions and identify which emotion was being expressed. The untrained judges quite accurately identified expressions of joy, sadness, surprise, and interest. They also identified expressions of fear, anger, and disgust (Izard, Huebner, Risser, McGinnes, and Dougherty, 1980).

The Interpretation

While parents and caregivers may have seen some of these emotions emerge on babies' faces, other expressions may have been surprising or perplexing. Once people are aware that babies can express eight emotions—joy, interest, distress, anger, disgust, sadness, surprise, fear—along with contentment and distress, it's fairly easy to take notice of the events that provoke them.

- **Joy.** When you enter the room after your child's nap, not only is joy visible on your child's face, but her body wiggles with joy as well. For most children, the emotion of happiness, pleasure, or joy is apparent many times a day, every day.

- **Interest.** Put your face in front of your baby while making popping sounds with your mouth, and you'll see interest written all over his face. Hang a mobile above a baby's head and he'll focus on and attend to the objects hanging overhead. Of course, you only want to try this when the baby is quiet and alert. If the baby is hungry, his interest is in his tummy and not on the delightful face or mobile in front of him.

- **Distress.** Hungry babies express distress by contorting their faces and using a wailing cry. The same expression will emerge when a baby receives an inoculation. Both pain and hunger evoke distress. Most parents recognize distress. Not only that, they'll do anything to relieve it because by doing so the parents themselves will feel relief as baby turns content.

- **Anger.** If distress isn't relieved fairly quickly, you'll see anger emerge. If a new caregiver is unprepared to deliver baby's bottle, her distress from hunger may shift into a loud and more intense cry expressing anger. Babies as young as four months old (as you'll read about in Chapter 12) will have temper tantrums when something they expect to happen no longer happens. When your child is a bit older, you'll see frustration on her face when she's first learning to button a button or zip a zipper; she wants to master the task but she may not have developed the dexterity to do so. Frustration too can lead to anger if it's unrelieved.

- **Disgust.** If your baby smells an offensive odor or perhaps when he tastes peas for the first time, you'll likely witness your baby's sensation of disgust. He may squeeze his eyes shut, wrinkle his nose, and purse his lips, indicating he is experiencing something unpleasant.

- **Sadness.** It's unlikely that you'll ever see your newborn sad. You'll indulge your baby when she needs interaction, cuddling, or quiet, thereby preventing sad feelings from ever welling up in your child. Kept fed and rested, with loving people and interesting objects around the house to watch and play with, your child will be content. However, if a child were left unattended and alone, sadness would emerge. Baby will cry or her eyes may just fill up with tears as she pouts. In an older baby you'll witness a sad face when he loses his beloved blanket or teddy bear. Once Teddy or blankie are found, a joyful expression will emerge instantly. When you first leave your older baby at child care, you may see distress, which will soon turn to sadness. After all, baby likes you best and will miss you, but it will only be temporary. Those tears will quickly dry up when a friend arrives or the teacher pulls out the play dough and the sadness is replaced by interest and joy.

- **Surprise.** When you turn a crank on a box and suddenly an object pops out, nothing but surprise will be revealed on your child's face. Her eyes will widen and her whole body may stiffen. Her initial reaction may be fear, but it will soon turn into delight as your child starts to anticipate an "unexpected" event.

- **Fear.** By age seven months you'll see fear on your child's face and in his eyes when he hears an extremely loud noise. You know instinctively to hold your child closely with comfort until the sound and feeling subside. Later, people in masks, Santa Claus, and dark rooms will likely frighten your child. When scared, your child needs reassurance that you'll protect him both physically and emotionally, no matter his age.

What Should Parents Do?

Most parents know exactly what to do. Identify the emotions, then name them by saying something like "Oh, you're sad that Daddy's leaving" or "Oh, you're so happy," "Boy that made you really angry," "Isn't that an interesting little car?" That's all it takes. You're validating the emotion by naming it and communicating empathy for your child's emotional state. Even very young children recognize the compassion in your facial expression and tone of voice if not the specific word that names the emotion. As important, you're practicing for when your child is older. With babies, your empathetic response comes easily. Hold onto this skill and make it a part of your parenting repertoire now and always. Expressing empathy for a child's emotions is a true expression of love and builds emotional intelligence.

Recognizing Emotions

Babies arrive expressing emotions, but when do they recognize the emotions of others? By around ten weeks of age, babies are already noticing the variations in emotional expressions of their caregivers, and responding accordingly (Haviland and Lelwica, 1987). Parents have a big impact on the emotional life of their children, starting in the first weeks of life. Later, by about five to seven months, babies can even discriminate between different facial or vocal emotional expressions of strangers (Bee and Boyd, 2007).

The Research

In one study, five-month-old babies looked at a picture of a woman making an emotional facial expression (happiness or anger) while listening to the woman's vocal expression of emotion (happiness or anger). For some of the babies, the facial expression matched the vocal expression (e.g., happy face, happy voice). For other babies there was a mismatch (e.g., happy face, angry voice). When the babies looked away from the picture, the sound was stopped and the picture occluded. After a brief pause, the same picture and sound combination was presented. The babies would look again for a while and then look away. This procedure was repeated until the babies habituated to the sight/sound combination (their looking time to a presentation had dropped to a certain criterion low duration).

At this point, the researchers presented the same picture again but changed the sound to a different emotional vocal expression (happy, angry, or sad). The babies perked up and took a new interest, looking longer at the picture of the woman now that it was accompanied by a new emotional vocal expression. This dishabituation of looking that accompanied a change in vocal expression led the researchers to conclude that five-month-olds can discriminate happy from sad, happy from angry, and sad from angry vocal expressions of a single female speaker (Walker-Andrews and Lennon, 1991).

A number of similar studies have found that babies can read facial expressions of emotions too. In one study, seven-month-olds were familiarized to happy facial expressions made by men and women. Then they were presented simultaneously with two pictures of a new person, in one picture expressing happiness, in the other expressing fear. The babies looked longer at the fearful face, which indicated that they could distinguish the two emotional expressions. In contrast, when the roles of the two emotions were reversed (babies were familiarized to fearful faces), the babies didn't look longer at the happy face than the fearful face. It seemed that the babies' interest in the novelty of the happy face did not overcome their basic interest in fearful faces.

To investigate this further, a new group of seven-month-olds were simply presented with the fearful face and happy face side by side. The babies looked overwhelming longer at the fearful face. These results indicate that not only can seven-month-olds tell that a happy face and a fearful face are physically different, but their differential responding to the two faces suggests that babies perceive that a happy face conveys different information than does a fearful face. Why do babies pay more attention to fearful faces? The babies didn't say, but researchers speculate that it could be a self-protection mechanism. The sooner a baby detects fear, the sooner he can become aware of a danger that is the source of that fear (Nelson, 1987).

The Interpretation

Your baby's skill at reading emotional expressions is another miracle to pay attention to. Your baby is watching your face and

listening to your voice, and in so doing, she picks up on your emotions. If you are happy, sad, or afraid, your baby senses it and
probably feels it too. Your emotions are contagious to her, especially while she is young and yet undifferentiated from you. So
know that if you get carried away by emotion, you are carrying
your baby along for the ride, which could be a strain on his sensitive system. Once your baby starts crawling, as he heads toward
the hot wood-burning stove, you might react with fear, which
could alert him that there is a danger, but he is too young to know
what the danger is or how to protect himself. Moreover, your fear
could cloud your thinking about how to handle the situation and
could condition your child to be fearful rather than cautious. If you
feel fear, observe it so it doesn't control you. It is best to remain
calm in the face of danger and take appropriate action. Move your
baby away from the stove while saying "That's hot." In time, he
will learn to keep a distance.

Your baby as yet doesn't understand every word you say, but
she can tell the difference when your face and your voice change
from happy to sad or from sad to surprised. This skill enables her
to read your mind without needing to understand your words or
talk herself.

What Should Parents Do?

Emotions are an important part of every person, even babies.
Freely express most emotions in front of your child. Babies learn
about what's going on with you and in their world by reading the
emotions that you're expressing on your face and in your voice. It
is confusing for a baby if you try to hide your emotions. Being very
sensitive, she picks up mixed messages. However, while authentic-
ity is important, keep in mind that emotions such as anger are
distressing to a baby. For baby's sake, and your own, be aware of

anger and resentment in yourself, so they don't get a hold on you, so that peace is the norm in your home.

Coordinating Emotional Faces and Voices

Now you know that babies sit up and pay attention when they hear or see a new facial or vocal expression, but they also know that a certain facial expression, say happiness, goes with a voice that sounds happy.

The Research

Researchers invited parents to come to a laboratory with their seven-month-old babies. While a baby sat on his parent's lap, the researchers presented two videos to the baby on two separate screens simultaneously. One of the videos was of an actress expressing happiness; the other was of the same actress expressing anger. Along with the visual displays, the researchers played the audio from either the happy video or the angry video. It is important to note that the audio was out of sync with the video by five seconds and was played through a speaker located centrally between the two visual displays. This meant that the voice audio matched one of the videos in emotional content only; the words spoken didn't match the lip movements. Consistently, the babies looked longer at the video that matched the audio. Because the two were out of sync, it was concluded that babies made the match based on emotional content only (Soken and Pick, 1992).

The Interpretation

Babies seek consistencies. By watching you and others, they learn which facial expressions go with what vocal expressions. Just as babies can coordinate bounces with *boing* sounds (see the research from Chapter 3), they are also able to coordinate emotional sounds with facial expressions.

What Should Parents Do?

Since babies are drawn to notice emotional expressions, parents need to embrace this interest by using words to describe everyone's emotion, whether it's joy, frustration, disgust, excitement, jealousy, disappointment, or love, to name only a few.

Also, when you're feeling an emotion, frustration for instance, make sure that your face, voice, and words mesh. Baby will be confused if you're feeling frustrated but masking it with a smiling face. Babies are looking for consistencies in their world even in regard to emotional expression.

Make conversation about emotions part of your parenting repertoire. By doing so, you're validating your child's innate interest in emotions and furthering her intelligence about emotions. For now, your child won't understand every word, but in time he will. You can get into the habit of bringing emotion into your everyday life, normalizing this important aspect of development.

Lullabies vs. Play Songs

Researchers were able to determine that along with being able to read emotional expressions, at about six months babies are so keen on sensing emotional sensations that they actually respond differently when hearing a lullaby such as "Rock-a-bye Baby" versus a play song such as "The Itsy Bitsy Spider."

The Research

Researchers recorded mothers singing a song to their six- to seven-month-old babies in a manner that would either put the child to sleep or in a manner that would be arousing and playful. Then they asked the mother to sing the same song in the opposite manner. For adults, determining the difference between the two types of songs is easy. Researchers found that adults listening to these songs were 100 percent correct in identifying whether each song was a lullaby or a play song. They rated the lullabies as more soothing, smooth, and airy, whereas they rated the play songs as more rhythmic, brilliant (like a trumpet), and clipped, having more smiling tone and more stressed consonants.

In a second experiment, neutral adults (not parents, grandparents, or caregivers) observed videotapes (without sound) of a new group of six-month-olds listening to alternating lullabies or play songs recorded in the first experiment. Most of the time, the observers could distinguish which type of songs the infants were hearing.

Why were the adult observers able to determine when the babies heard a play song as opposed to a lullaby? Because the six-month-olds responded to lullabies by focusing inward: looking toward their own bodies, toys they were playing with, their clothing, their pacifier, or the chair they were sitting in. With the play songs, they focused outward, directing their attention away from their immediate environment and often toward their caretaker (who was wearing earplugs so as not to bias the baby's responses) (Rock, Trainor, and Addison, 1999).

The Interpretation

Babies as young as six months are able to read the emotional expressions in songs and clearly know the difference and so respond differently to play songs and lullabies. Babies sense the soothing, smooth, and airy affect of lullabies and respond by focusing inward. They also pick up on the rhythmic, brilliant, clipped, smiley tone and stressed consonants of play songs and respond appropriately by focusing outward.

What Should Parents Do?

It's likely that you sing both lullabies and play songs to your baby. As you sing, have you noticed a difference in your baby's response to these different types of songs? If so, you've noticed exactly what researchers discovered in the laboratory setting.

Since babies obviously sense the emotional difference between play songs and lullabies, use each to help regulate your infant's states and to communicate emotional information. You probably know the song "If you're happy and you know it, clap your hands." Add more emotions to this song by singing sadly, "If you're sad and you know it, say boo hoo," and angrily, "If you're mad and you know it, stomp your feet." Your baby will love to watch your facial and vocal expression mesh with the music.

Also be sure to sing differently when trying to communicate that it is time to sleep versus time to play. You communicate this difference in the melody, tone, and style (not in the words). The lullabies quiet your child; play songs stimulate, entertain, and engage her.

Music's distinct beat—whether waltzes or musical nursery rhymes—coordinate emotional states between parents and children. Bounce your child on your lap while singing, "Hey Diddle Diddle" to your baby. Then waltz around the room while singing "Goodnight, Irene," "The Tennessee Waltz," or "My Darling Clementine." With each different type of music, you can easily coordinate your emotional state, developing an emotional synchrony between you and your baby.

Babies Sense Conflict

Along with babies' ability to feel the different emotions conveyed by a play song and a lullaby, they are also able to pick up on emotions that are not directed at them but occur between the people in their immediate environment; they're amazingly sensitive to the emotional mood that surrounds them. Your baby senses when Mom and Dad are happy and when a conversation goes from a discussion to an argument. Just as people, and that includes babies, are affected by secondhand smoke, all people (babies too) are sensitive to the emotions between others in their environment.

As most parents are fully aware, babies bring such joy, but simultaneously, baby's arrival brings tense moments too. Parents feel stressed, particularly when they're deprived of sleep. It's frustrating as parents try to determine just what baby needs to reach contentment. At the same time, parents express a mix of emotions toward each other: happiness, bliss, interest, and care, coupled with frustration and anger, sometimes resulting in tears, tantrums, or shunning, all of which baby senses. What most people don't realize is that baby senses the difference between these emotional moments, and he's affected by them (Cummings and Davies, 1994).

The Research

In one study, researchers trained a group of mothers of one- to two-and-a-half-year-old children to act as observers and record the responses of their children to naturally occurring emotional incidents. The mothers reported, on average, 363 incidents of naturally occurring anger and 144 incidents of naturally occurring affection that each child witnessed during a nine-month period. For each incident, the mothers recorded onto tape a narrative description of the event, the child's responses, and any consequences that might have occurred.

The mothers' recording practices were monitored by the researchers who visited the homes every three weeks. To assess reliability, during those visits the researcher or mother would simulate an expression of anger, pain, or minor physical discomfort (like coughing) in the presence of the child. Both the mother and the researcher would then make a recording for that event. When the recordings of the mothers and researchers were compared there was very high agreement, indicating a high level of reliability of the mothers' recording practices.

The mothers also took part in ten simulated emotional events in the presence of the child, spaced out over the nine months of the study. Five of the events were affection simulations, which consisted of the mother and father hugging and kissing. The other five events were an adult (the mother or a researcher) pretending to be angry with someone on the phone.

The data revealed that the children were not only aware of others' emotional interactions, but were also likely to react to them emotionally. Anger and distress were the most common types of responses to naturally occurring anger, occurring more than 70 percent of the time. The children's angry behaviors included hitting, pushing, scolding, and unfocused yelling. Signs of distress included crying and expressions of concern. Crying was the single most common response, occurring 22 percent of the time (Cummings, Zahn-Waxler, Radke-Yarrow, 1981).

In another study, even ten-week-old infants showed distress when their moms displayed anger. Experimenters gave mothers instructions for the facial and vocal expressions they would be asked to display to their young infant. They showed the mothers examples of happy, sad, and angry facial expressions based on a theoretical standard, pointing out between the different expressions the appearance changes of the brow, the eye, and the mouth regions. The mothers practiced making happy, sad, and angry facial expressions with a mirror and were asked to imagine happy, sad, or angry situations while they made the facial expressions. The mothers were instructed to start each expression while turned away from their baby, then to turn to face the baby while maintaining the expression and not reacting to the baby's responses. Finally they were instructed to continuously say, but without dramatically lowering or raising the voice, "You make me so happy (or sad or mad)" during the expression. With signals from the experimenters, each mother presented four fifteen-second episodes of each of the three expressions, with a twenty-second turn away between each expression. Neutral observers judged that the mothers presented emotional expressions that were clear and accurate.

The infants' responses were coded, second by second, for mouthings and nonmovement as well as signs of interest, anger, joy, sadness, fear, and surprise. The analysis of the data revealed that while the babies did at times mirror their mothers' expressions, it was clear that they weren't simply imitating, they were having an emotional response. When their mothers expressed happiness, the infants initially reflected the joyful expression of their mother. The infants showed more signs of interest or excitement than joy in the subsequent happy presentations. During the maternal sad presentations, the infants did not match the mothers' expressions. Instead they responded with lip and tongue sucking and pushing their lips in and out, probably a self-soothing behavior and one that didn't occur frequently in the happy or angry presentations.

In response to the first anger presentation of their mothers, four of the sixteen babies participating began crying intensely and had to be removed from the testing room for soothing—it was that distressing to them. The data for the remaining twelve infants showed that when the mother's expression was angry, the infants' expressions of interest decreased and their expressions of anger increased over the four presentations, perhaps as a sign of increasing anger induced in the infants when the mothers continued with an angry display. There were also more periods of nonmovement during the angry expressions, which indicated a change in the emotional state of the infant, perhaps a genuine fearful freezing behavior (Haviland and Lelwica, 1987).

The Interpretation

Numerous studies confirm that witnessing anger between others or being on the receiving end of anger—verbal or nonverbal—is a stressor for kids. There's no way to eliminate all stress from a home, nor would you want to. Moderate stress, which occurs occasionally, exercises the baby's developing brain and nervous system; however, frequent intense stress is harmful to this delicate development.

Children's responses to stress are varied but evident. Some cry, others freeze, and some show distress in their facial expression. Researchers have also detected increases in stress hormone (cortisol) levels and changes in heart rate, blood pressure, pallor, and perspiration in children when they are witnessing angry episodes.

What Should Parents Do?

There's no way to make your home atmosphere frustration- and anger-free. But you can work on your relationships so that when you're feeling overwhelmed or anxious you don't attack your parenting partner or escalate the emotions of the moment by turning angry. While you don't need to put on a happy face twenty-four/ seven, you do need to find a way to iron out your differences with others, especially your spouse. Once you've made up, make sure that your children—and this includes babies—are aware that the conflict is over. While research has shown that witnessing anger increases a child's stress level, the authentic resolution of conflict and a return to peace is the best remedy to alleviate that stress (Cummings and Davies, 1994).

Social Referencing

You now realize that babies pick up on the emotional climate that surrounds them. Beginning around the time your child turns one year old, look for your child to adjust her actions depending on your emotional response to a person, object, or event. This behavior is called social referencing. Your child references your emotional reaction when she is uncertain about a situation. Let's say an unusual object is sitting out in baby's reach; it could be a new and peculiar-looking windup toy, a large unopened box, or a freestanding electrical heater at Grandma's. Because your baby is curious, she'll likely approach the object with the idea of exploring it. But now, at one year old, she'll look at you first before touching it, as if asking, "Is this object safe or dangerous? Should I touch it or not?" If you smile with encouragement, your baby will proceed with her investigations. If you look fearful, your baby will stop immediately, at least temporarily.

The Research

Researchers conducted an experiment in which they examined the social referencing behavior of fourteen- and eighteen-month-olds. Researchers had an adult look into two boxes while one child after another watched. The children couldn't view the contents of the boxes. When peeking in one box, the adult said, "Wow! I've found something! Wow! I can see it! Wow!" while looking happy, as if seeing the object evoked joy. When peeking in the other, the adult said, "Eww! I've found something! Eww! I can see it! Eww!" while looking disgusted as if smelling or seeing something abhorrent. All of the necessary controls were in place. For example, half of the children saw the happy expression followed by disgust, the others saw disgust first.

Then the children watching the adult had the opportunity to open the boxes and look inside themselves. Which box did they check out first? Most of the children first chose the one that had provoked a smile from the adult, demonstrating that children as young as fourteen months old knew the meaning of another's emotional communication, correctly identified the target of it, and adjusted their own behavior accordingly (Repacholi, 1998).

The Interpretation

While your child is highly curious about windup toys, unopened boxes, and freestanding heaters, he's also determined to survive. He doesn't trust himself to know of the dangers the world presents, so by turning to you, his protector, he reads your emotional expression and in doing so will act on it by either going forward to investigate this unusual object because you've communicated that it's safe or backing off because you've communicated that it's dangerous. If you smile and nod, he'll proceed. If you look horrified, he'll stop cold. He'll do so with respect to new, strange, and wonderful objects, and new, strange, and wonderful people he encounters as well. Children learn about the world through firsthand experiences and have their own emotional responses to what they are discovering, but they also learn about people, creatures, and objects by watching how others relate to them.

What Should Parents Do?

If your child is approaching that electrical freestanding heater at Grandma's house, and glances at you while doing so, let her see horror on your face. Don't fake a smile and use a sweet voice, saying, "Sweetheart, don't touch the heater, it's hot." To prevent any confusion, it's important to mesh your body language, tone of voice, words, and actions by saying firmly, not harshly, "NO! I'm not going to allow you to touch the hot heater," while moving toward your child and blocking her from moving any closer to it. Research shows that babies (and most likely all of us) discriminate emotions best when they're communicated and received consistently and simultaneously on many channels—such as when they see fear in a facial expression while hearing fear in the adult's voice (Berk, 2009).

Emotional Eavesdropping

There is another way that babies use their emotional antennas. It's called emotional eavesdropping, and it occurs when they witness emotional situations between others. If your toddler hears your sister yell in anger at her son for poking the dog with a stick, your child will be drawn to notice his aunt's angry emotions and will avoid poking the dog with a stick—at least when his aunt is present.

The Research

Eighteen-month-olds were brought into the laboratory one at a time. While seated on their parents' laps, the toddlers watched a woman experimenter play with a toy, demonstrating a certain action with it.

Then another woman entered the room and sat down to read a magazine. When the experimenter said to the new woman, "Nina, look at this," and showed her the action with the toy, "Nina" responded with an angry face and voice, saying something like, "That's aggravating!" The experimenter maintained a neutral demeanor throughout. The children in the research study observed the interaction carefully.

Angry "Nina" then adopted a neutral expression and either left the room or silently remained in the room, not looking directly at the child, but seated with her face visible to the child.

Next, the toddlers were offered a chance to play with the toy.

If the angry woman exited the room, the children without hesitation played with the toy and often imitated the action with the toy that had been demonstrated by the experimenter. If the angry woman stayed in the room, the children were reluctant to pick up and play with the toy, spent less time touching the toy, smiled less, and spent more time monitoring the angry woman.

A second experiment was conducted, identical to the first, but this time after the angry outburst toward the experimenter, Nina changed to a neutral expression and either turned away from the child, going back to reading her magazine, or silently watched the child with "friendly interest." The results were very similar to the previous experiment. If Nina's back was turned, the child played happily, but if she was watching them, the children hesitated to touch the toy, touched it less, imitated less, and monitored Nina carefully (Repacholi and Meltzoff, 2007).

The Interpretation

Children, even toddlers, are smart enough to realize what provokes anger. Not wanting to have Nina's anger directed at them, the toddlers didn't play with the toy if Nina was watching. The anger disturbed them and interfered with their natural desire to explore a new object and imitate actions on it. Instead, the babies watched and worried about when the anger might erupt again.

What Should Parents Do?

It's important to understand that when babies witness anger it affects them. Children are naturally joyful and curious, but the anger in the environment causes them to become wary and worried. It also demonstrates how anger doesn't accomplish what the parent wants—for the child to learn to avoid a dangerous situation when the parent is not around. It may even do the opposite. Clearly, it's the parent's job to keep toddlers away from dangerous situations, but as the children get older, parents serve their children best by guiding them with patience and kindness, not anger.

For instance, if older brother attempts to stick a screwdriver in an electrical outlet, you yell at him while seizing the screwdriver and strongly reprimanding him in your younger one's presence. The likelihood is great that your younger child will learn not to poke screwdrivers in outlets so as to avoid provoking your anger.

But if you're out of the room or have your back turned, he might locate the screwdriver and stick it in an outlet. Why? He's highly curious about electrical outlets and as yet doesn't have the self-control to stop himself from copying his brother's behavior when you're not watching. That's why toddlers must be watched all the time and dangerous objects kept out of their reach.

When your child is a baby, it's fairly easy for you to be responsive when she exhibits an emotion. Your child hears a loud noise, automatically you'll say, "I can tell that loud noise scared you." As your child travels the developmental years, when she expresses an emotion, your response needs to be exactly the same. If a toddler expresses fear upon seeing Santa Clause, you offer the same sort of empathy, "I can tell Santa really frightens you." If your teenager appears fearful the first day of high school, your response will be similar, "I can tell starting high school is scary for you, I remember a similar feeling my first day too."

Too often parents try to talk their children out of their emotions, hoping that by doing so the emotion will dissolve. Instead of an empathetic response, they might say, "There's no need to be frightened of Santa" or "You'll be fine your first day of high school, don't worry about it." While such responses seem reassuring or encouraging, such lines actually make children hold onto the emotion even more. By naming the emotion, you're validating what the child is feeling and then most often the emotion disappears. Not only that, you create intimacy between you and your child as your child feels comforted and understood.

Each time your child expresses an emotion, do your best to identify it by naming it. Doing so increases your child's feeling vocabulary, and then as your child ages, he won't need you to identify the emotion, he'll do it for himself, thereby nurturing himself through the situation by thinking, "I was nervous up on that stage. That's a normal emotion. My mom feels nervous sometimes. This feeling will pass."

If you don't know what your child is feeling, you can always ask, "What's going on? How are you feeling?" Your child won't always have an answer, but at least she knows that you care and that you're interested in what she's feeling and that you're not going to ignore her emotions or talk her out of her emotional state.

Your goal is to guide your child on the road to emotional strength. Children who don't have parents who coach them through emotional situations find themselves emotionally crippled, covering up emotions with drugs, sex, or alcohol, or are paralyzed when they feel an emotion such as disillusionment, betrayal, or loneliness for the first time.

Just because you validate your child's emotional state does not mean that you allow any negative accompanying behavior. A toddler jealous of her baby brother is not allowed to hit the baby. The feeling of jealousy is expected, along with feelings of affection and interest toward the baby. A child feeling overwhelmed with homework needs those feelings validated. Once the feeling subsides, she then needs to complete her assignments. A twelve-year-old disappointed about not making the basketball team still needs to go to school the next day.

It's also important in such situations for parents to look at themselves. You only need to ask, "Have I been impatient with my older child and so he's acting it out by hitting the baby?" "Is my child overwhelmed with homework because he feels pressure from me to perform and succeed or is he overscheduled with school, trumpet lessons, and soccer practice?" You'll be a more effective parent if you adjust yourself and your feelings toward your child before responding to your child's emotional state.

In this regard, it's important to be aware that your emotions affect your children's, and that emotions are contagious. When children are upset, check with yourself and ask, "Have I created a disturbance in the environment that's affecting my child?" It's easy to feel resentment when exhausted from taking care of a baby, which will show on your face and in your behavior (even if you're trying to hide it). Children, even babies, read the resentment and then turn upset themselves. At such times, it's best to recognize that the problem is yours, not your child's, settle your emotions, correct your behavior, and apologize. Children are naturally so innocent and forgiving that this will usually resolve the upset immediately. Even before children understand all the words, they will get the gist of what you're saying and will register your change of emotion. The truth of the matter is that you can only help your child with her emotions if you're not the cause of her emotional upset. If the parent is not the cause, and he is not in judgment of or wanting to control the child's feelings, then he can offer help. If the parent responds to a child's upset with her own upset that will only escalate the emotions of the moment. Managing your own emotions in the face of parenting your children is likely the toughest part of your job.

Not only do children wear their emotions on their sleeves, making it easy for you to tell what they're feeling and respond, little children make it perfectly clear when they are referencing your face. As your children get older, they're more subtle about seeking you out as a reference for social situations. Besides, there will be others whom they'll reference: peers, teachers, and the media, to name a few. But let it be known, children are always interested in their parents' take on events and situations and are interested in their opinion. Therefore, speak up. If there's a newscaster on the TV telling of a situation that you disagree with, let your child or children know where you stand. If a peer tells your child something that you know to be untrue, set your child straight. If a teacher expresses a value that you don't agree with, be sure to speak to your child about it and you may need to talk to the teacher as well.

Now, your child may not always choose your influence over another's, plus your child has a mind of her own and so will mesh your opinion with the opinions of others, including yours, and come up with her own thoughts and ideas, but you at least want your child to know where you stand. So if a person asks your child at age fourteen how his parents feel about drugs, alcohol, or sex, you want your child to be able to reiterate your opinions.

A child being able to explain her parents' opinions says that the parents see themselves as a viable reference and that they have taken it upon themselves to communicate opinions and facts to their child. Now, your teenage son may be disinclined to say, "Thanks, Dad, I really appreciate hearing your take on that," but your son may quote you to teachers or friends without listing his source.

Realize that you are now, and will be for many years to come, an important reference for your children regarding what's safe, what's dangerous, what's right, what's wrong. For now it's hot stoves and electrical outlets. Later the issues get more complicated, but children continue to look for your opinion all the years they develop; don't hesitate to offer it.

REFERENCES

Bee, H., and D. Boyd. 2007. *The Developing Child, 11th Edition*. Boston, MA: Pearson Education, Inc.

Berk, L. E. 2009. *Child Development, 8th Edition*. Boston, MA: Pearson Education, Inc.

Cole, M., S. Cole, and C. Lightfoot, 2005. *The Development of Children, 5th Edition*. New York, NY: Worth Publishers.

Cummings, E. M., and P. Davies. 1994. *Children and Marital Conflict.* New York: The Guilford Press.

Cummings, E. M., C. Zahn-Waxler, and M. Radke-Yarrow. 1981. Young children's responses to expressions of anger and affection by others in the family. *Child Development* 52: 1274–82.

Haviland, J. M., and M. Lelwica. 1987. The induced affect response: 10-week-old infants' responses to three emotional expressions. *Developmental Psychology* 23: 97–104.

Izard, C. E., R. R. Huebner, D. Risser, G. C. McGinnes, and L. M. Dougherty. 1980. The young infant's ability to produce discrete emotion expressions. *Developmental Psychology.* 16: 132–40.

Nelson, C. A. 1987. The recognition of facial expression in the first two years of life: Mechanisms of development. *Child Development* 58: 889–909.

Repacholi, B. M. 1998. Infants' use of attentional cues to identify the referent of another person's emotional expression. *Developmental Psychology* 34: 1017–25.

Repacholi, B. M., and A. N. Meltzoff. 2007. Emotional eavesdropping: infants selectively respond to indirect emotional signals. *Child Development* 78: 503–21.

Rock, A., L. Trainor, and T. Addison. 1999. Distinctive messages in infant-directed lullabies and play songs. *Developmental Psychology* 35: 527–34.

Soken, N. H., and A. D. Pick. 1992. Intermodal perception of happy and angry expressive behaviors by seven-month-old infants. *Child Development* 63: 787–95.

Walker-Andrews, A. S., E. and Lennon. 1991. Infants' discrimination of vocal expressions: Contributions of auditory and visual information. *Infant Behavior and Development*, 14: 131–42.

Chapter 7

Reading Your Mind

As you know, your baby realizes that people move themselves, and people move objects. Also, he watches you closely and imitates your behavior. Then at some point he begins to observe and be aware of not just your movements and actions, but also where you look. He seems to realize that what you look at is important, so he follows your gaze. He's beginning to understand that where you're looking is directed by your interests, which then influences your actions. As your child follows your gaze, he's trying to get inside your mind. Determining where you're looking leads to understanding your thoughts, beliefs, and ideas on whatever it is that you're directing your gaze. He wants to share your mental experience by looking where you're looking and thereby thinking about what you're thinking and ultimately learning from you.

In time he'll be so good at reading your mind that if you toss a piece of paper into the trash can and miss, leaving it on the floor, he might copy your actions, but when he does, he'll perform the act correctly because he was able to read your intentions.

There is more that researchers have learned about children's capacity and limitations in following people's gazes. For one thing, children don't understand peripheral vision. If you're reading a magazine, your child believes that with your gaze directed toward it and not him, you won't be able to keep track of his actions. However she can tell the difference between when you're looking at something and when your head is just turned in a certain direction.

Once a child is efficient at tracking your gazes, she will soon begin to point, as if saying, "Lookie here, I'm interested in this, tell me about it." She may point to a fly as if asking, "What's that?" In time she'll say the words for herself. Not only will you say, "That's a fly," but you will explain a little about the insect to the child.

Your baby—like all of us—is interested in what's going on within other people's minds. A preschooler might ask, "How do you know that?" While no one knows perfectly what others are thinking, we all try to second-guess one another, attempt to decipher what others are thinking, and predict what others will do. We'll ask ourselves, "Why did he do that?" or "What was she thinking?" or "Was she telling the truth?" All people, including babies, seem to share an interest in and capacity to read minds. We develop a *theory of mind*, as researchers call it, recognizing that people are psychological beings with mental states such as beliefs, desires, emotions, and intentions that underlie behavior. We then work with this theory in social situations.

Over the first year of life, infants demonstrate an implicit understanding that people have mental states that govern their behavior. After age two, children will frequently verbalize their understanding of the thoughts, feelings, and desires of themselves and others, demonstrating a clear awareness of an inner self. If a child sees someone pour orange juice on her cereal, she may comment, "He thought it was milk." Their theory of mind becomes more explicit around this time, and then, like any good scientist, they gather data and test it. From reading his father's facial expression, a child may realize that his daddy is mad. Then another day he realizes that Daddy turns angry when he, the child, touches the TV's remote control, changing the channel. The child will nevertheless need to try out his theory a few more times to make sure he's accurate as to what provokes his father's anger. Children revise and elaborate their theory of mind over the years based on what they learn.

Following Your Gaze

It's between ten and eleven months of age that babies begin to follow people's gazes. We all do it, so why wouldn't a baby? If you're looking out the window at the neighbor's new car, your spouse will notice that you're looking at something interesting and will want to see the event or object for himself. If you're holding your baby, she'll notice your gaze too and follow the direction in which your eyes are looking and look in the same direction to see what you're seeing.

Realize that your baby sees you as a font of knowledge; she wants to know what you know. She realizes that where you're looking is the window into your mind. It's not just what you touch and where you walk that are of interest to her, but where you direct your gaze.

Babies make use of gaze following to learn words. Say you are looking out the window at the neighbor's new car and say the word "car." If your baby can follow your gaze to that object, he can make the connection between the word "car" and the four-wheeled object it references. If your baby is not able to follow your gaze or doesn't yet know to do so, he would not necessarily know to what object the word "car" referred. Your baby at nine months might look at the window with you and hear you say "car," but because at this age his gaze following is immature, he may not know exactly what it is you are looking at. As far as he can tell the word "car" could refer to anything he sees out the window—a bush, tree, driveway, sidewalk, street, or house. Beginning at about ten or eleven months, your baby will be able to follow your gaze and know what you are looking at when you say "car," thus having an opportunity to learn the meaning of the word.

The Research

Researchers assessed new gaze followers, babies at ten and eleven months of age. One by one, these babies were brought into the laboratory and seated on their mother's lap at a table. Across the table sat an experimenter who engaged with each baby by playing until the baby seemed comfortable in the setting. Next, the experimenter placed two identical objects on the table, one to the right and the other to the left. Then the experimenter made eye contact with the infant to direct the child's attention straight ahead and to make sure that the child could see the experimenter's face. Then, without saying a word and with a neutral expression, the experimenter would gaze either to the right or the left at one of the placed objects for six-and-a-half seconds. This test was repeated three times with play in between each.

The infant's behavior was observed and recorded during each of the four tests. Sometimes the babies looked at one of the objects, and sometimes they looked down or elsewhere, but overall, when the babies looked at an object, it was more often at the same object at which the experimenter was gazing, thus demonstrating their emerging new skill.

The researchers also measured how long the infants looked at the object after following the experimenter's gaze to it. The look time varied from child to child. What did this mean? Well, in this longitudinal study, the researchers found that the longer the look time during gaze following at ten or eleven months, the larger the spoken vocabulary at two years (Brooks and Meltzoff, 2008).

The Interpretation

When children follow gazes, it's as if they're saying, "He's looking at that for a reason and I want to be in on it." Children recognize your intelligence; by following your gaze, they learn from you. Once you realize that your child is looking where you're looking, she'll benefit from doing so if you explain what you're looking at and why. It's likely that if you do, your child's vocabulary will be enhanced.

What Should Parents Do?

When you notice that your child is following your gaze, pause along with your child. Talk about what you're seeing and what your baby is now looking at along with you. While there's no way to force a child to look longer at an object than the child deems necessary, you can support your child's interest in following your gaze by giving him the time to do so and by describing the event. "Mr. Smith has a new car. It's a fancy red convertible."

Also, you can return the favor. If your child is looking at something, look at it too and describe it. "You see the birdie flying into the tree. He lives in a nest up there."

It's gratifying to all parents when children start using language. It's wonderful when they can say, "Birdies fly" or "Balls bounce." While children acquire language at different rates and ages, some sooner than others, parents want to do what they can to support language development. Therefore put language to whatever it is you're looking at, particularly when your child follows your gaze, and when you follow your child's gaze describe what he's looking at as well.

Headbands vs. Blindfolds

When your child seems to follow your gaze, you might wonder, "Does she actually take notice of what my eyes are seeing or is she just following my head as it turns toward something?" Researchers wondered the same thing and discovered a developmental progression in a child's understanding of what another person sees.

The Research

Using a procedure much like the previous study, researchers examined the gaze following of nine- to eighteen-month-olds. After a little warm-up play, the experimenter placed identical objects, one on each side of the child, made eye contact across the table, and then turned her head and gazed for six-and-a-half seconds at one of the objects. The child's behavior was observed and the test was repeated three times.

What differed from the previous study was that for half of the children in this study, the experimenter moved her head in the same way as if she was gazing at one of the objects during the test, but in fact her eyes were closed. The results showed that the children who were ten months of age and older were monitoring the experimenter's eyes: those in the open-eyes condition followed her head turns significantly more often than those in the closed-eyes condition. In contrast, the nine-month-olds followed the experimenter's head turns just as often whether she turned with eyes open or closed, indicating that they were not following her gaze.

In another experiment, the same procedures were used to examine gaze following of twelve-, fourteen- and eighteen-month-olds, except that instead of the experimenter keeping her eyes open or closed to manipulate whether or not she could see the target object, she used a bandana either as a headband or a blindfold.

The fourteen- and eighteen-month-olds recognized that the blindfold blocked the experimenter's view. Those in the headband condition followed her head turns significantly more often than those in the blindfold condition. The toddlers weren't just watching the researcher's head turn toward an object, they were noticing her eyes. If the eyes were covered by the blindfold, the babies usually didn't bother to glance in the direction the researcher was facing, but when a headband was in place and the eyes revealed, the children were more likely to look where her eyes were gazing.

The twelve-month-olds' behavior differed from the older children. They followed the experimenter's head turns just as often whether her eyes were covered by the bandana or not. The previous experiment demonstrated that twelve-month-olds can recognize that another person cannot see a target object when her eyes are closed. This experiment, however, shows that they do not recognize that a blindfold will also block a person's vision.

The researchers theorized that at twelve months of age, a child has enough personal experience with his own eyes to know that closing them blocks his vision, and he realizes that other people have eyes that work the same way. However, at this age a child does not yet have much experience with other visual occluders such as a blindfold. Could it be this lack of personal experience that explains the results? To test this idea, the researchers gave a new group of twelve-month-olds some blindfold training prior to their participation in the gaze-following experiment. The infants learned that when the blindfold was held in front of their own eyes, their view was blocked. These infants behaved like the older children in the first blindfold experiment, they followed the experimenter's head turns more often in the headband condition than in the blindfold condition. Their personal experience had made a difference in their behavior (Brooks and Meltzoff, 2002; Brooks and Meltzoff, 2005; and Meltzoff and Brooks, 2007).

The Interpretation

This research shows us that young children are learning that the eyes determine what a person is looking at and possibly thinking about and interested in. A baby wants to share in what others are seeing. From nine to fourteen months, she is learning about how to do that. First, she knows to follow your head turns, later she knows you can't see anything with your eyes closed, and then she figures out that other things, like blindfolds, can block vision as well. By fourteen months she knows there is no reason to follow a person's gaze or turning head if the eyes are covered or closed.

What Should Parents Do?

Understand that your child is very interested in what you're looking at. By seeing what you see, he begins to learn what you know because he's realizing that your eyes are the window into your brain. His curiosity about all that you do related to what you're seeing is difficult to deny.

Let's say you'd like to answer a few e-mails, so you set out toys to occupy your child while you work. Unfortunately your plan probably won't work and now you know why. Your child will be interested in what you're looking at and doing and will want to get involved. It's not only that he loves you the best and wants to be with you constantly; he is following your thinking by watching what you're looking at and getting involved with what you're doing.

Limitations of Gaze Following

Even though they can identify the target of a person's gaze quite well, toddlers demonstrate in the next piece of research that their understanding of what another person can see or be aware of is still primitive in some ways. They don't seem to realize that while a person is gazing at one thing, the person could be paying attention to something else. If you're reading a magazine, a toddler doesn't realize that you can still see her out of the corners of your eyes, and you can listen, and be aware of what she is doing.

In the last chapter you learned how children soak up information relating to emotional incidents that they're eavesdropping on. If a person sternly reprimands another for touching a toy, the person reprimanded will be reluctant to touch the toy again, but the child who eavesdropped on the emotional situation will also hesitate to touch the toy while the reprimander is looking. But what if the reprimander is distracted, reading a magazine, while still facing the child? What would the child do then?

The Research

Researchers wanted to find out, so they conducted an experiment very similar to the emotional eavesdropping experiment described in the previous chapter. As an eighteen-month-old sat on his mother's lap at a table, an experimenter seated across the table demonstrated a target action with a novel toy, something of great interest to the toddler. Then another adult (the emoter, "Nina") entered the room, was introduced to the child, sat down, and started reading a magazine. After a short amount of time, the experimenter said, "Nina, look at this," and demonstrated for her the same target action on the toy. Nina immediately expressed anger toward the experimenter.

Next, Nina's expression became neutral and she silently stood up, sat down again, oriented her body toward the child and held her magazine open in front of her at chest height. The experimenter offered the child the toy by putting it on the table in front of the child and saying, "Here." For the next twenty seconds, Nina's face was visible to the child and her eyes were gazing either toward the magazine (giving the impression that she was reading with interest) for the full twenty seconds, or toward the tabletop in front of the infant (giving the impression that she was monitoring what the child was doing with the toy with friendly interest) for the full twenty seconds. The child's behavior was observed and recorded during the twenty-second period. Then the experimenter retrieved the toy and said good-bye to Nina who left the room.

This procedure was repeated three times with three different toys for each child. Some of the children were assigned to the "Nina distracted" condition in which Nina read the magazine each time and others to the "Nina attentive" condition in which Nina watched them with the toy each time.

When offered the toy, the children in the "Nina attentive" condition were hesitant to touch it, less likely to perform the target action, and spent more time monitoring Nina compared to the children in the "Nina distracted" condition. Indeed, the behavior of the children in the "Nina distracted" condition was indistinguishable from the behavior of a control group of children who went through the same procedure except that Nina responded neutrally to the experimenter instead of angrily: they eagerly touched and played with the toy, often imitating the target action.

The toddlers' behavior indicates that they expected Nina to become angry if they played with the toy, but only if she could see them, and they assumed she couldn't seem them when she was reading a magazine. They didn't seem to appreciate the fact that, even while gazing at a magazine, Nina could be attending to their actions on the toy, she could look up any time, or she could be alerted by sound to what the child was doing (the children appeared to make no attempt to silence the toys, each of which made a noise when the target action was performed) (Repacholi, Meltzoff, and Olsen, 2008).

The Interpretation

From this research it's apparent that young children's understanding about vision and attention is limited. They believe that people only see and pay attention to what they are gazing at directly; they don't understand that people can divide their attention and use peripheral vision and hearing to be aware of more than what's going on in the direction of their gaze. That's why the children would play with the toy when the emoter looked at the magazine.

There's more, however, that's important about this research. Remember that in the emotional eavesdropping experiment, the children didn't play with the forbidden toy because they had eavesdropped on the emotional interaction between the emoter and the experimenter and wanted to avoid provoking a similar response directed toward themselves.

It's important to understand that when toddlers keep themselves from touching an object that's forbidden, it's a strain. Given the high level of interest in the toys, it was no small feat for the children in the "Nina attentive" condition of the experiment to inhibit their natural exploratory behavior. They did so because their desire to avoid having the anger directed at themselves was so strong it outweighed their desire to pursue their natural interest. Their natural inclination is to thoroughly explore objects and toys that they encounter, satisfying their curiosity as they learn to master their environment. To hold back from doing what's appropriate to their age and development causes children undue stress.

What Should Parents Do?

A toddler is programmed to explore his world—that is how she learns and develops. If you ask her nicely to not touch something, she won't likely be able to comply, not because she's naughty or doesn't respect your request, but because her self-control is limited and her drive to explore is strong.

Now, a parent could exploit a young child's interest in avoiding emotional reprimands by yelling at him or others when approaching a breakable statue or a wood-burning stove, but doing so would cause the child stress. The anger puts stress on the child, and then there is the added stress of trying to inhibit his impulse to explore. To avoid putting such stress on a toddler, it's better to put the statue out of reach and barricade the wood-burning stove. By doing so you're avoiding overtaxing your child's ability to keep away from precious or dangerous objects when you're looking at him. Plus, if your eyes glance away from your child while he's in the vicinity of the statue or stove, he'll think you can't see him, so he may go for the statue, breaking it, or for the wood-burning stove, burning himself. His limited understanding about what you are aware of allows him to go for these forbidden objects when you're focused on your knitting.

Children are not being sneaky by keeping away from forbidden objects when parents are constantly monitoring them and going for them when parents glance at a magazine, wash dishes, or stitch on a piece of needlework. It's healthy curiosity, limited self-control, and immature cognitive development that's working here.

Down the developmental road a bit, as your child approaches age three, she will have developed some impulse control as well as better cognitive and communicative skills. She'll be better able to understand why she shouldn't touch the wood stove and to control any impulse to do so that might arise. She'll be able to comply with your prohibitions even when you're not looking directly at her and won't be stressed when doing so, as long they are given with patience and not anger.

Pointing

Right around your baby's first birthday, look for him to be pointing at various objects around the house and elsewhere. Once he starts to talk, he'll add words to the pointing gesture saying, "Whas'at?" Now, you might think that pointing is only about learning various words. Certainly it is, but it's much more. Your child attempts to get inside your head by pointing.

A young baby engages solely with you or with an object. He'll focus on a rattle he's holding without pulling you into his interest in the rattle. Even if you talk in parentese about the rattle he's holding, he simply can't create a triangle that involves you, him, and the rattle; he's only able cognitively to focus on you or the rattle. Once your child is one year old, however, he expands his ability to focus by looking at an object and then drawing you into what he's interested in by pointing at it.

The authors of the book *The Scientist in the Crib* call this pointing phenomenon the cognitive triangle. The baby points to an object, creating a triangle with its three corners being her, the object, and the parent. This triangle makes learning so much more efficient. A child could learn things on her own, but by pointing she draws you into what she's interested in, and when you respond with a thoughtful, informative, yet age-appropriate response, she acquires information quickly.

One-year-old babies usually don't point to familiar objects; they point to unusual and unfamiliar items and in doing so are asking about the object's function, safeness, and uniqueness.

The Research

Pointing is produced more frequently than any other type of gesture over the second and the third years, and it is supported by the parents' verbal and nonverbal responses. At first, children point at objects in close proximity to them and then, a couple of months later, to objects in the distance.

In a study in Spain, a researcher videotaped children during play, bath, and dinner in their own homes with their mothers present. The study lasted twelve months, with the researchers visiting the homes every three months. At the beginning of the study, half of the children were one year old and the others were two years old.

The researchers transcribed from the videotapes the instances of the children using pointing gestures and/or verbal means to indicate a specific target. While the frequency of these instances varied considerably from child to child, on average they occurred about once every two minutes for the younger children and once per minute for the older ones. The data also revealed the following about the specific means the children used to indicate a target:

- Pointing combined with a preverbal vocalization (like *ga*) was typical from twelve to twenty-four months of age.

- Pointing alone was also evident from twelve months on.

- Pointing combined with a content word such as "doll" or "horse" emerged at eighteen months and continued during the third year.

- Pointing plus a deictic (showing or pointing) word such as "there," "that," "this," and "here" emerged at twenty-one months and continued during the third year.

- Pointing was used widely across ages, especially combined with speech, and even after a child was able to use a deictic word alone.

Why is pointing so prevalent across ages? The researchers suggest three reasons. First, pointing is easy to do and conveys localization information efficiently (both direction and distance). Second, pointing plays an important role in early language development: it draws another person's attention directly to an object to be named. Third, even after a child can use a deictic word alone to indicate a target, pointing along with the word can help with localization, especially if the target is difficult to locate, such as when it is fully or partially hidden. (Of course, adults do this too.)

In this longitudinal study, the mother's support was clear. She tended to actively work with the child to specify the reference by visually searching for the target as well as by looking at the child's face. Once a mother identifies a target that her child is referencing, the foundation is laid for naming and discussing the target.

The researchers speculated that those deictic words (like "that" or "this") or content words (like "ball" or "dog") used by older children when pointing seemed to play a key role in the transition from single-word to multiple-word sentences, from "That" or "Ball" to "That's the ball."

They also suggest that once children learn to use deictic words, they have at their disposal a useful communicative device that supports further language acquisition. They can tag individual objects that are moving or changing or part of a large group of similar objects (e.g., a particular fish swimming in an aquarium is "*that* fish") and can point their parent's attention to the object of interest, allowing for further communication about it. By pointing and saying "this" or "that" at the same time, the child efficiently communicates about targets, thereby young language learners are able to connect language directly with objects and derive meaning from the ensuing communication with the parent (Rodrigo, Gonzalez, de Vega, Muneton-Ayala, and Rodriguez, 2004).

In another experiment, with twelve- to eighteen-month-old children, researchers had interesting objects—a radio-controlled model car, a doll whose arms and legs moved, a telephone, and a musical toy—for the children to see at different times during the experimental procedure. When the doll was visible, it was placed at a distance from the child. When the telephone and musical toy were present, they were demonstrated by an experimenter and then left on a nearby table just out of reach of the child. When the car was visible, it moved from a position far from the child to a position near the child. The researchers observed and recorded the pointing and reaching behaviors of the child. They also took note of when the child looked to his mother, seated nearby.

The researchers wondered: Do pointing and reaching serve different purposes? Or do they serve the same purpose, but reaching is used more by younger children and pointing by older children? The results showed that the children, even the youngest ones, didn't reach for the distant doll, they pointed at it. In contrast, the children did more reaching than pointing when it came to the just-out-of-reach toys on the table. These results indicate that pointing and reaching serve two different purposes. Pointing refers another per-

son to an object or event ("Look at that!" or "What's that?").
Reaching demonstrates an interest in handling an object ("I want
that.") Pointing does not substitute for reaching.

The results did not indicate that children, as they got older,
pointed significantly more and reached less. What did vary with
age was frequency and timing of the looks to Mother while pointing. The proportion of gestures associated with visual checking
tended to increase with age for pointing, but remained stable for
reaching. Also, a timing shift occurred. The twelve-month-olds
mainly looked at their mothers *after* pointing, the fourteen-month-
olds mainly looked *while* pointing, and the sixteen- and eighteen-
month-olds more often looked *before* pointing. The pattern for
reaching was different. The twelve-month-olds looked equally
often before, during, and after reaching. The older children looked
almost only during reaching.

The researchers speculated that the older children, of sixteen to
eighteen months, did more planning with respect to their involvement in pointing, because first they checked for their mother's attention, then they pointed, and then they vocalized an internal state
such as a feeling, perception, or belief about the object of interest.

The different patterns of visual checking for pointing versus
reaching reflect the different purposes for that checking. When the
child is reaching, he looks to his mother or other social partner as
a means to achieve an object. When the child is pointing, he looks
to his partner to gain her attention in order to share reference to
the object and often to gain information about that object.

The researchers suggest that getting someone's attention and
then sharing something with her by pointing indicates some awareness that the other person has a mind of her own and can feel
interest, amusement, or other emotions. Included in this research
article, the authors note that young children who are autistic, a
disorder characterized by profound deficits in understanding the

minds of others, rarely direct the attention of another person to an object or event (Franco and Butterworth, 1996).

The Interpretation

When children point, it's as if they're saying, "Look at that!" It's a directive for another person's attention. Deictic (showing, pointing) words are also useful for attracting and keeping the attention of the person whom the child is addressing, particularly because mothers are busy and easily distracted by other events.

Just as fine finger exploration helps the infant find out details of various objects, pointing might have the same exploratory function, except it is applied to distant objects and involves a social partner. When pointing, children are taking responsibility for their own learning, asking another to offer information about what they're pointing to. They realize that their pointing partner has thoughts inside her mind about the object of interest. Pointing relies on some awareness of a psychological process between people, which includes attention sharing between another person and the self. It's as if the child is asking his social partner, "I would like you to communicate to me the name of that thing over there and tell me about its function or purpose" or "That thing over there is interesting to me. I want to show it to you. Is it interesting to you too?" Pointing plays a role when seeking information and demonstrates a social awareness, in that another person is being asked to shed light on an object of interest and possibly share that interest. Pointing is a highly socialized gesture.

What Should Parents Do?

A twelve-month-old may see a fly on the window, fold her thumb over her middle, ring, and baby fingers while extending her index finger toward the fly, and then look at her first and most important teacher—you. That point of the index finger is your cue to respond. Even if the child does not say, "Whas'at?" you can see the question written all over her face. The parent just knows to say, "That's a fly." Your child is relying on you to figure out her world, and she wants to share her joy of discovery with you. So many things that are common and familiar to you are new and full of wonder to your child. Your sense of wonder will be renewed as you look at the world anew through your child's eyes, share her interests and communicate with her about them. In so doing, you will be supporting your child's learning and at the same time learning new things yourself (one mother of a young boy now knows the difference between a front-loader, backhoe, and excavator) and developing your relationship with your child.

Take notice of the difference between pointing and reaching by observing your child. The following example will give you an idea about what to look for. A nineteen-month-old child at a pizza restaurant pointed to an unusual looking jar well within her reach while asking, "Whas'at?" The mother answered as she moved the jar out of the toddler's reach, "Those are pepper flakes; they're hot." The child heard the name and that it was not something for her to try. Then she eyed her older sister's juice box. This time she didn't point and ask, "Whas'at?" she simply reached for the box. She knew what it was and didn't hesitate going for it.

Understanding Another's Intentions

As your child moves into his second year, there's so much more that he's aware of regarding your mind and brain and thinking processes: he knows that your gaze is important and so follows it; he knows that where your eyes look is the thoroughfare to your thoughts and interests; and he points at objects to gain your attention and pull words and ideas from your mind to his.

There's more that your child knows about in relation to you; he's beginning to understand your intentions. If you pour cream from a small pitcher into your coffee mug and miss your target, the cream spilling on the table, he'll notice and possibly say, "uh-oh." Given the chance to pour cream into his own cup, he won't miss his cup as you did; he'll try his utmost to pour the cream into his cup without spilling. He will have picked up on the gist of what you were trying to do and so will imitate that, rather than what you actually did.

The Research

In a research experiment, eighteen-month-old children, one at time, watched as an adult tried and failed three times to perform a target action with an object. Next, the child had a chance to handle the object. This procedure was repeated four times with different objects. The toddlers watched as an adult tried but failed over and over again to pull the ends off a wooden dumbbell. They watched an adult try to hang a nylon cord necklace on a prong, with the adult trying again and again to complete the task but ultimately failing. They watched an adult try to activate a buzzer on a box using a stick, trying over and over to hit the target with the tool but missing. They also watched adults try and fail to perform two other target acts on different objects. At least, this is the way it appeared. Of course, the adult in each case was an actor and his actual intent was to give the impression that he was trying to produce a certain target action with each set of objects.

After each tried-and-failed demonstration, when the toddlers had their chance to handle the objects, they didn't imitate the "failed" actions (the actual behavior of the adult), but instead completed the actions correctly: they pulled apart the wooden dumb-bell, hung the necklace, and activated the buzzer. In fact, their performance was indistinguishable from that of another group of eighteen-month-olds who went through the same procedure but witnessed the adult perform the target acts correctly.

To make sure that the performance of target acts was not something that the toddlers would do spontaneously with the ob-jects, but was indeed the result of watching the demonstrations, the researchers included a control group in the study. The toddlers in the control group handled the objects without first witnessing demonstrations of successful or failed attempts at target acts. These toddlers produced significantly fewer of those target acts compared with the children who witnessed the demonstrations (Meltzoff, 1995).

The Interpretation

Be aware that your toddler picks up on and gets the general idea of what others are attempting to do. It's just one more amazing attribute of preverbal children. This research shows that at least by eighteen months, children interpret human acts not as mere move-ments in space, but ones with deeper meanings. When they see an action, they read beyond what was literally done and infer the goal that's behind it.

What Should Parents Do?

Live your life naturally, knowing that even when you goof up, your child learns from what you were actually intending to do in the situation. When you spill milk, drop a book, or misplace keys, your child will know that you weren't intending to do these acts but instead wanted to pour the milk into the glass, hold onto the book, and keep track of your keys. You and significant others in your child's life are often hurried and do not act perfectly. Nevertheless, your toddler will respond to what you're meaning to do rather than what you actually do.

Not Understanding Objects' Intentions

While children pick up on your intentions when you attempt an act but fail, they don't seem to have the same capacity for understanding the inaccurate movements produced by an inanimate object. In another experiment, they didn't imitate and correct the missed efforts of a mechanical device.

The Research

The same researchers built a device that did not look human but nevertheless mimicked the movements of the person in the previous research experiment trying to complete one of the tasks. The device had pincers that grasped the dumbbell on each end (just as the human hand did) and then pulled outward. The pincers then slipped off one end (just as the human hand did), and because they were spring-loaded, closed immediately (just as the fingers of the human hand did).

One group of eighteen-month-olds watched a human try and fail to pull the dumbbell apart, the other group watched the mechanical device "try" and fail. The toddlers in both groups were riveted by what they saw. There appeared to be no difference in reaction to the human versus the machine demonstration. However, the two groups behaved very differently when they had a chance to handle the dumbbell. The toddlers who saw the human's failed attempt were six times more likely to pull the dumbbell apart, thus producing the intended target act, compared to the toddlers who watched the mechanical device.

Since the movement patterns of the human and those of the mechanical device were very similar, it is not likely that the movement patterns alone suggested the pulling apart of the dumbbell. The movements were interpreted differently when performed by a human versus a machine.

The data suggests that children at eighteen months, if not exactly aware of intentions, are at least thinking in terms of goals that are connected to people and not to things. They are making sense of human behavior in terms of a psychological framework including the goals of acts, if not the intentions of actors (Meltzoff, 1995).

The Interpretation

By eighteen months, as your child sees what people actually do, he is aware that there is a deeper level to that behavior. He understands the movements of objects in terms of physics, but knows that physics alone does not account for human actions. There are psychological reasons behind the behavior of people. Intentions and goals are used to explain the behavior of persons, not things.

Your toddler's not about to follow around the lawn mower and copy its grass-cutting abilities. In the same regard, she's not going to read and duplicate the intentions of that lawn mower when it's not working properly. With people, children read into the invisible goals or intentions behind a situation, but of course there are no intentions when mechanical devices are involved.

What Should Parents Do?

Your child is beginning to comprehend that intentions and goals are used to explain the behavior of persons, not things. Last year, your child grasped that objects require assistance to move whereas people move on their own. Now, she's applying a much deeper meaning to the differentiation between people and things: as a human and not an object, you and others have internal, unseen motivations that make you do what you do. Even though she can't actually see you thinking about what you're going to do next, your child knows there are deliberate reasons to your actions, even if your attempts at them fail. And if you attempt these actions, so can she, because she realizes that she's human too.

As this study shows, children sees themselves to be like you and not like the machines or objects around them, and so your actions and not machines' are the ones your child is interested in imitating. Your child has learned that there are actual physical reasons for explaining objects' actions as compared to psychological reasons for explaining the behavior of people. Young children come to understand that car keys don't lose themselves, people misplace them. Likewise, a sippy cup doesn't just fall from a table on its own, and a toy on a high shelf requires some help if it's going to get down to the ground.

There's more to pointing than the mere act of using one's index finger to locate a target, then look at someone and say, "What's that?" If a child points at a clock and says, "Whas'at?" any parent will say, "It's a clock." For now the child is satisfied, but eventually the child will want to know more about clocks and time. He'll want to know about the second, minute, and hour hands; he'll want to know that there are twenty-four hours in a day and 365 days in a year. When older, he'll be curious about the seasons, leap year, how the earth goes around the sun, how the earth tilts on its axis, and the winter and summer solstices. You can see how one object takes a child's learning deeper and deeper into a topic. The human brain allows for such learning on many, many subjects.

It's important to keep in mind that the essential thing is the relationship between parent and child. Reading minds, following gazes, and pointing is about understanding each other, building a relationship, and sharing interests. Learning works both ways: the child may be learning the name for an insect, and the parent may be learning to see the insect in a new way and, more generally, learning to be childlike again.

You'll be your child's teacher on many topics, but teachers, coaches, peers, books, television, and the Internet will also contribute to your child's learning as he delves into a subject that interests him, whether it's sharks, submarines, or sex. You'll want to stay on top of your child's interests, making sure that his sources and those other people influencing him are positive and productive and not negative and destructive.

REFERENCES

Brooks, R., and A. N. Meltzoff. 2002. The importance of eyes: How infants interpret adult looking behavior. *Developmental Psychology* 38: 958–66.

Brooks, R., and A. N. Meltzoff. 2005. The development of gaze following and its relation to language. *Developmental Science* 8: 535–43.

Brooks, R., and A. N. Meltzoff. 2008. Infant gaze following and pointing predict accelerated vocabulary growth through two years of age: A longitudinal, growth curve modeling study. *Journal of Child Language* 35: 207–20.

Franco, F., and G. Butterworth. 1996. Pointing and social awareness: Declaring and requesting in the second year. *Journal of Child Language* 23: 307–36.

Meltzoff, A. N. 1995. Understanding the intentions of others: Re-enactment of intended acts by 18-month-old children. *Developmental Psychology* 31: 838–50.

Meltzoff, A. N., and R. Brooks. 2007. Eyes wide shut: The importance of eyes in infant gaze following and understanding other minds. In R. Flom, K. Lee, and D. Muir, eds. *Gaze Following: Its Development and Significance*. Mahwah, NJ: Erlbaum.

Repacholi, B. M., A. N. Meltzoff, and B. Olsen. 2008. Infants' understanding of the link between visual perception and emotion: "If she can't see me doing it, she won't get angry." *Developmental Psychology* 44: 561-74.

Rodrigo, M. J., A. Gonzalez, M. de Vega, M. Muneton-Ayala, and G. Rodriguez. 2004. From gestural to verbal deixis: A longitudinal study with spanish infants and toddlers. *First Language* 24: 71–90.

Chapter 8

Sorting Objects and Using Tools

By now you may be thinking that there's little more that can dazzle you about your child's developing mind and brain. Yet truly as your baby becomes a bit older, there's much more that will amaze you. You'll see your baby demonstrate an important skill she'll use her entire life: categorization. One day you may see your child put cars in one pile and trucks in another. Not only that, she'll also begin to use tools. Not tools like a hammer or a saw—those tools are too challenging, and dangerous—but she may use a stick as a tool to retrieve a ball from under the sofa, or she may use a blanket to pull Teddy around the room. You'll witness your child actually thinking and planning in order to solve baby-sized problems.

Categorizing Objects

Think about how complicated learning would be if the human brain didn't allow us to create categories. We learn about foods and remember their various names and types by putting them into categories. Beans and carrots go with other vegetables, and apples and oranges go in the fruit category. Breads, grains, meats, and beverages have their own categories.

When learning a new vegetable—artichoke or asparagus, for example—a child will examine it and likely classify it along with other vegetables. By doing so, he'll remember its name more easily and make comparisons with other vegetables regarding shape, taste, and texture.

If people were not able to categorize, they would need to learn about each food item individually. Categorization helps all of us, and that includes young children, make sense of daily experiences by reducing the enormous amount of new information we encounter every day and slotting it into categories so that we can understand it and recall it efficiently.

Babies are able to make inferences about objects, events, sounds, animals, and people that they have never experienced by fitting them into categories they've previously experienced. A young child who encounters a dog and learns that it barks, when coming across another dog, slots it into the dog category and assumes it will bark too. She does not need to learn anew that this dog barks; she expects that it does.

The Research

Researchers showed three- and four-month-olds twelve pictures of different cats, two at a time. The infants watched with great interest from the first to the last presentation, not habituating, presumably due to the level of complexity and degree of variability of the cat pictures. Next came the test trial: A novel picture of a cat was presented along with a picture of a dog. Even though the other cats had all been very interesting to look at, the babies looked reliably longer at the picture of the dog, indicating that it was more novel. How was the dog more novel? It was from a different category. The preferential looking at the dog picture indicated to the researchers that the children knew that the dog didn't belong with the group of cats (Quinn, Eimas, and Rosenkrantz, 1993).

In another experiment, with nine- and eleven-month-olds, researchers assembled a group of three-dimensional miniature replicas of animals and vehicles. The objects all differed substantially from one another in appearance. In the animal category there was a horse, a bird, a turtle, a rabbit, and an elephant. In the vehicle category there was a motorcycle, a train engine, a school bus, an all-terrain vehicle, and a cement truck. All the objects were sprayed with a nontoxic plastic coating so that texture wouldn't hint at categorical membership.

Each baby was given four objects from one category, one at a time, to handle and examine (e.g., horse, bird, turtle, rabbit). Those same four objects were presented again, one at a time. Next, a fifth object from the category was given to the baby, one that they hadn't yet seen (e.g., elephant). Finally, an object from the other category was presented for hands-on exploration (e.g., motorcycle). None of the objects were verbally labeled by the experimenter. (As we'll see in Chapter 10, adding labels helps babies form categories, but in this experiment they wanted to see if the babies could do it without any help.)

Most of the children spent more time examining the last object, the one from the different category, than they did the second-to-last object, the one from the familiar category. The babies hadn't seen either object before, but they took a greater interest in the one from the different category, indicating that it was more novel to them. This showed that the babies had formed conceptual categories for animals and for vehicles. A repeat of the experiment showed similar results for seven-month-olds.

After finding that the nine- and eleven-month-olds could separate animals and vehicles into categories, next the researchers wanted to see if children this age could still make the categorical distinction when the animals and vehicles were more similar to one another in appearance. In this case they repeated the experiment but used birds and airplanes. The birds had outstretched wings, like the planes. Some of the airplanes had painted-on mouths, teeth, and eyes (WWII Flying Tiger markings), whereas for several of the birds such features were not prominent. All in all, the birds and the airplanes looked very much alike. Again the objects were sprayed with the plastic coating, so their surface texture was also the same. The results showed that the similarity of appearance did not make the categorization task too difficult (Mandler and McDonough, 1993).

In another research setting, experimenters gave fourteen-month-olds four balls and four blocks of various colors, patterns, sizes, and textures. Two of the blocks and two of the balls were made of compressible material (foam rubber or flexible plastic); the other two blocks and the other two balls were made of rigid material (wood or hard plastic). By observing the sequence in which the babies touched the objects, the researchers knew that the babies (some more than others) were able to classify the objects into their respective ball and block categories. Then an experimenter demonstrated the compressibility of each of the objects. The babies who were more advanced in language and categorization ability were able to quickly reclassify the objects into categories of compressible versus rigid (Ellis and Oakes, 2006).

As dexterity improves, around sixteen months, toddlers will spontaneously arrange objects into a single category such as gathering all the balls together from a set of balls and boxes. A month or two later, when given a set of balls and boxes to play with, toddlers will sort the objects manually into the two respective catego-

ries (more details about this study later in the chapter) (Gopnik
and Meltzoff, 1987).

The Interpretation

The results of these research experiments show how skilled babies
are when it comes to putting objects into categories. Even when
the objects were similar in appearance, the categorization tasks
were not too difficult for the children. Of course, the children became more skilled as they advanced in age from three months to
fourteen months. The children demonstrated that they had a conceptual category for objects as similar as birds and airplanes. Then
as their knowledge of categories and verbal labels expanded, the
babies in the experiment with blocks of various colors, patterns,
sizes, and textures had acquired the ability to categorize with more
flexibility: they could categorize items one way, then rapidly recognize a different way of grouping them.

What Should Parents Do?

Give your child sorting tasks. For instance, mix together spoons
and forks in a pile. You can begin the task by separating out a
spoon and fork from the pile and then encouraging your child to
join in the game. Sorting laundry, emptying the dishwasher, and
putting toys away all involve categorization. Since your child loves
being right by your side, you might as well include her in these
sorting tasks.

When grocery shopping, involve your child in the task of buying items from different categories. Vegetables, fruit, canned soup,
baby food, and cleaning supplies are all categories that your child
can come to know.

Your child also learns to categorize items through play. When, in a few years, your child plays store, he'll sort various grocery items into their categories as he sets up his store all on his own.

Categories and Their Accompanying Actions

When your child plays with vehicles, it will be obvious to you that she's able to sort trucks, motorcycles, SUVs, sedans, and station wagons into individual categories. During such play sessions children also display the knowledge that items belonging to one category may act in a way that wouldn't be appropriate for items belonging to another category—for example, animals drink and vehicles don't.

The Research

In a research study with fourteen-month-olds, an experimenter modeled actions with little replicas of real-world objects while the child watched. The experimenter modeled a dog drinking from a cup while saying, "Sip, sip, umm, good." She also modeled the dog going to sleep in a bed while saying, "Night, night." With a miniature car, the experimenter modeled starting the car with a key and giving a person a ride. After each modeling demonstration, the experimenter did not give the child a turn to play with the dog or car that had been used. Instead she gave the child a different animal or vehicle along with the prop used in the demonstration, and watched to see what the child would do.

When the child observed the experimenter model a dog drinking from a cup, and then was given a cat, rabbit, fish, bird, anteater, or armadillo along with the cup, the child typically acted out the animal having a drink. If the child was given a vehicle, he did not make the vehicle drink. Similarly, when the experimenter modeled a car being started with a key, the infants imitated this action with other vehicles (truck, bus, motorcycle, airplane, forklift, and power shovel), but not with animals. They didn't just repeat what the experimenter had done; the children imitated selectively according to what they knew about actions of real animals and vehicles. In another experiment, these researchers found similar results even for children as young as nine months of age (McDonough and Mandler, 1998).

The Interpretation

At fourteen months, and even as early as nine months, the children knew that a vehicle wouldn't take a drink but an animal would. The children knew that the dog, rabbit, and cat and even the less familiar animals, the anteater and the armadillo, were in the animal category, and so they did similar things, such as drink and sleep. The children recognized members of the vehicle category and knew that vehicles didn't drink or sleep, but they started with a key and could give a person a ride. The children's behavior revealed their awareness of the fact that certain actions are appropriate for animals but not vehicles and vice versa.

What Should Parents Do?

For fun, collect a key, a toy car, and a doll. Pretend to start the car with the key and then have the car move across the floor as if the key got the car moving. Now put the key to the doll's tummy, turn the key as if to start it, and pretend to have the doll walk across the floor. See if your fourteen-month-old child looks perplexed or amused. While you don't want to fool your child into believing that the doll started walking from the key, it's fun to see if your child knows that this situation is impossible. You can say, "The key can't start the dolly walking." If by chance you own a doll that winds up and then performs some movements, introduce it to your child. By doing so, you encourage your child to put this doll into another category of objects that move when wound up by a key. Such activities engage and challenge your child's thinking skills, plus they're enjoyable for both of you.

Transferring Categorical Knowledge

There is yet another way children put objects into categories. Let's say your child has a pop-up toy. It's the kind where four doors open revealing various Disney characters—Minnie Mouse, Donald Duck, Mickey Mouse, and Pluto—that pop up when the doors open. Your eighteen-month-old loves the toy and plays with it again and again.

One day at Grandma's, your child eyes your mother's pop-up toy. Hers, though, is a slightly different type. The little doors open using a different mechanism, popping up a dog, cat, pig, and cow. Your toddler sits on the floor at Grandma's and pops up each of the four animals.

What a smartie. Your child didn't see the second pop-up toy as a totally new and different toy, he recognized the similarity between the two toys and determined that since they looked alike, they must work alike, and so was able to figure out how the second one worked based on his experience with the first. He had developed a pop-up toy category and applied what he knew about it to Grandma's version of the toy.

Research tells us that your baby mentally put the two toys in the same category because each toy had four doors, opening mechanisms, and attractive characters that pop up.

Recall the experiment in Chapter 5 with the wailing can? Once children discovered through hands-on exploration that a can wailed when shaken and tilted, the nine- to sixteen-month-olds in that study shook and tilted other cans of the same shape, expecting them to wail also. They categorized the cans and generalized that if one had the property, the others would too.

Even without the opportunity to practice, your child at about eighteen months can watch someone use an object, remember how that person used it, and apply that use to other similar objects. She does so by categorizing the slightly different objects into the same category, assuming and then testing out that they'll work the same.

The Research

Researchers conducted the following experiment with twelve- and eighteen-month-olds. The children watched an experimenter place a puppet over her hand and perform three target actions with the puppet: she took a mitten off the puppet's hand, shook the mitten, ringing a little bell that was inside, and then put the mitten back on the puppet's hand. The babies were not given the opportunity to play with the puppet themselves. Half of the children saw the actions demonstrated with a pink rabbit puppet wearing a pink mitten. The others saw a gray mouse puppet with a gray mitten.

The next day, the researchers gave the babies a puppet different from the one they had seen the researcher use previously. The children who had seen the pink rabbit were given the gray mouse, and vice versa. The eighteen-month-olds knew exactly what to do with this puppet. On average, each child performed, or attempted to perform, two of the three target actions (removing the mitten, shaking the mitten, putting the mitten back on). They remembered what they had seen the adult do with the first puppet, put the new object in the same category and used it appropriately.

In contrast, the twelve-month-olds showed no evidence of having learned from the previous puppet demonstration what to do with the new puppet. They very rarely performed or attempted a target action. In fact, their behavior was indistinguishable from that of a control group of children who hadn't seen any puppet demonstration. It was not for lack of ability. When the twelve-month-olds were given the same puppet they had seen previously, they readily performed or attempted one or two of the target actions, showing that they had learned and remembered what they saw and could apply it to the same object. However, they weren't able to generalize to the new puppet (Hayne, Boniface, and Barr, 2000).

The Interpretation

By eighteen months, when children play with an object or even if they only see another person use an object, they know how to use another similar one because of their ability to categorize. Your child knows that you'll read her the book that you just checked out from the library, because she slots that library book in a category with other library books. She also knows that that book in the library category goes on a special shelf so as not to have it mixed up with books of her own.

A new coat will go in the closet with all the other coats. Being able to remember, imitate, and place new objects, events, and actions into already established categories makes learning so much more efficient and the child so much more competent as he enters new and ever-expanding environments: friends' and family members' homes, playgrounds, libraries, and children's museums, to name only a few.

What Should Parents Do?

There are times when children can transfer knowledge from one situation to the next. If you've always taken your child to the same grocery store where you've developed a routine and a set of standards for behavior, when going into a different grocery store, your child will apply that same set of standards and fall into your established routine in the new grocery store.

But what happens if you take your child into a completely new environment? Let's say you're taking your child on an airplane trip for the first time. Your child has no airplane traveling category to draw from. In this situation you'll do lots of work, establishing routines and standards for behavior that are appropriate to your child's developmental age. The first time is the most difficult; then it gets easier as your child develops a mental category for airplane travel that she applies from one trip to the next.

Manually Sorting Objects

Up until about sixteen months, sorting objects is mostly an intellectual proposition for your child. Next, you'll see your child manually sort objects into categories all on his own. One grandmother watched her granddaughter put ornaments on the Christmas tree. She grouped all the stars in one section of the Christmas tree, all the bells in another, the snowmen in another, and the Santas in another. The grandmother was amazed at her granddaughter's skill at sorting and categorizing. As it turns out, most toddlers are equipped to take on such tasks.

The Research

Over the course of several months, researchers examined how the sorting ability of twelve children matured. At the beginning of the study, the children were fourteen to eighteen months old. Every three weeks, each child was brought into the lab and given eight objects, four of one type and four of another. In one task there were four flat yellow rectangles made of masonite and four brightly colored plastic humanlike figures. In the second task there were four pillboxes made of hard plastic, and four balls made of red play dough. In the third task there were four plastic Raggedy Andy dolls and four red plastic cars. The eight objects were placed on the table in front of the child in a predetermined random arrangement. Then each child was told, "Play with these things" or "Fix them all up." The experimenter placed his hands on the table, palms upward. Another adult observed the child's behavior, recording each time an object was touched or objects were grouped.

The researchers wanted to see if the children placed four objects of one kind together. The children did not need to manipulate the other category. This was the first level of categorization behavior. A second level of categorization was achieved when the child touched or manipulated first the four objects from one group and then the four from the other group. The third type of categorization was when the child grouped the objects into two distinct categories. This third level of categorization was achieved if the child sorted all eight objects by moving them from their original locations and putting them into two groups or piles.

The results were as follows: single-category grouping first occurred at about sixteen months; manipulating two kinds of objects at about sixteen-and-a-half months; two-category grouping at a little over seventeen months. These were average ages; there was typically a five-month range of ages at each level of achievement.

However, no matter the age at which it was begun, the sequence of achieving level one categorization, followed at a later date by level two, then, still later, level three, was the same for all but one child (Gopnik and Meltzoff, 1987).

The Interpretation

This research tells us that there's a natural progression that children travel through as they advance in their ability to categorize. First, if given four toy dogs and four toy cats, they will pull out just one of the categories, the dogs or the cats, not both. The next step is when they pull out first one category and then the next. The last is when they sort the toys into their proper category as they come, as if saying, "Here's a dog, it goes into this category; here's a cat, it goes into this category," and so on until all the animals are placed in their correct category. It's an orderly progression that children follow no matter when they start on the road to physically sorting objects into groups.

What Should Parents Do?

Because your child regularly puts toy vehicles in one pile and toy people in another, it's obvious that he's interested in organizing his world, and he proves it by sorting objects. It's a satisfying mental exercise that most children perform all on their own.

Since most children at about eighteen months sort objects into categories, assemble some boxes, baskets, and bins in the area where your child plays. Designate a box for dolls, a basket for blocks, a bin for toy vehicles. Make sorting toys the preamble to your bedtime routine. Do so by sorting the toys scattered on the floor into their appropriate categories designated by the boxes, baskets, or bins. Involve your child. Make it fun, not a forced event.

This activity meets your child where his learning lies—plus you acquire a neater space, be it living room, den, playroom, or basement. Also, you create a positive habit relating to tidying up before bed.

There's an item that you can purchase from an education toy source called "attribute blocks." These blocks are of different shapes, colors, and sizes. Mix up the blocks and set them out for your child to play with; then resist interfering. Watch your child as she goes from single-category grouping, to two-category grouping, to multiple-category grouping. As a child's mind advances in its ability to categorize, it's fun for parents to take time to watch it happen.

Using Tools

Toward the end of your child's first year, along with putting objects and events into categories, look for her to use tools. People use tools every day. Hairbrushes, pencils, rakes, vacuum cleaners, silverware, and computers are among the most common that children observe parents use daily and so copy their usage. Even though children copy what you do with tools, they are actually able to invent ways to use tools all on their own.

Let's say your nine-month-old has a problem; she wants her doll who is sitting on a blanket. Now, the baby could crawl over to it, but then she has a flash of brilliance: "Why crawl when all I need to do is pull this corner of my blanket to retrieve my dolly?" The child is using the blanket as a tool to retrieve her doll. As early as nine months, parents will see their children use tools for reaching goals.

The Research

Researchers tested nine-month-olds' ability to use tools. They put a sponge block in front of each child in the experimental group, who was seated on Mother's lap at a table. A cloth was laid out behind the block, and as the child watched, the experimenter placed an attractive object on the far end of the cloth, out of reach of the child. The block wasn't big enough to obstruct the child's view of the toy at the end of the cloth, but it was in the way of the child reaching the near end of the cloth. The same procedure was used for children in a control group, the only difference being that the toy was not placed on top of the cloth, but instead just beside it.

The infants in the experimental group typically tossed or placed aside the sponge block, grabbed the cloth, and pulled to retrieve the interesting toy. The infants in the control group typically picked up the block and played with *it*. They manipulated the block, banged it on the table, and mouthed it. Apparently they knew they couldn't get the toy, and they made do with what was available: the block. They rarely touched the cloth, let alone pulled on it. It seems they knew that in order for the cloth to work for them as a tool, the desired object must be sitting on top of the cloth. Since the toy was not on top of the cloth, they didn't bother trying to pull it (Willatts, 1984).

In another experiment, researchers introduced ten-month-olds to a few basic tools: a cloth, a string, a hoop, a crook, and a stick. On, attached to, or near the tool was a fuzzy buglike mechanical toy creature that bounced and clicked when wound.

The toy and a tool were presented to the babies one at a time. The babies were highly interested in the toy, which was out of reach. They turned to the tool to use it to retrieve the toy. The experimenters recorded the children's ability to use the various tools to reach their goal.

If the colors or textures of the toy and the tool were different, it was easier for the children to solve the toy retrieval problem. The researchers concluded that the color or texture difference helped the ten-month-old children recognize that there were two distinct objects, one of which was the tool to help them acquire the toy.

The better the contact between toy and tool, the easier for the child to reach his goal. The toy sitting on the cloth and the toy attached to the string were the easiest problems for the ten-month-olds to solve. The babies had more difficulty when using the hoop or crook, with the toy placed inside and touching the curve of the tool. The biggest challenge was when the crook or stick was placed beside the toy. In the report of their experiment, the researchers noted that even many eighteen-month-olds will have difficulty using a stick to obtain an out-of-reach object (Bates, Carlson-Luden, and Bretherton, 1980).

The Interpretation

At first your child needs a little help making the intellectual connection that she can pull a hoop toward her to acquire the toy sitting inside the hoop. Let's say you take a small hula hoop and place an interesting toy inside it. The hoop is within your child's reach; the toy is not. With a ten-month-old, you might need to set the toy inside the small hoop and make sure that the toy and hoop are different colors for the child to figure out how to use the hoop as a tool. You might even need to demonstrate how to use the hoop to bring the toy toward your baby. By eighteen months, however, you won't need to do so. If your child is sitting on the floor and can't reach a toy, but can reach the hoop, he'll likely determine all on his own that he can use the hoop to lasso the desired toy.

As toddlers encounter problems, they seek to solve these problems many times by using tools; it's part of the human condition. It's as if they're inventing such usage all on their own. You'll see joy on their faces when they do so.

Let's say Grandpa's cane is lying on the floor next to the sofa. Your child's windup car has rolled out of reach under the sofa. Your child sees the car, can't reach it, whines, and points at it. Once he realizes that both you and Grandpa are occupied with other activities, he'll likely look intently at the situation, obviously thinking about it, and then suddenly, as if a lightbulb is going on over the child's head, the child will take the cane and use its crook to pull the car out from under the sofa.

What Should Parents Do?

Watch your child's use of tools and see what you can do to enhance her play. Provide a cart for your child to load up toys so that she can deliver the goods to another spot in your home. A wagon to pull up and down the sidewalk is another example of a tool used for delivery and distribution purposes. Allow your child to use scoops, shovels, and buckets when playing in the sandbox. As she plays, she determines the tools' use and makes up ways to use them all on her own. In time she'll apply such usage to other similar situations. Later your child will use marking pens, a glue stick, and scissors as tools to complete craft projects.

Allow your child to solve some problems for himself. Resist always stepping in and solving problems for your child. Realize that he's able to figure out some of them on his own, so permit him to do so, because when you do you're supporting his ingenuity. Usually all he needs is a little time to analyze the problem and then think about how to solve it using a tool.

Analogical Problem Solving

Remember in the last section on categorization the example where the eighteen-month-old child knew how to use one pop-up toy and then, with his memory at work, applied the information from that experience to another slightly different pop-up toy? Toddlers complete similar actions when using tools; researchers call it analogical problem solving and it emerges between ten and twelve months. It's nothing more than recognizing that two problems are similar and transferring a solution strategy from one to the other.

The Research

In one study, twelve-month-old babies were given three similar problems, one at a time. The underlying structure of each of the three problems was the same: The child saw an attractive toy that was out of reach. Between the child and the toy, two cloths were laid out side by side. Beyond the child's reach, there were two strings, one on each cloth, and one of the strings was attached to the toy. To get the toy, the child had to pull on the correct cloth to bring the string attached to the toy within reach and then pull on that string.

What differed between the problems was the surface features, including the type of toy, the color of the cloths, the type of string, which of the two strings was attached to the toy (left or right), whether the infant was seated on the floor, standing while supported at the hips, or seated on Mother's lap.

When the child was presented with the first problem, the experimenter and the parent said, "Can you get the toy?" and "You can get it." If the child didn't solve the problem in a short amount of time, the parent demonstrated the solution two times. The materials were replaced, and the child was encouraged to imitate the actions the parent used: pulling the correct cloth and then pulling the string to get the toy. Some of the children succeeded in getting the toy and others didn't. Next, the child was guided to the second problem at another location. Remarkably, the babies obtained the toy more readily with each additional problem. If they solved the first problem on their own, it was mostly through trial and error, but once they had solved it or had seen their parent solve it, they transferred that solution strategy to the next two analogous problems. This was evident by the fact that their approach to the second and third problem was goal-directed, intentional, and efficient. Obviously they had caught on to the method of using the cloth and then the string to pull the toy and quickly applied it to obtain the next and then the next toy (Chen, Sanchez, and Campbell, 1997).

The Interpretation

At the end of the first year, when infants use tools, they're not simply using trial-and-error experimentation or imitating others. When they find a solution to a problem by using a tool, they remember doing so and then apply its use in new situations with similar objects, demonstrating some flexible thinking.

What Should Parents Do?

We use tools for so many things. Brooms to sweep floors, hammers to pound nails, shovels to dig holes. When you're about to sweep the floor, ask your child, "I need to sweep the floor, what can I use?" Do the same when you're about to pound a nail or dig a hole in your garden. You'll see that your child is able to understand which tool works for which project, whether at home with familiar tools or at Grandma's or child care with slightly different tools used for the same purpose.

Tool Use Progression

When it comes to using tools such as silverware and hairbrushes, it will take your toddler some planning and problem-solving time before she readily masters using each tool.

There appears to be a progression that your child will follow as he masters using tools. It's fun and interesting to watch as your child gradually learns to skillfully use a tool. Here's what to look for: First, he'll explore a tool; next, he'll use it haphazardly in the task without any apparent planning involved. Then, over time, as he becomes more familiar with the tool and task, he'll take more time to perform the task, obviously planning his actions in order to use the tool with more efficiency. With lots of practice, his actions become quicker and more automatic. This level of mastery will occur at different ages depending upon the tool and task but, for most simple tools, not before your child turns two, as the next piece of research shows.

The Research

Researchers presented nine-, fourteen-, nineteen-, and twenty-four-month-olds with tools and encouraged them to use each. The researchers invited each child to perform the following tasks:

- Feed himself applesauce with a spoon

- Use a spoon to pretend to feed a toy lion

- Brush her own hair with a hairbrush

- Brush the lion's mane, coat, or tail

- Use a hammer to pound pegs

- Pick up an object using a magnet attached to the end of a handle

When necessary, an experimenter demonstrated a task before giving the child a turn to try it. The children were given several opportunities to try each task, and the researchers observed and recorded their behavior during each trial. (The children seemed to like the sweet applesauce and wanted to keep eating it, so there were many trials of that task!) The researchers found that the youngest children (nine-month-olds) were usually able to use the spoon to feed themselves the applesauce; however, they generally did not use the other tools for their designated purpose. They typically only picked them up and explored and played with the objects as babies do. The older children (fourteen-, nineteen, and twenty-four-month-olds) could accomplish all of the tool tasks and did so about 80 percent of the time. Although these children could usually complete the tasks in one way or another, they hadn't yet mastered using these tools.

The researchers found that the older children tended to be more efficient in their use of a tool when the task was self-directed (feeding themselves or brushing their own hair). It was considered an efficient use of a tool when the child gripped it correctly and then applied it appropriately. The children were more likely to need to make an adjustment to their grip when attempting a task that was not self-directed. Also, the children tended to reach and grasp a tool more slowly when performing a self-directed task. These results indicated to the researchers that the children did more planning before acting in the self-directed tasks. They took more time at the beginning in order to accomplish the task more efficiently.

The researchers expected that as the children get older (beyond twenty-four months), additional practice with self-directed tasks would lead to quicker and more automated performance. Further development would also lead to the ability to plan actions with the less familiar, externally directed tasks (pounding pegs and using a magnet to pick up objects). With planning, performance on these tasks would also become more slow and deliberate, before becoming more automated later through practice (McCarty, Clifton, and Collard, 2001).

The Interpretation

Putting together the results from the research presented so far on tool use, here's what to look for as your child attempts to use and eventually masters the various tools at his fingertips:

- Nine-month-olds can pull a cloth to retrieve a toy (Willatts, 1984) and can feed themselves with a spoon (McCarty, et al., 2001).

- Ten-month-olds will pull a string or a cloth (toy attached), but will have more difficulty with a hoop or a crook (toy touching) (Bates, Carlson-Luden, and Bretherton, 1980).

- Fourteen-month-olds can use many simple tools both self-directed and externally directed (McCarty, et al., 2001).

- Even by twenty-four months, simple tool tasks are not completely automatic; more practice is needed (McCarty, et al., 2001).

- Children ages fourteen to twenty-four months show evidence of planning on self-directed tasks (McCarty, et al., 2001).

As children develop, they do more planning before acting. They start out planning when approaching simple tasks that are already familiar, like self-directed hair brushing and spoon using. Planning is revealed by the fact that they move slowly as they reach for and grasp a tool. The benefit to the planning is that their tool use is more efficient. For example, they plan how they'll approach the tool, then grasp it correctly and use it. Without planning, they might grasp the tool incorrectly then, once they notice it doesn't work that way, adjust their grip on the tool before using it. Either way they'll eventually use the tool correctly, but the planning makes its use more efficient, which with practice leads to mastery.

Let's say you've purchased a new cell phone. At first you may simply explore it using trial and error to reach some success. Then when using it you employ much planning and use your problem-solving skills, and then practice these skills. You may also resort to reading a manual or asking a friend to demonstrate how some part of the phone works. Then in time you become a proficient user. Your progression to mastery with this new tool is not so different from that of a child who is seeking to master the use of more basic tools.

What Should Parents Do?

Offer your child child-safe and child-sized tools to use as she moves through her daily routines: a stool in the bathroom to reach the sink to wash her hands and brush her teeth with her very own toothbrush; a small, gentle hairbrush; spoons and forks that fit her hand. If your child insists on using the egg beater when you're cooking, allow him to do so. The world is full of tools. The more proficient your child is at using them, the better equipped he'll be to tackle the challenges of each environment he enters. Challenge yourself to teach, guide, and train your child in the use of tools. Call on your patience as you do so. The only downside is that occasionally tool use brings about a mess. Using a spoon to learn to eat applesauce is a perfect example. While the first attempt is the worst, the child does get more proficient with time and practice. It's worth it because your child is proud to be feeding himself along with the all the people seated at the table.

It will certainly take time for your toddler to refine her ability in the use of more complicated tools, such as picking up objects with a magnet or pounding a nail with a hammer, but once accomplished, these skills set the stage for even more precise tool use: sewing needles, knives, and screwdrivers are yet to come.

Also be aware that problem-solving toddlers are not apprised of the peril they might encounter when using tools. One mom told us of the following tool-related event: For his second birthday a little boy received a music box from his aunt. The mom demonstrated how the music box worked, which, of course, fascinated this little boy. Then the mom put the music box (she thought to keep it safe) in a glass cabinet that contained her crystal glassware. She didn't realize how interesting and attractive the music box was to her two-year-old son, and how determined he was to play with it and explore it. One day when emerging from the bathroom, much to her horror, the mom saw that her toddler had pulled his high chair into the dining room and opened the cabinet to retrieve the music box. Thankfully he had left the uninteresting crystal glassware alone. He had used the high chair as his tool to reach his goal.

Although it's amazing how children's minds develop, they often need a little help as they try to make sense of this world. Watch out for children overcategorizing. One day a four-year-old said to his mother, "Daddies work and mothers stay at home." Now, wouldn't it be easy for a child to understand how the world works if he could slot all people into such categories? What's interesting about this situation is that the mother worked part-time out of the home, and, of course, she worked inside the home too, taking care of her children, as well as managing the household and various volunteer projects. The dad in the family worked outside the home at his law office every day, but also contributed to the household by mowing the lawn, doing the dishes, and caring for the children. Nevertheless with categorization on his mind, this preschool-age child tried to slip his parents into simplistic categories from his own experience, which involved dad going off to work each morning to an office and mom being at home most of the day even though she worked part-time out of the home.

The mom explained that some dads work outside the home part- or full-time, but they also work at home. And some moms work inside the home, but some also work outside the home part- or full-time. So when children make generalizations about erroneous categories that they've created inside their own minds, it's important for parents to challenge their thinking.

Another area children could use some guidance in is the use of tools. It's important to be aware that like all children, those between eighteen months and two years can get into trouble using tools. Keep in mind that they are able to slot various tools into categories, they remember how they're used, and they copy your behavior. So let's think how the seemingly innocent behavior of combining these skills can lead to household problems.

Let's say that only a day or two ago you finished painting the nursery for your new baby. Your older child, while you're busy with a phone call, finds her markers and starts coloring on the wall. You're angry, aghast, bewildered. Why did she do this? Well she wanted to copy your painting behavior, which she obviously remembered, didn't have access to paint (thank goodness), so then generalized the painting task to a similar tool at hand, the markers. It's brilliant when you think about it, but now the mess is there for you to clean up. You had better put the markers up out of reach unless you're available to monitor their use. Your job is to teach your child the appropriate place to use markers—which is at the table with paper. While your child has the mental capacity to imitate, remember, and use tools, and to categorize, she has not acquired self-control, which emerges between ages three and five.

REFERENCES

Bates, E., V. Carlson-Luden, and I. Bretherton. 1980. Perceptual aspects of tool using in infancy. *Infant Behavior and Development* 3: 127–40.

Berk, L. 2009. *Child Development.* Boston, MA: Pearson Education, Inc.

Chen, Z., R. P. Sanchez, and T. Campbell. 1997. From beyond to within their grasp: The rudiments of analogical problem solving in ten- to thirteen-month olds. *Developmental Psychology* 33: 790–801.

Ellis, A. E., and L. M. Oakes. 2006. Infants flexibly use different dimensions to categorize objects. *Developmental Psychology* 42: 1000–11.

Gopnik, A., and A. N. Meltzoff. 1987. The development of categorization in the second year and its relation to other cognitive and linguistic developments. *Child Development* 58: 1523–32.

Hayne, H., J. Boniface, and R. Barr. 2000. The development of declarative memory in human infants: Age-related changes in deferred imitation. *Behavioral Neuroscience* 114: 77–83.

Mandler, J. M., and L. McDonough. 1993. Concept formation in infancy. *Cognitive Development* 8: 291–318.

Mandler, J. M., and L. McDonough. 1998. On developing a knowledge base in infancy. *Developmental Psychology* 34: 1274–88.

McCarty, M. E., R. K. Clifton, and R. R. Collard. 2001. The beginnings of tool use by infants and toddlers. *Infancy* 2: 233–56.

McDonough, L., and J. M. Mandler. 1998. Inductive generalization in 9- to 11-month-olds. *Developmental Science* 1: 227–32.

Quinn, P. C., P. D. Eimas, and S. L. Rosenkrantz. 1993. Evidence for representation of perceptually similar natural categories by 3-month-old and 4-month-old infants. *Perception* 22: 463–75.

Willatts, P. 1984. The stage-IV infant's solution of problems requiring the use of supports. *Infant Behavior and Development* 7: 125–34.

Chapter 9

Understanding Hidden Objects and People

Want to engage a baby and do so in a way that's meaningful? Play games that involve hiding and finding. Why? Because doing so meets a baby where his learning lies. During the first year, babies grapple with the fact that objects and people disappear and reappear, and that they continue to exist even when out of sight. Babies learn about the permanence of objects gradually, in steps.

Noticing an Object's Disappeared

One day a dad was dressing his two-month-old daughter. As he was putting a shirt over his baby's head, this multitasking dad bent down out of her vision to put a soiled diaper in the diaper pail. Once her eyes were uncovered and her shirt was in place, his daughter expected to see her daddy's face. When she didn't—when her expectation was violated—she wasn't surprised as much as angry and began wailing. Once Daddy reappeared and comforted her, her tears evaporated, and she quickly turned joyful and smiley once again.

Parents will notice their newborn's rudimentary ability to keep objects and people in mind in other situations as well. Let's say you're at a friend's house and your baby is engrossed in watching a light fixture that twinkles in the sunlight. When it's time to leave and you carry him away, your baby may be a bit surprised that he can no longer see the sunlight glistening through the crystal lamp, but that surprise is temporary; quickly he'll fixate on your glasses as you put his coat on and wrap him in a blanket. In a few months, he may protest furiously if you take him away from an object that's holding his interest and satisfying his curiosity. Parents learn quickly to either allow their child time to finish observing an item before moving him on to the next event, or when they can't, at least to give the child fair warning that you'll both be moving along soon. By doing so, you allow the child time to adjust to the transition that's about to come.

The Research

Researchers showed two-month-olds a toy, and then they put a solid screen in front of it, so that the baby could no longer see the toy. Then they quickly removed the toy, and then the screen. Upon seeing no toy, the babies showed a surprised expression because the toy was not behind the screen as expected. Even though the babies expressed surprise when the toy was not where they expected it to be, they didn't look for it elsewhere. Their surprise lasted only briefly (Bee and Boyd, 2007).

The Interpretation

Babies as young as two months begin to grapple with the concept of disappearance. They're taking notice of appearing and disappearing objects and people. They've actually developed a rule regarding physical things: when objects and people disappear, their expectation, although fleeting, is that they're to be found where last seen. Two-month-olds don't hold the disappearance thought in their heads for very long, and they don't search for the toy either, but some researchers believe, based upon experiments such as these, that they have a rudimentary understanding of the permanence of objects and so are surprised when they disappear unexpectedly.

What Should Parents Do?

There isn't much that parents should do about this. Just know that babies are paying attention as objects and people come and go. Even though babies will be perplexed from time to time as they struggle to keep track of people and objects as they disappear and reappear, they are fascinated when it happens and will actually seek out such occurrences.

For example, let's say one day you decide to clean out your walk-in closet. You set your baby in her infant seat with toys to look at and listen to as you get to work. The toys don't catch her attention, you do. Your child will be engrossed in watching you and clothing go in and out of your closet. If she could talk she'd say, "There she is with a pile of clothes." "Oh! She's gone again." "Now she's here again."

Babies are trying to come to terms with the fact that objects and people still exist when out of sight and to learn as they do so that there are rules that dictate physical phenomena. Over their first year of life they'll be determining what these rules are, and eventually they'll be able to predict when and how objects come and go and learn to rely on these rules.

Disappearing Objects:
Part of Baby's Intellectual Agenda

Some parents, caregivers, and other people interested in babies may think that babies just sit in their infant seat randomly gazing around the room. Babies are doing much more than that, particularly when it comes to trying to determine the consistencies in their environment regarding disappearing and reappearing objects and people.

The Research

Clever researchers devised an experiment using a large and a small cardboard carrot, in a vertical orientation, that moved behind a solid yellow screen and then reappeared on the other side of the screen. The three-and-one-half-month-old babies watched both the large and small carrot take turns moving behind the screen, disappearing on the left side and reappearing on the right side. They watched the carrots do this over and over until they tired of seeing it.

Then the researchers showed the babies another event, but first they changed the color of the screen to blue to make sure that the babies would take notice that there was a window on the top half of the blue screen. The window was too high for the short carrot to be seen as it moved behind the screen. So the babies in the study didn't flinch when they couldn't see the short carrot through the window, they just waited for it to reappear on the other side of the screen. All was well and good by the babies.

Then the babies saw the tall carrot move behind the left side of the solid screen. The researchers had devised the experiment so that the tall carrot didn't appear in the window either, but then it did reappear on the right side of the screen, as if it had passed behind the screen as normal. (Unbeknownst to the babies, they used two identical carrots, one on each side). The carrot was tall enough so that the babies should have been able to see it through the window, but they didn't. The babies looked longer at this event compared to the short carrot event, which researchers took to mean that it wasn't what they expected and that they were perplexed (Baillargeon and DeVos, 1991).

The Interpretation

Babies are learning that objects continue to exist when out of sight, but the awareness of the permanence of objects takes months to mature. Some researchers conclude, based on experiments such as the one described above, that even these young three- to four-month-olds are showing an awareness of the permanence of objects. Other researchers using similar procedures have had different results, concluding that awareness of object permanence doesn't start to emerge until around eight or nine months. Even though it's not certain exactly when babies fully learn that objects continue to exist even when out of sight, it's clear that babies are watching for when objects appear and disappear from a young age and are trying to establish rules for themselves for how such events consistently take place. They're perplexed when the top half of a tall carrot isn't seen when a short screen is moved in front of the carrot, because it violates rules they've developed for appearing and reappearing objects.

As baby is learning about object permanence, she is like a little scientist noticing that there are certain conventions that objects and people disappear and reappear by, and she is trying to determine what they are. Think how alert a person would need to be if objects and people would come and go with no regard for physical order. If objects popped in and out around a room or if a person went out a door leading to the outside of the house and then showed up by coming in from a closet, we would all have difficulty determining the laws for such systems. Such inconsistencies would be confusing, alarming, and stressful. As babies' cognitive skills develop, they become aware of the operating rules that objects and people come and go by. When predictable rules are violated, their curiosity is provoked, so they look longer at such events.

What Should Parents Do?

Play games with your baby that involve appearance and disappearance. Peekaboo is the most obvious. You can play peekaboo with people or objects. Children seldom tire of this game. They want to play it over and over in as many situations as possible, and each time they do they're affirming their theory that objects continue to exist when out of sight.

Keeping Track of More Than One Object

Not only are babies interested in one object going away and returning, they can actually keep track of three objects. Let's say that you come home from the grocery store and set your baby on the kitchen table in his portable car seat, and then set a bag of groceries on the table along with your purse. Then the phone rings. While your baby is watching you talk, your spouse sets a box delivered from the post office on the table next to the grocery bag and your purse. When your baby looks back at the table, he's alerted to the fact that an object has been added to the other two sitting on the table. Call it primitive arithmetic if you like. Regardless, babies as young as five months old have demonstrated the ability in the research laboratory to tell the difference between quantities of one, two, and three objects and add and subtract those numbers.

Now it's not adding and subtracting in the abstract sense of two plus one equals three, or three minus one equals two, using the numerals, 1, 2, and 3, and the plus, minus, and equal signs. But when a baby sees two objects and then sees one taken away, he expects to see one remaining, and if the situation is different than what he expects, he looks perplexed.

The Research

Here's how the researchers discovered this phenomenon to be true: Five-month-old infants saw one toy animal, which researchers then placed behind a solid screen. Next each baby watched as an experimenter's hand holding another toy animal moved behind the screen and then came away empty. Then the experimenter removed the screen, revealing the two objects. The babies were interested but somewhat blasé, as the babies were expecting to see exactly what they did see in this situation: two toy animals.

Then to see if these five-month-olds were actually keeping track of the number of objects, the researchers proceeded as before by having the babies witness as a screen covered one toy animal and then a hand added another toy animal. This time, however, the experimenter would sneak an item away without the baby seeing him do so, and then remove the screen, revealing one fewer item than the baby expected. The babies looked longer at this "impossible" situation than the previous one, which indicated that what they were seeing was not what they had been expecting. The children were perplexed and curious.

In a similar regard, when babies saw two items sitting on the table, then a screen was put in front of them and a hand took an item away, they would expect to see only one item remaining. When the researchers surreptitiously added a toy animal back to the scene and then pulled away the screen, the babies again looked longer at this unexpected situation as compared to the expected one. They had witnessed one item subtracted from the two-item display, but when the screen was taken away, they saw two items instead of just one as expected. It didn't add up, so to speak, and the babies knew it (Wynn, 1992).

The Interpretation

Babies are watching as objects and people come and go, and we now know they can keep track of at least three: three people standing around the room, three items sitting on the kitchen counter, or three toys on their blanket. Again, it's all about looking for consistencies in the environment that baby can predict so that she can gradually become more competent at keeping track of items as they come and go, appear and disappear, following certain rules that dictate physical phenomena.

What Should Parents Do?

Should you take your child to a baby math class and drill him on simple arithmetic? No, there's no need. Just know that your baby is watching when you put three apples on a plate, take one away, and eat it, leaving two. When you hand Grandpa and Grandma each a cup of coffee, your baby is likely watching. If you bring your own cup to the table, he's now keeping track of three cups. You know your baby is alert to the events around him, and now you know that he's aware of three items as they're added and subtracted to a situation.

In the course of daily living, your child is learning the basics of mathematics. You can play adding and subtracting games with your child, but don't trick your baby as the experimenters did in the research study; doing so will only confuse and frustrate your baby's need to understand consistent numerical events that occur daily around the home environment.

Following an Object's Trajectory

You realize that your baby is watching items as they come and go. She notices when her brother zooms one toy car across the floor and then later zooms two of them. She tracks the path that the car takes as it rolls across the floor and then behind the sofa. What does she do next? Do her eyes follow the car's trajectory while it is hidden and anticipate where it will emerge? That's a question researchers set out to answer.

The Research

Researchers rolled a ball behind a solid screen. As long as the ball was out of view only briefly, four- to five-month-olds would move their gaze to the far edge of the screen in advance of the ball reappearing there. Not only are babies at this age able to track visible moving objects, they seem to be able to predict the future path of a moving object based upon its current direction and speed. The fact that the object disappears for a bit doesn't seem to faze them (Meltzoff and Moore, 1998).

In another experiment, researchers moved a toy on a track back and forth behind a screen and five-month-old babies moved their gaze each time, anticipating where the toy would emerge, following its trajectory. After a rest, the researchers showed the babies the toy moving back and forth behind the screen twenty more times, but in half of the trials, the toy emerged much sooner than would be appropriate given the object's constant speed while it was visible. When the toy emerged too soon, the babies' visual tracking was disrupted, and they tended to take their eyes off the visible object that had emerged and to look back to where it had disappeared or to look away from the display entirely.

The babies were perplexed. They might have been thinking, "That toy appeared too quickly, therefore it can't be the one that was originally moving behind the screen." The researchers concluded that one of the rules that five-month-olds follow is that an object must maintain its unique trajectory of motion in order to be judged the same object as it disappears and reappears (Moore, Borton, and Darby, 1978).

The Interpretation

Keeping in mind that babies are driven to survive, once they understand and can predict how objects move, it makes sense that they'll be able to relax and therefore be unstressed. A toy moving at an unpredictable speed alerts a baby to the situation; she perks up and takes notice of the inconsistency. Once the baby can predict how an object moves, in what fashion and at what speed, he relaxes. Therefore, if an object goes behind a screen and then speeds up coming out from behind the screen too quickly, baby is perplexed and curious.

What Should Parents Do?

Conduct your own experiment. Most likely your baby recognizes how you move through the house. Maybe your gait is typically quick. Now change it. Hop through a room while your baby is watching. See if your baby takes notice. Next, trot, then skip or crawl. It's just a little something fun to do that will prove to you that your baby is paying attention to not only how toys scoot across the floor but how people do too.

Gradually Keeping Track of Objects and People

Researchers and observant parents note that by about six to eight months babies will look over the edge of a crib for a dropped toy. Their minds have developed to the point where they won't forget about a toy as it drops out of sight; they now follow it. If babies are crawling at this age, they'll follow parents as they move from room to room (Bee and Boyd, 2007). Soon they will look for partially hidden objects.

The Research

In two experiments, researchers sought to discover at what ages babies would uncover or look for partially hidden and fully hidden objects.

In the first experiment with babies just under nine months old, the researcher would play with the toy himself and then allow the child to play with it, taking turns back and forth. Then, on some of his turns, while baby watched, the researcher would partially hide the toy by placing a vertical screen in front of half of it or by covering half of it with a cloth. On other turns he would hide the toy completely.

Most of the babies successfully recovered a partially hidden toy; some pulled at the toy, while others removed the cloth or screen. However, all but one of these same babies did not reveal the toy when it was fully hidden, though they had the manual ability to do so, as they demonstrated with the recovery of the partially hidden toy.

In the second part of this study, ten-month-olds as well as just-under-nine-month-olds were tested. Also, the experimenters added sound to the fully hidden objects on some trials. The older babies were more successful than the younger babies at finding a fully hidden toy, especially when it made a sound (Moore and Meltzoff, 2007).

The Interpretation

By about nine months, babies will uncover partially hidden objects. They're interested in revealing the entire object because they want to prove to themselves that the rest of the object is hidden by the cloth or the screen. They won't, however, uncover a fully hidden object; to them the object is out of their mind if it's completely out of sight. Most ten-month-olds are starting to understand that objects continue to exist even when not visible, so they will uncover a fully hidden object, but they are more likely to do so if it makes a sound. The sound gives the child a clue that something is lying under the cloth or hiding behind the screen.

What Should Parents Do?

Since you now know that during your baby's first year of life she's grappling with the issue of the permanence of objects, play games that involve disappearance.

Have a cadre of balls on hand to roll around the floor, behind chairs, and under your sofa. It's one of the best ways to entertain baby for an afternoon.

Be aware that when your baby is sitting in a high chair it's likely that once his tummy's full, he'll drop food to the floor to test if that food will vanish. Of course, it instead ends up on the floor. One opportunity with a cracker isn't enough for a baby to gain full understanding of this phenomenon. Babies are compelled to drop macaroni and cheese, toast, and banana slices over the edge of their high chair tray to see if each individual item ends up, as predicted, on the floor. If, by magic, the food disappeared, baby would wonder why.

This messy game of food dropsy may put you over the parenting edge, so go ahead and end it, but if you're willing, play dropsy with toys, which are much easier to clean up. In time, your child's interest in dropping toys and food will wane, but it won't be until he realizes that all dropped items end up on the floor and continue to exist.

Also play peekaboo at first with six- to eight-month-olds by only partially hiding items, whether toys or people. It's fun and an appropriate way to engage your baby exactly where her learning lies. When at home, hide yourself behind the sofa but have your foot sticking out in view. Your child will be excited to find all of you behind the sofa. When your child reaches ten months, hide yourself behind a curtain and make a noise, see if your child can find you.

Let's say you're at a restaurant waiting for your food. Take your spoon and hide most of it under your napkin. Your baby will be delighted to lift the napkin again and again to find the entire spoon underneath it. This game will likely entertain your baby until the food arrives.

Playing peekaboo is not a silly pastime but a way for babies to discover that people and things continue to exist even when hidden behind a blanket, drapery, or door.

As you now know, researchers determined that by ten months, babies eagerly look for fully hidden objects. If you completely cover a spoon with your napkin, baby may find the spoon, but this game is not enough for babies to know that all objects, as well as people, continue to exist when out of sight. Therefore, they must experiment with all sorts of objects. Realize that children are little scientists determining for themselves the complexities of the world.

One mom reported that son Drew, age eleven months, set up his own experiment using a rug and a section of toy train track. Drew likely hypothesized that the track would still exist even when covered up by the rug, but he needed to test his hypothesis. He took the piece of track, hid it under the rug, waited a little while, and then uncovered it. He conducted this experiment several times a day for a week or so. He did so with no prompting from Mom or Dad. He searched for the truth regarding the permanence of this object and confirmed for himself that indeed the object still existed even when he couldn't see it.

A child's fascination with hiding and finding continues until about age twenty-four months, when the concept of object permanence takes hold completely.

While you can support your child's interest in disappearance by playing peekaboo and by purchasing a Jack-in-the-box—or any pop-up toy for that matter—and playing with it over and over again with your baby, also realize that if you never did so, your child, like Drew, would probably play such games all on her own as she discovered for herself that objects continue to exist even when covered up by something like a rug. Games relating to disappearance mesh with your child's intellectual agenda; therefore, when you do play them with your child, you're not only helping your child establish rules that objects exist by, but you're solidifying your relationship with your child as well, because your child sees you as a conduit to understanding and becoming competent in the environment in which he lives.

Enjoy Hide-and-Seek

For months babies will continue to play peekaboo, and love it. Once a baby turns twelve months old, the game of hide-and-seek will come into play. What's the difference? The game of peekaboo involves one object or one person that's hiding in one place. You cover your head with a blanket; your baby unveils your face. You cover a toy with a cloth; your baby finds it, over and over again, much to her delight. Again and again a child will squeal when Jack pops out of his box.

After your child's first birthday, the game takes a more complicated approach; it's hide-and-seek that brings squeals of joy. If you first hide behind a curtain, and then move yourself behind the sofa, your baby will look for you there. If you move when he's not watching you, he knows you're somewhere, so he will keep searching until he finds you.

The Research

When researchers repeatedly hid an attractive toy under an easy-to-reach lid, ten-month-old babies typically reached toward that lid in search of the toy. Then the babies watched as the researchers hid the toy under a second equally easy-to-reach lid. Even though the babies saw the toy moved, most of them reached for the first lid. They looked for it where they had found it previously, rather than at the new location where it had most recently disappeared.

Twelve-month-olds, however, did not make this error. They reached for the first lid when they saw the toy hidden there, and then later, when they saw the toy hidden under the second lid, they reached for the second lid (Smith and Thelen, 2003).

In another experiment, researchers set an attractive toy on a table and then covered it with a cloth. The majority of babies at ten, twelve, and fourteen months succeeded in uncovering the hidden toy. In another situation using the same babies and the same toy, the researchers took the toy in their hand, moved their hand under the cloth, depositing the toy there, then removed their empty hand. In this event it was not until fourteen months that a majority of infants were successful in looking for and finding the toy under the cloth. Why? The researchers speculate that the younger babies expected to find a toy in the place it disappeared, in this case the hand. They typically demonstrated no awareness of what had happened under the cloth, and so they didn't look there for the hidden toy (Moore and Meltzoff, 1999).

The Interpretation

Such research is fascinating because researchers and parents can actually witness a child's mind advancing. At ten months babies look for fully hidden objects. They're now able to hold the object in their minds, remembering it even though they can't see it. They know it's under the cloth. But then they're fooled if the object is moved; even if they see it moved to a second hiding place, they look for it under the first place it was hidden. By fourteen months their mental ability has advanced enough to keep track of an object when moved by a hand from one spot to another.

What Should Parents Do?

Have fun with your child's newfound ability. When you're at a restaurant, hide a penny under a napkin, then move it under your plate. See if your child can find it.

Knowing that objects continue to exist keeps us looking for missing keys, hats, or teddy bears. It's what keeps us fascinated with magicians, because although it seems the magician made a rabbit disappear, we know it can't be, so we wonder how the magician made it look that way.

Protruding Shapes

Once your child fully understands that objects continue to exist when covered up by a cloth, he'll then look for items when moved from under one cloth or box to the next. In addition, he can also read clues about the object, such as how much it causes a covering to protrude. Hide behind a curtain and your child will easily find you in a game of peekaboo because he sees a protuberance in the curtain the size of your body.

The Research

To determine if babies understood that the amount of protrusion of a cloth determines the size of the object hiding underneath, researchers covered two identical small toy dogs with two identical cloths. The babies could only see the two cloths protruding with something under each one. Then the researchers set a solid screen in front of one of the covered dogs. The other covered dog remained visible, providing a reminder to babies of the size of the screen-hidden cloth-covered object. Next, a hand reached behind the screen and pulled out first the cloth and then the small toy dog. The hand then held the dog next to the visible cloth-covered item, allowing a size comparison if the infants were so inclined. This was the "possible event."

Next, those tricky researchers performed a sleight of hand, creating an "impossible event" to see how the babies would react. They did the same thing but rather than pulling out a small toy dog, they pulled out one much bigger, too big to have been fully covered by the cloth. Nine-and-a-half-month-old babies didn't seem to mind. They tended to look at the impossible event as long as at the possible one. At twelve-and-a-half months, however, the babies looked longer at the impossible event, suggesting that they knew the big toy dog was too big to have been the thing that caused the protrusion in the cloth behind the screen (Baillargeon, 1995).

The Interpretation

At nine-and-a-half months, babies don't take the clue of how much an object protrudes under a cloth into consideration. Even though the small cloth could not have covered up the large toy dog, the babies didn't seem to notice this impossibility, as was determined by their looking time. They were just happy to see the dog appear from under the cloth.

Then as their mental ability advanced, by twelve-and-a-half months they realized that the amount of the cloth's protrusion needed to be consistent with the size of the object. The babies at this age knew that the size of the protrusion determined the size of the object that was hiding underneath the cloth.

What Should Parents Do?

Play peekaboo by putting different sized and shaped objects under blankets and behind curtains. Since your baby is not only learning that objects and people continue to exist when out of sight, but that size and shape send clues about what's hiding under or behind blankets and curtains, these soft coverings increase your child's interest in the game of peekaboo and so are more cognitively compelling than simply hiding yourself behind a door or hiding Jack inside his box.

When you're playing hide-and-seek with your child, she will hide her eyes, count to ten, and in that time you'll hide. Your child will then seek you out. She knows you exist somewhere in the house, and she will work to prove this to herself through the game of hide-and-seek. At first she's happy to find you in obvious hiding places; later, the more complicated your hiding spots, the more interesting the game.

Stop for a moment and think about the time, practice, and game playing that was involved as your child learned the concept that people and objects continue to exist even when out of sight. As she went about her day, your child was watching as people and objects moved or zoomed out of sight, and as people went off and then returned. Then at around eighteen months your child mastered the concept.

There will be other concepts your child will master. He'll learn that people have likes and dislikes different from his own. At first he believes that all people like applesauce as he does; then he'll realize that someone else may prefer bitter-tasting cauliflower. These differences fascinate him, and he'll set out to understand just where people are like-minded and where their desires differ. He'll set up little experiments of his own and conduct them over and over again until he fully grasps the concept that people can feel differently about different events, activities, and objects than he does. He'll desire to touch a glass vase and will be amazed that you have a different opinion about him doing so.

Your child will be interested in the properties of water and other substances in her environment be it mud, play dough, or glue. She'll need to play with these over and over until she grasps an understanding of their properties. Your child will be interested in balls, balloons, and birds. How they bounce, float, and fly. He'll set out to understand their properties, and sometimes he'll use you as a resource to understand how such phenomena operate.

No matter what your child is learning, keep in mind the need for him to practice what he's learning, the importance of play that supports what he's learning, and that he needs time to master each one of these concepts.

REFERENCES

Baillargeon, R. Reasoning in infancy. In M.S. Gazzaniga, ed. *The Cognitive Neuorsciences*. 1995. Cambridge, MA: MIT Press.

Baillargeon, R., and J. DeVos, J. 1991. Object permanence in young infants: Further evidence. *Child Development* 62: 1227–46.

Bee, H., and D. Boyd. 2007. *The Developing Child, 11th Edition*. Boston, MA; Pearson Education, Inc.

Meltzoff, A. N., and M. K. Moore. 1998. Object representation, identity, and the paradox of early permanence: Steps toward a new framework. *Infant Behavior and Development* 21: 201–35.

Moore, M. K., R. Borton, and B. L. Darby. 1978. Visual tracking in young infants: Evidence for object identity or object permanence? *Journal of Experimental Child Psychology* 25: 183–98.

Moore, M. K., and A. N. Meltzoff. 1999. New findings on object permanence: A developmental difference between two types of occlusion. *British Journal of Developmental Psychology* 17: 563–84.

Moore, M. K., and A. N. Meltzoff. 2007. Factors affecting infants' manual reach for occluded objects and the genesis of object permanence. *Infant Behavior and Development* 31: 168-80.

Smith, L. B., and E. Thelen. 2003. Development as a dynamic system. *Trends in Cognitive Science* 7: 343–48.

Wynn, K. 1992. Addition and subtraction by human infants. *Nature* 358: 749–50.

Chapter 10

First Words

In Chapter 2, you read about child-directed speech—parentese, and babbling and cooing, which are precursors to speech.

Remember from Chapter 3 the parent's natural inclination to teach words not only by taking an object such as a doll and labeling it using the senses of sight and sound, but by moving the doll and touching the child with it? This multimodal strategy that comes naturally to most parents is another method by which children learn words more readily.

In Chapter 7 we discussed a child's ability to understand the intentions of others. As you may recall, children watched as an experimenter failed to complete several tasks. Then, when given the opportunity to complete the task for themselves, the babies did so successfully because they were able to read the intentions of the experimenter. This ability to read another's intentions also leads to competency in language as toddlers use this skill to figure out what others are talking about (Golinkoff and Hirsh-Pasek, 2006).

Another way children prepare to speak is by playing games. The give-and-take you use while playing—"I give the spoon to you, you give it back to me," "I roll the ball to you, you roll it back to me," and "I hide, you find me, peekaboo!"—provides children with opportunities to practice taking turns, which carries over into conversation. Conversational turn taking actually began with the babbling and cooing stage, but now it includes the child understanding your words and then using words herself. Playing games while vocalizing with the child promotes the process (Rome-Flanders and Cronk, 1995).

In Chapter 7 you read that ten- to eleven-month-olds notice the precise direction in which others direct their gaze. As older babies follow another's gaze, that person in turn usually talks about what the person is looking at. In a similar regard, most adults follow a baby's line of vision and comment on what the baby sees. As babies begin pointing around one year of age, they actively seek opportunities to share reference to an object or event and communicate about it. A baby points at an object then looks back toward the parent or caregiver to indicate that he wants the adult to speak about it, explaining what it is and its function. These episodes of verbalization in the context of joint attention promote children's ability to sustain their attention, comprehend language, produce meaningful gestures and words, and acquire vocabulary (Carpenter, Nagell, and Tomasello, 1998, as referenced in Berk, 2009; Flom and Pick, 2003; Silven, 2001).

If a child wants a cookie, she points to it and, with an accompanying whine, stomp, or *uh, uh* sound, gestures clearly to the parent that she wants the cookie. The parent responds by saying, "Oh, you want a cookie? Here it is." The child soon learns that gestures lead to desired results. Children rely on gestures to expand their ability to communicate while their vocabulary is small, then they gradually replace gesturing with words (Capirci, Contaldo, Casellie, and Volterra, 2005).

There are gestures other than pointing that parents teach and children learn: waving bye-bye, blowing a kiss, asking for more, expressing the desire to be picked up or put down, requesting a person to get something, expressing that mealtime is over, expressing the need for a hug, nodding yes or shaking the head to communicate no. Learning to read a child's gestures, having common words for them, and saying the words as the child uses the gestures—all contribute greatly to early language.

There's more to learn about language learning, however. You'll realize quickly that children comprehend a word's meaning ahead of their ability to say a word for themselves. A parent may say, "Give me the doll," and the child will do so on cue. It could be another five months until the child can say along with the appropriate gesture, "doll," meaning, "Give me the doll." One study, as we'll see later in the chapter, showed that a five-month lag exists between children's comprehension of fifty words at about fourteen months and production of fifty words around nineteen months (Menyuk, Liebergott, and Schultz, 1995).

Children usually say their first words around twelve months and at first add to their vocabularies slowly, one to three words per week. Then it accelerates to one to two words per day between eighteen and twenty-five months. As you'll learn, some children go through a spurt in rate of word acquisition, others increase their rate more gradually (Berk, 2009).

One of the words that your baby is attuned to early on is his own name because he hears it spoken frequently.

Recognizing Her Own Name

You'll be fully aware that your child comprehends ten words at eleven months, and produces ten words at fourteen months. Since your child comprehends more language than he can produce, when you ask, "Where's the ball?" your eleven-month-old baby will likely pick it out among the other toys in a bin. If several of his favorite people are sitting around the table—Mommy, Daddy, Uncle Jerry, Auntie Christy, Grandma, and GG (that's Great-grandma)—and you say, "Where's Uncle Jerry?" your child will likely point to the correct person. Not only that, if you say, "Where's Flora?" naming your child, your child's ears will likely prick up. She probably won't point to herself, but she'll know you're talking about her.

Research has shown that babies as young as four-and-a-half months will recognize their own name when spoken in a quiet set-ting (Mandel, Jusczyk, and Pisoni, 1995, as referenced in Newman, 2005). Recognizing their own name spoken amid background noise is a more difficult task and babies get better at it as they get older.

The Research

Researchers put children ages five, nine, and thirteen months in a sound booth, sitting on their mother's lap, one at a time. There, each infant heard a woman's voice repeat a name. In some trials, the name belonged to the infant being tested; in others, it was a random name.

As the woman repeated the name, nine different female voices spoke simultaneously in the background, emulating real-life listen-ing situations. The researchers wondered if the babies would listen longer to trials in which the voice repeated their own names versus trials in which the voice repeated other names. If so, this would indicate that the babies recognized their own names. The experi-menters measured the child's listening time as the amount of time he spent looking at the source of the sound, a loudspeaker. All the names were called in a lively, animated parentese voice that children readily pay attention to.

When the intensity of the voice calling the child's name was high compared to the background babble, the five-month-olds listened longer when their own name was being spoken. They recognized their name in this situation where it stood out fairly well from the background noise. However, when the intensity of the voice calling the child's name was not so high compared to the background noise, only the thirteen-month-olds recognized their own names among the mix of other talking voices. The younger babies did not (Newman, 2005).

The Interpretation

It's exciting to know that the name you picked out and pondered over prior to your child's birth now holds meaning for your child. She knows herself by her own name. Even in the buzz of sounds that occur around the home, your child is learning to pick out and tune into his own name, thereby knowing when he's the topic of conversation. This skill is about familiarity with his own name, but it's also about identity of himself as a person.

What Should Parents Do?

Language is a powerful tool supporting and reinforcing behavior. Let's say your child helped you put toys away and that night at dinner you tell your spouse about it using the child's name. Be aware that your child knows when she's the topic of conversation and that such communication reinforces the behavior; the likelihood is great that your child will repeat this positive behavior.

A mom reported that on the phone one day, she was telling a friend about her toddler, who had colored on the wall. Then as she was talking, the toddler located another crayon and started marking the wall in exactly the same fashion. Because she was the topic of the conversation, and knew what the conversation related to (remember that even if your child can't say a word like "crayon" or "wall" yet, she can understand it), she went about, much to her mother's dismay, repeating the exact same negative behavior. The mother talking about the negative behavior brought it to the child's mind and so the child went about repeating it.

So be careful what you reinforce when your child is in the vicinity of your conversation, because early on children recognize their names and know when parents are talking about them. When you're talking about your child and what he's done, you're inadvertently reinforcing the actions you're describing; therefore, brag to Grandma over the phone about positive actions but talk in private with others about the negative and perplexing behaviors your child exhibits.

Earliest Words

Your baby's correct responses to "What does the cow say?" or "What does the kitty say?" are certain to impress Grandma. It's so gratifying once your child can point at a puppy and say, "Woof, woof." It's exciting to point to a ball while asking your child, "What's this?" and have your child answer by saying, "Ba." You'll be pleased when your child holds up his cup and says, "Ju" and you know he wants more juice. As you've learned, there's much more in the big picture of language learning that's paving the path to conversation and intellectual verbal exchanges between your child and others. Once language learning takes off, parents who tune in feel as if they're seeing their child's mind at work, which is actually the case.

The Research

When your child speaks her first words, make note of what they are. In the first fifty words that your child speaks, you'll likely hear some of the following:

- Important people, "Mama" and "Dada"
- Familiar animals, "doggie" or "kitty"
- Familiar objects, "bed," "cup," or "doll"
- Things that move, "car" or "ball"
- Favorite foods, "juice" or "apple"
- Actions, "bye-bye," "look," or "up"
- Familiar states, "hot," "dirty," or "wet"
- Descriptions, "big," "blue," or "mine"
- Questions, "what" or "where"
- Assertions, "no," "yes," or "want"

(Hart, 2004; Nelson, 1973)

There are other words that you'll hear your baby speak that relate to a concept that the child is attempting to comprehend.

The Link Between Language and Cognition

As children come to terms with the fact that objects continue to exist when out of sight, they'll use the word "gone." Your child will cover up a key with a napkin, and when revealing the still existing key, the child will likely say "gone." It seems peculiar that the child says "gone" when she's meaning to say, "The key still exists even when covered up by the napkin." It appears that as your child grapples with the concept of disappearing and reappearing objects combined with limited expressive language, she'll label that concept as "gone."

When children accomplish a task, they'll use the word "there," "done," or a familiar word to convey that they've completed a task to their satisfaction. Listen for "there" when your child stacks one block on top of another or fills a bucket to the brim with sand. When the child then knocks the blocks over or dumps the sand out of the bucket, you'll likely hear "uh-oh." "Uh-oh" can apply to any mishap—spilled juice, a coat on the floor, or a purse's contents dumped out on the table.

The Research

Researchers launched a longitudinal study with thirteen- to nineteen-month-olds to investigate the relationship between achievements in linguistic and cognitive development. Over time, they repeatedly provided the children opportunities to engage in tasks relating to two different cognitive achievements: (1) understanding object permanence and disappearance and (2) using insight to solve means-ends problems.

If a child was able to succeed at the following two tasks, it indicated to the researchers the child had a full understanding of the concept of object permanence.

In the first task, the experimenter hid an object in his hand. The hand was placed under one of three visible cloths and the object was left there. To succeed at this task, the child had to search under the correct cloth to find the object.

In the second, again the experimenter hid an object in his hand. But this time the hand was placed under one cloth, then a second cloth, and then a third. The object was left under the third cloth. To succeed at this task, the child had to search under all three cloths or search directly under the third cloth.

Later in the study, if a child was able to succeed at the following four tasks, it indicated that the child had developed the ability to use insight to solve means-ends problems:

- Pull an object with a string

- Use a stick to obtain an item

- Drop a necklace into a bottle

- Stack a set of rings on a post, avoiding one solid ring

Over the course of the study, the researchers also monitored the word acquisitions of the children based on questionnaires filled out by the parents. They noted at what age each child began to spontaneously use disappearance words like "gone" and success/failure words like "there" and "uh-oh."

It turned out that at whatever age the children were able to successfully complete the disappearance tasks, such as find an object hidden under a cloth, the children acquired a word like "gone" around the same time. Near the time the children were able to successfully complete all the means-ends tasks, such as retrieve an object with a stick, they started using success/failure words like "there" and "uh-oh." Each cognitive achievement was linked to the acquisition of related words (Gopnik and Meltzoff, 1986).

The Interpretation

These one-word usages are more about understanding concepts and less about describing precisely what each child had actually accomplished. These toddlers weren't able to express, "I'm so proud of myself because I can drop a necklace into a bottle," so after completing the task, they simply said "There." It's as if mastery provokes a word to describe what they've learned. This need to find words to describe a discovery exists whenever people master a new task or come to a new understanding.

What Should Parents Do?

Provide tasks for your child to complete that are within his skill set and play hiding and finding games. Listen for the words "there" and "gone" to emerge. Clap and smile and expand on the experience: "Oh boy, look at you, you separated all the yellow, blue, green, and red balls into the different boxes." Or, "I'll hide Teddy, then you can find him. Hurray, you found him behind the door, good for you!"

When your child says "gone," respond by saying, "Yes, the key was gone under the napkin, but it's still there!" When your child spills juice on the floor and says "uh-oh," respond with "Yup, the juice is on the floor. I'll wipe it up, you can help."

Another first word you'll likely hear is some version of "What's that?" like "Whas'at?" or just "That." It comes with pointing and the creation of the cognitive triangle as your child brings you into his intellectual interests. Remember this information from Chapter 7? Such pointing evokes from you a response and explanation about the object, event, or person the child points to. The concept involved here is that the child realizes that he can learn much more efficiently by including you in the learning process and does so by pointing and soon thereafter using the phrase "whas'at?" to gain your attention, in order to acquire information about the object of interest (Gopnik, Meltzoff, and Kuhl, 1999).

For all those "Whas'ats?" first provide an answer: "clock," "garbage truck," or "cell phone." Your job, however, is to offer more than a one-word response. Your child doesn't want to know only the name of the round object on the wall with numbers and hands, she wants to know what it does and why it's there. She wants to know what the garbage truck is doing and what the garbage collector is doing. Her pointing to your cell phone (which she likely sees many times a day), accompanied by a "whas'at," may mean that she wants to try it out for herself. Allow her to do so as you say, "Let's call Daddy" or "Who's calling on the phone?"

Words Help with Categorization

Think about the world and all the objects in it. If people didn't slot objects into categories, it would make learning so much more complicated. Each object would be its own separate entity that a child would need to learn about, remember, and determine the unique place in the world for. Since objects fit into categories and people are equipped to categorize, learning is much more efficient.

In Chapter 8 there was research about how children learn to put objects into categories. Such grouping facilitates language learning. Cats go in the animal category, cars go with all vehicles, dads go in the men category, birds and airplanes, although they both fly, can be put in separate categories because one is made of biological material, the other mechanical material. As children hear a new word, they place it in a category, thereby making it more easy to remember through recognition or recall.

Children realize that circles, squares, and rectangles go in the shape category. So when a parent points out a triangle by saying, "This is the shape of a triangle," the child automatically slips the triangle into the same category with other shapes. Facilitating the process even further, a parent can say, "That piece of pie is in the shape of a triangle." Researchers discovered that when children hear a new word, they naturally seek to put it into a category and consider its relationship to words they already know.

The Research

Children ranging in age from nine to twenty months participated in a research study to examine how words spoken to children influence their categorization of objects. Each child was presented with four different toys that all fell into a particular category (such as a dog, lion, duck, and bear, all of the *animal* category, or a hammer, wrench, pliers, and saw, all of the *tool* category). For half of the children, each toy was presented with a category word label ("Look, an *animal*!"). For the other half of the children, no category word label was used: The experimenter just said, "Look what's here!" with each toy presentation.

After this familiarization phase, the experimenter said "Look!" and presented the children with both a new member of the category presented previously (e.g., animal) and an object from a novel category (e.g., vehicle). This was the test phase of the experiment. The researchers determined how much attention the children paid to each of the two toys. Attention was measured as the amount of time the child spent looking at, touching, handling, banging, or mouthing the toy. The researchers reasoned that, because children have a preference for novelty, if a child had formed an object category during the familiarization phase, that child would pay more attention to a toy from a new category than one from the now-familiar category. For example, after seeing four animals, the child would pay more attention to a vehicle than another animal, but only if that child had formed an animal category.

Amazingly, the children who had been given a word for the category did show evidence of having formed that category: On average, they paid more attention to the novel-category toy. The children who had not been given a word for the category paid about the same amount of attention to each of the two toys, showing no evidence of having formed a category. The researchers argued that the use of a common label focused the children's attention on commonalities among the objects and, in so doing, helped them to form a conceptual category (Waxman and Markow, 1995).

The Interpretation

With the category *animal* identified, nine- to twenty-month-old children can recognize other animals as members of that category; without a word, they're challenged to do so. Words have power and apparently promote children to make comparisons among the various objects they encounter. When doing so, they discover the common features among members of the category and easily place a new and different animal along with the others in the category.

What Should Parents Do?

Think in terms of categories and then think out loud:

"That's a daisy, it's a flower."
"We're having salmon for dinner, it's a fish."
"We're going to buy a new table; we need some new furniture."

"That car is a station wagon."
"That ball with the holes in it is called a bowling ball."
"I need some new clothes, I think I'll buy a blouse."

Doing so helps your child learn words more quickly and make better sense of the world around him.

Fast Mapping

Another approach to language learning characteristic of children in their second year is called fast mapping. Fast mapping refers to the skill that children apply when they hear a new word; it's the ability to learn and retain new words with only minimal exposure.

Let's say you pull out a bulb baster from a drawer in the kitchen, demonstrate its use, and say just once, "This is a bulb baster." At about a year-and-a-half this word for the object will become a permanent part of the baby's vocabulary. Having mapped the name to the object, weeks or even months later, your baby will most likely identify the bulb baster (Gopnik, Meltzoff, and Kuhl, 1999).

Though the initial understanding of the fast-mapped word is incomplete, it is often sufficient to allow the child to recognize the word the next time she hears it. Then, with repeated exposure over time, the child gleans additional information that expands her understanding of the word. Apparently word use leads to more word use. Just as the more an older child uses an atlas, the more quickly he can locate new places on a map. When fast mapping, children start to form networks of related concepts and words, which contributes to an increased rate of word learning.

The Research

A researcher showed each child in a study an oddly shaped plastic ring, identifying it with the nonsense word "koob," but only once during a game: after the child had been asked to hide two familiar objects (a pen and a fork), the child was asked to hide the koob. The only remaining object to be hidden was the oddly shaped plastic ring. Nearly all of the children in the study knew what the researcher meant. They hid the koob.

Their comprehension of the word was demonstrated further. When the researcher put two unfamiliar items beside the pen, fork, and koob and then asked for the koob, the children gave her the correct object. Children as young as two years picked up the word's meaning with minimal exposure (Dollaghan, 1985).

In another experiment, researchers brought sixteen- to eighteen-month-olds into the laboratory each week for twelve weeks. Half of the children (the experimental group) were given extended training on names of a set of unfamiliar objects (e.g., crab, toucan, trumpet) in the twelve weekly sessions by showing each child pictures and talking about word meanings. ("See the crab. The crab lives in the ocean.") At the end of each session, the children were tested by asking them to point to the correct picture when an object was named. ("Where's the crab?") The other half of the children (the control group) went through the same procedure except that the words presented were known from the start (e.g., dog, baby, car).

During the final session of the study, both groups of children were trained and tested on a new set of novel words, words that were new to all the children. After training on these new words, the toddlers in the experimental group correctly identified 71 percent of the new words, whereas the toddlers in the control group correctly identified only 38 percent. The previous extended training on novel words had given the children in the experimental group a fast-mapping advantage when learning a new set of words.

Not only that, the children who received extended training on a set of novel words progressed from learning just one word per session at the beginning of the study to learning many new words at once in the final session. Knowing some words appears to make it easier for children to learn more (Gershkoff-Stowe and Hahn, 2007).

The Interpretation

It appears that the more words you use with children, the more words they're likely to learn. Intentionally expose a child to one word, the child will likely learn it and then another that you add casually. Thoughtfully teach your child two words and she'll probably pick up four from you or someone else. A child's capacity to learn words seems to be multiplied rather than simply added.

What Should Parents Do?

Expose your child to new words. Don't hold back when it comes to using a broad range of vocabulary words. When on a trip to the zoo, name as many of the animals as possible. If you see an orangutan at the zoo, don't refer to it simply as an ape. Call it an orangutan. Your child will be able to learn the more complex name if given the chance.

Read books to your child and read the same ones over and over at your child's request. Use any new vocabulary words from these stories in everyday conversation with your child. This way they'll be incorporated into your family's vocabulary and your child will call upon her ability to fast-map these words.

Any new experience provides an opportunity for a child to increase her vocabulary of words. There's no reason to hold back word learning; your child's mind is primed to learn words and use them. However, while it's beneficial to add new words as you speak to your toddler, keep sentence structure simple.

When playing with a toy farm set, say, "Here's a horse. He lives in the barn (put the horse in the barn). The farmer is going to ride the horse (put the farmer on the horse's back) and jump over the fence (demonstrate the horse jumping the fence)." With this approach, in one play session your child will likely add the words "horse," "barn," "farmer," "jump," and "fence" to his vocabulary.

If you can take your child to a farm or if you live on one, your child will acquire words relating to a farm setting quickly. The cow grazing in the pasture, the chickens sitting on nests and laying eggs, and the tractor plowing the field—putting language to such experiences is your part; soaking up the experience along with the words connected to it and eventually saying those words is the child's part.

Also, as you do something with an object, describe what you are doing:

"I'm beating the eggs with the egg beater."
"I'm hammering the nail with the hammer."
"I'm digging a hole with a shovel."
"I'm writing with a pencil."

With this approach, your child not only learns the name of the object, but also the action word that describes its use.

More Skills Applied to
Learning Language

By about seventeen months, children actually use a process of elimination to determine the names of objects. You do the same. Let's say your friend is talking about traveling to Germany, France, and England, including the cities London, Heidelberg, and Blois. You know where London and Heidelberg are, but not Blois. Through a process of elimination you determine that Blois is in France. The children in the fast-mapping study used the same skill to figure out that the word "koob" referred to an oddly shaped plastic ring. Here's another piece of research that demonstrates the emergence of this skill:

The Research

Children ages fourteen to eighteen months observed two monitors that presented three-dimensional images of objects. In some trials a cup would appear on one monitor and a ball on the other. In other trials it would be a car on one side and a phototube on the other. The cup, ball, and car were all familiar to the children; the phototube was unfamiliar and was referred to as a "dax" in this experiment. On each trial, two objects would appear for three seconds, one on each of the two monitors. Then a voice would label one of the two objects (e.g., "Look at that cup. Cup!"). Then after four more seconds, the labeled object "danced" on the screen to music.

The results showed that when the voice said, "Look at the cup. Cup!" the children at each age tended to look at the cup and watch it "dance." They did the same for the ball and car. However, when the car and the dax were presented and the voice said, "Look at the dax. Dax!" the behavior depended on the age of the child. The younger children (around fourteen months) tended to look at the car, the middle group (around sixteen months) showed no preference, and the older children (around seventeen months) correctly looked at the dax. The researchers were unable to explain the surprising behavior of the fourteen-month-olds without more research. But the study did reveal that by around seventeen months, children have developed an effective process-of-elimination word-learning strategy. It's as if the child is thinking, "That's a car, so the other thing must be the dax" (Halberda, 2003).

The Interpretation

Researchers showed in this study that children employ a process of elimination when learning some words. You can set up your own situation similar to what the researchers did. Let's say your child loves fruit salad. Typically you include in the salad bananas, oranges, and apples, all of which your child knows the names of. At the grocery store one day you buy a mango and include it in the fruit salad. Ask your child, "Please give me a piece of mango." See if she'll pick out the correct fruit. If she does, she will have used a process of elimination to identify the piece of fruit you're requesting. "She doesn't want a piece of banana, orange, or apple, so it must be this she's wanting and it's called a mango."

What Should Parents Do?

Use this process of elimination to teach new words. For instance, if you're building a birdhouse, you'll be using several tools—hammer, nails, and saw—all of which you'll talk about. Then on another day, when you're building something else using the same tools plus a screwdriver, ask your child for the screwdriver. Because your child knows the other objects already, when you name the screwdriver, your child will easily go through a process of elimination to know which item you're talking about.

Comprehension Before Expression

Psycholinguists, like most parents, realize that a young children's receptive language (what they understand) exceeds their expressive language (what they can actually say). A toddler can follow directions before he can express those same words in his own speech. The following research study examined this comparison in detail.

The Research

Researchers followed the language development of fifty-three children over a thirty-month period; half the children began the study at birth, the others at nine months. Many aspects of cognitive and language development were carefully recorded and observed. One of the aspects measured was word acquisition. Each set of parents kept a diary of the words their child could comprehend and those their child produced until the child comprehended one hundred words and had produced fifty. Such diaries made by parents have been shown to be quite accurate.

When the children reached one year, all could communicate in some way, but the means they used varied. One child could already comprehend fifty words and say ten. Another child had not yet learned ten words, but he showed great intention to communicate through pointing, reaching, and vocalizing, so there was no concern about his linguistic development. During the second year, all the babies were using words. Though some of the children started producing words around ten months of age, others began at fourteen or fifteen months. Of the later starters, many quickly acquired fifty words and the others moved along more slowly.

On average, the children comprehended ten words at age eleven months and were able to produce ten words at age fourteen months—comprehension preceded expression by three months at this stage. On average, the children comprehended fifty words at age thirteen-and-a-half months and produced fifty words at age eighteen-and-a-half months—comprehension preceded expression by five months at this later stage. Not only did comprehension precede expression, but the rate of acquiring new words was faster in comprehension than in expression.

As a side note, the effects of prematurity were of interest in this study, so half of the children selected were premature and the others were full-term. Interestingly, the premature children as a group performed just as well as the full-term children as a group on language comprehension and production (Menyuk, Liebergott, and Schultz, 1995).

The Interpretation

Most likely, before your child can say all the words "give," "me," "the," and "ball," she will understand when you tell her, "Give me the ball," and many other words and phrases. Parents tend to be very aware of the early words that their child can understand and later can say. It is a joyful experience to witness when your baby starts to communicate using language.

What Should Parents Do?

Notice your child's early words, those he understands and, later, those he expresses. Keep a diary if you like, noting the ages at which your child comprehends ten and then fifty words, compared to the ages at which he can express that many words. Keep in mind that each child learns at his own pace; there is a wide range of what is normal and healthy language development.

Acquiring More Spoken Words

The typical child speaks his first word somewhere between eight and fourteen months. Maybe it is "Mama" or "Dada" or "car" or "kitty" (perhaps pronounced *tar* or *ki-ki*). Then the child slowly adds words to his vocabulary. The children in the previous study went from speaking, on average, ten words at about fourteen months to fifty words four months later. But the more words the child knows, the more quickly she acquires more (remember fast-mapping?). That initial slow rate of word-learning increases, and children can go from fifty words at eighteen months to an astounding three hundred on average by the end of their second year (Fenson, Dale, Reznick, Bates, and Thal, 1994, as referenced by Ganger and Brent, 2004).

If you're going hiking and pull out your visor, fanny pack, and hiking boots, and then put them on while talking about each item, your almost-two-year-old child will likely be able to name each item when you go on your next hiking excursion. Today it's your hiking boots, visor, and fanny pack; tomorrow when gardening he'll remember the names for your shovel, gloves, and hose.

It has been widely assumed that most children go through a so-called vocabulary spurt or naming explosion at some point in their second year, when their vocabulary is somewhere around fifty to one hundred words. Believed to be motivated by an underlying jump in cognitive development, this spurt is characterized as a slow word-learning rate that suddenly jumps to a fast word-learning rate. However, recent research, as we'll see next, suggests that what is more typical is not a jump, but simply a gradual, albeit dramatic, increase in rate. Whether it is a spurt or a gradual increase, toddlers amaze their parents with how quickly they add words to their vocabulary.

The Research

Researchers asked the parents of twenty children to keep a daily journal of the words their child expressed, noting which words were immediate imitations and which were spontaneously produced. Only the words produced spontaneously were credited as being part of the child's vocabulary. At the beginning of the study, no child had more than a twenty-word vocabulary. The average age of the children was fifteen months when the parents began keeping journals.

The researchers represented the data for each child with the number of words acquired each day as a function of the size of the child's growing vocabulary. Using statistical analysis computer software, the researchers tested which of two models best fit the data for each child. One model represented a vocabulary spurt, the other a gradual increase in word acquisition.

The vocabulary spurt model was characterized as a low rate of word acquisition that jumped to a higher rate at some point. An example of a spurt is the following: acquiring one to two words per week up to a vocabulary of thirty-five words, then over a brief span of two weeks, jumping up to a rate of fourteen words acquired per week that continues for a period of time.

An example of the other model, representing a gradual increase, is the following: acquiring one to two words per week at twenty words, acquiring three words per week at thirty words, five words per week at forty words, seven at fifty, ten at sixty, fourteen at seventy, and so on.

In both models, the child reaches a fourteen-word-per-week rate, but in the case of the spurt, it happens suddenly, and in the other case, it happens gradually.

Of the twenty children that were considered in the study, only five showed evidence of a vocabulary spurt. The data from the other fifteen children was better modeled by a gradual increase in word acquisition (Ganger and Brent, 2004).

The Interpretation

If your child doesn't seem to be a spurter with words, there is no need to worry. First of all, for those children who do have a vocabulary spurt, the age at which it happens varies greatly. It could happen at fourteen months or twenty-two months (Reznick and Goldfield, 1992). Second of all, this recent research tells us that most children don't exhibit a spurt at all; instead they build their vocabularies at a gradually increasing pace.

What Should Parents Do?

Use language yourself, as doing so brings about better language skills, behavior, and thinking skills on your child's part.

Here are three ways:

- Identify your toddler's wants. When your child points at the crackers in the cupboard while whining, don't just give her one. Instead, first ask, "Do you want a cracker?" By doing so, you'll encourage her to soon ask, "Cracker?" rather than inarticulately whining for one.

- Speak as you hope your children will speak. Remember that children are mimics; this fact pertains to words as well as actions. If you're occasionally harsh when speaking around your child or swear from time to time, curb your inappropriate language ways. If you don't, don't be surprised when you hear your child soon say, "I just can't get the damn remote to work!"

- Expand on your child's one-word utterances. If you child points to the kitty and says, "Ki-ki," respond by saying, "That's the kitty. Do you think she's hungry or do you think she needs to go outside?"

Turn reading into a dialogue between you and your child. Rather than picking up a book and reading straight through a story, you will benefit your child's language development by making the book-reading experience more like a conversation.

Keep in mind that children over the age of twelve months create a triangle with the points of the triangle being you, an object, and the child. Reading to your child is a perfect example of this cognitive triangle. Just as a child points to a bug while saying "whas'at?" and expecting you to not only name the bug but offer some information about it, while reading a story, your child will point to various pictures and inquire using the same combination of pointing and the "whas'at?" question as you page through the book. Parents who engage their child in dialogue as they read a book benefit their child's development in verbal skills.

As you read to your child, realize that young children typically interrupt, ask questions, and page back and forth. They don't yet follow the story line, but they are interested in what's on each page and what the people or animals on each page are doing. Some parents go along with the young child's approach, making it a shared, interactive experience. They pause, point out various pictures on the page, ask questions, answer their child's questions, and converse about what's going on on each page, while listening to their child's input.

While any kind of reading experience is beneficial to children, particularly as you surround your child with love and nurturance, creating a positive association with the reading experience, this approach, referred to as "dialogic reading," is particularly effective at supporting the development of a child's language skills. It makes reading more like a conversation between the two of you.

The Research

Researchers recorded parents reading picture books to their two- and three-year-olds. When the recordings were analyzed, they found that the parents commonly read aloud moving straight through the text without conversing with the child about the pictures, action, and story line. The researchers counted few instances of the parents using the skills involved in dialogic reading, including inquiring about the book's characters and situations, offering the listener praise, repeating and imitating the child's utterances, and following the listener's lead in the reading experience. Neither did they take opportunities to expand on what the child said, or to ask open-ended questions about what they were reading.

The researchers then set out to teach the parents the skills involved in dialogic reading. They developed a video that defined and demonstrated each reading technique and encouraged daily reading using the dialogic style. They instructed parents to increase the use of the dialogic skills they learned, which invite and maintain the child's active participation, and to avoid behaviors during reading that minimize or exclude child participation, such as reading without engaging the child, asking yes/no questions, asking questions that could be answered by pointing, or criticizing the child. Some of the parents received in-person instruction, others watched the video at home and then had follow-up phone calls from researchers, and some only watched the video.

No matter the method of instruction, the parents later demonstrated that they were able to follow the instructions. They had learned and were using the skills involved in dialogic reading, and moreover, their children responded positively! The toddlers showed a significant increase in verbosity, that is, more speaking, and an increase in the length of their utterances during reading sessions compared to their behavior during reading sessions at the beginning of the study (Huebner and Meltzoff, 2005).

The Interpretation

So what's the connection between dialogic reading and improved language skills for your child? Multiple studies have documented that dialogic reading provides benefits above and beyond those of typical, less interactive reading. In the first such study, participating parents were told that the researchers were investigating the potential importance of picture-book reading in children's language development. Half of the parents (the experimental group) were given brief instruction in and were asked to use dialogic reading techniques. The other half (the control group) were not told to change any behaviors.

After one month, children whose parents had used dialogic reading techniques scored significantly higher than the children in the control group on standardized tests of expressive language ability. This was true even though the control group parents were motivated and read to their children as frequently as the dialogic-reading parents did during the study. Nine months later, follow-up testing revealed that the dialogic-reading advantage persisted.

Why does dialogic reading help children improve their expressive language skills? Two possible reasons: the child gets more practice speaking, and the responses and feedback provided by the parent offer language learning opportunities (Whitehurst, Falco, Lonigan, Fischel, DeBaryshe, Valdez-Menchaca, and Caulfield, 1988).

What Should Parents Do?

So how do you become a more engaged book reader to your child? Let's take a favorite book, *Where's Spot?* by Eric Hill, to illustrate dialogic reading:

- Ask "what" questions: "What's Spot doing?"

- Ask questions about function: "How does the door open?"

- Ask questions about attributes: "What color is the snake?"

- Use praise: "You found all the animals! Good for you!"

- Repeat what your child says: if your child barks like Spot, saying "bow wow," you say, "Yes! That's what Spot says, 'bow wow.'"

- Imitate your child: after your child makes a barking sound, bark yourself.

- Follow your child's lead: if your child wants to skip the dialogue while moving through the book quickly, playing peekaboo with all the hiding animals, go along with her approach.

- Expand on what your child says: if your toddler says some semblance of the word "penguin" as he locates them inside the trunk, respond by saying, "You found the penguins! They were hiding in the trunk."

- Ask open-ended (rather than yes/no) questions: "How do you think the turtle got under the rug?"

What's the downside of dialogic reading? It takes more time. But it's probably better to read one story using the dialogic approach than to read three books quickly.

Your child will speak first using one-word sentences ("Doggie" means "There's a dog"), then two-word sentences ("Doggie run," which means, "The dog is running down the street"), and eventually complete sentences emerge ("A dog is in our yard. He's chasing our cat.") Some children seem to talk nonstop, almost in a stream-of-consciousness style of speaking, describing everything they do and asking lots of "why" questions. Most parents are gratified once their child learns to speak, because now she can use words instead of pointing, whining, or throwing a tantrum to communicate; the child's words now communicate her needs. Nevertheless, at this stage, some parents report, "My child is chattering nonstop and it is irritating." If you feel this way, observe yourself to identify the source of your irritation. Maybe you're stressed, with a lot on your mind. Perhaps if you realize that as your child speaks, he's refining his language skills (which takes lots of practice), you'll be more patient, because who is better for your child to practice with than you? Right now you're the focus of your child's communicative interests; later, friends will take your place.

As your child uses language, questions may arise: Should I be worried that my child doesn't pronounce r's and l's perfectly? Should I correct my child's grammar? My child seems to stutter, should I be concerned? My child seems to have several ear infections each winter, will this tendency affect his speech? How can I enhance my child's ability to communicate?

Let's tackle each issue briefly.

Should I be worried that my child doesn't pronounce r's and l's perfectly?

- No. If by age eight your child still isn't saying them correctly, seek testing from a speech therapist. For now, be a good model by saying those letters correctly yourself. When your child says, "Let's go to the paak" (as if he's from Boston), you say "Okay, let's take your shovel and bucket with us to the park and play in the sandbox."

Should I correct my child's grammar?

- No. Simply say your child's sentence back to her using the correct usage. If your child says, "Me go to the park," you respond by saying, "Oh, you want to go to the park? I want to go to the park too." When you're home from the park, if your child says, "We goed to the park," simply repeat back his statement using the correct grammar for this irregular verb, "Yes, we went to the park, wasn't it fun?" With time, your child will correct his grammar all on his own.

My child seems to stutter, should I be concerned?

- Most children repeat the initial sounds of words as they learn to speak. Give your child time to complete her thought, exercising lots of patience as she does so. If you're concerned, see a speech therapist.

My child seems to have several ear infections each winter; will this tendency affect his speech?

- Sometimes ear infections can obstruct hearing, which can hinder language development. Talk to your physician about your child's chronic ear infections.

How can I enhance my child's ability to communicate?

- Expand on what your child says. If your child says, "Grand-ma's car," you say, "Yes, that's Grandma's car. She's coming for a visit."

- Ask questions. If your child says, "My dolly's tired," you say, "Are you going to put her down for a nap or rock her to sleep?" Also ask questions that relate to your child's senses: hearing, smelling, feeling, tasting, and seeing. After a trip to the ocean ask, "What did you see at the ocean?" The child may respond by saying, "I see big water."

- Put your child's body language and emotions into words. If your child is stomping his foot insisting on another piece of pie, say, "Boy, I can tell you really want another piece of pie." If you do so, your child will eventually say, "I really want another piece of pie." And then you can say, "No, one piece is enough for each of us." If the child looks disappointed, say, "I can see you're disappointed. You can have another piece of pie tomorrow."

- Read stories using the dialogic method described in this chapter.

- Sing play songs and recite nursery rhymes. Doing so boosts language development as such activities act as verbal gymnastics to coordinate the movement of the lips, tongue, and mouth.

- Once your child begins to draw pictures of objects and events that you recognize or that she identifies, write down what your child says as she describes what she's drawn. One four-year-old drew a picture of her favorite dessert, and once she described it, Mom wrote underneath the picture, *Strawberry Shortcake*. Putting the written word to the spoken word promotes reading. Some children are inspired to read by reading their own words first, whether it's a story of make believe or an illustrated recollection about a trip to an aquarium or zoo.

Teachers teach children to read; parents contribute to children reaching this developmental milestone by nurturing the love of reading. It all begins with the spoken word. It's important to understand that if you have concerns about language development, you can have your young child's speech tested through the public school system. Though some problems will disappear all on their own, it's better to tackle as early as possible speech issues that won't go away naturally.

REFERENCES
Berk, L. 2009. *Child Development*. Boston, MA: Pearson Education, Inc.

Capirci, O., A. Contaldo, M. C. Caselli, and V. Volterra. 2005. From action to language through gesture. *Gesture* 5: 155–77.

Carpenter, M., K. Nagell, and M. Tomasello. 1998. Social cognition, joint attention, and communicative competence. *Monographs of the Society for Research in Child Development* 63 (4 Serial No. 255) as referenced in Berk, 2009.

Dollaghan, C. 1985. Child meets word: "Fast mapping" in preschool children. *Journal of Speech and Hearing Research* 28: 449–54.

Fenson, L., P. S. Dale, J. S. Reznick, E. Bates, and D. Thal. 1994. Variability in early communicative development. *Monographs of the Society of Research in Child Development* 59 (5, Serial No. 242) as referenced by Ganger and Brent, 2004.

Flom, R., and A. D. Pick. 2003. Verbal encouragement and joint attention in 18-month-old infants. *Infant Behavior and Development* 26: 121–34.

Ganger, J., and M. R. Brent. 2004. Reexamining the vocabulary spurt. *Developmental Psychology* 40: 621–32.

Gershkoff-Stowe, L., and E. Hahn. 2007. Fast Mapping skills in the developing lexicon. *Journal of Speech, Language, and Hearing Research* 50: 682–97.

Golinkoff, R. M., and K. Hirsh-Pasek. 2006. Baby wordsmith: From associationist to social sophisticate. *Current Directions in Psychological Science* 15: 30–3.

Gopnik, A., and A. N. Meltzoff. 1986. Relations between semantic and cognitive development in the one-word stage: The specificity hypothesis. *Child Development* 57: 1040–53.

Gopnik, A., A. N. Meltzoff, and P. K. Kuhl. 1999. *The Scientist in the Crib: What Early Learning Tells Us About the Mind.* New York, NY: Morrow Press, then HarperCollins.

Halberda, J. 2003. The development of a word-learning strategy. *Cognition* 87: B23–34.

Hart, B. 2004. What toddlers talk about. *First Language*, 24, 91–106.

Huebner, C. E., and A. N. Meltzoff, A.N. 2005. Intervention to change parent-child reading style: A comparison of instructional methods. *Applied Developmental Psychology* 26: 296–313.

Mandel, D. R., P. W. Jusczyk, and D. B. Pisoni. 1995. Infants' recognition of the sound patterns of their own names. *Psychological Science* 6: 314–17, as referenced in Newman, 2005.

Menyuk, P., J. W. Liebergott, and M. C. Schultz. 1995. *Early language development in full-term and premature infants.* Hillsdale, NJ: Erlbaum.

Nelson, K. 1973. Structure and strategy of learning to talk. *Monographs of the Society for Research in Child Development* 38: (1–2, Serial No. 149).

Newman, R. 2005. The cocktail party effect in infants revisited: Listening to one's name in noise. *Developmental Psychology* 41: 2005.

Reznick, J. S., and B. A. Goldfield. 1992. Rapid Change in Lexical Development in Comprehension and Production. *Developmental Psychology* 28: 406–13.

Rome-Flanders, T., and C. Cronk. 1995. A longitudinal study of infant vocalization during mother-infant games. *Journal of Child Language* 22: 259–74.

Silven, M. 2001. Attention in very young infants predicts learning of first words. *Infant Behavior and Development* 24: 229–37.

Waxman, S. R., and D. B. Markow. 1995. Words as invitations to form categories: Evidence from 12- to 13-month-old infants. *Cognitive Psychology* 29: 257–302.

Whitehurst, G. J., F. L. Falco, C. J. Lonigan, J. E. Fischel, B. D. DeBaryshe, M. C. Valdez-Menchaca, and M. Caulfield. 1988. Accelerating language development through picture book reading. *Developmental Psychology* 24: 552–59.

Chapter 11

A Mind of Their Own

Once your toddler turns eighteen months old, you'll witness an interesting and significant phenomenon in his life and, therefore, your life as well. As your toddler heads toward a forbidden object, let's say an electrical outlet, he'll turn to look at you as if to say, "What are you going to do about the fact that I'm heading toward this dangerous object?" Parents may think, "He knows not to touch that, I've told him a thousand times, but there he is going after it again. What's even more maddening, as he does so, he checks my response."

Some parents are perplexed, while others become infuriated, and some go as far as to punish the child by sitting her on a chair for a time-out, thinking that the threat of punishment will deter her from touching outlets in the future. The punishment rarely manifests this result. More typically, after sitting on the chair designated for time-out—which most of the parents had to actually wrestle their child into—she'll be right back again going after that dangerous object and then looking again for Mom or Dad's response.

It's important to understand that a child's curiosity about the outlet coupled with his fascination that the two of you can feel differently about the same object, overrides his interest in pleasing you or staying out of the time-out chair.

In some households, it's the family's cat that comes under attack by the toddler. The child realizes that you don't want her to bother the animal while she herself relishes the prospect of exploring him and thereby satisfying her curiosity about the pet. What the child has discovered and is fascinated by is that you and she have differing opinions about what she should and should not be investigating: she wants to examine the kitty and you don't want her to do so.

Most toddlers find interest in dropping food on the floor. They're fascinated by comparing how applesauce versus macaroni falls on the floor. Before eighteen months this event was nothing more than a scientific study of gravity, but now there's an added element involving your response. The child realizes that between the two of you there's a conflict: she desires to continue her experimentation, while you desire her to stop it.

Not only is your child a little physicist experimenting to discover the cause and effect of many phenomena around the house, but he's also a little psychologist experimenting to discover whether you're like-minded regarding various events that occur or if you're in conflict. If you would prefer that your child stop dropping the macaroni or applesauce on the floor, consider that the meal is over, wipe his face and hands, and get him down from his high chair.

The bottom line for parents is to not take this period of psychological experimentation personally. While your child is certainly pitting herself against you in a battle of wills, she's not doing so out of spite or simply to be naughty or necessarily to win. She is just trying to come to terms with the fact that you have a mind different from hers.

Now, of course, you know that people think and feel differently than you. With your friends, family members, and colleagues, you probably have fewer conflicts than with your toddler, or do you? One person likes spinach, another doesn't; you accept this fact as a matter of personal preference. One family member might be a Democrat, another a Republican. While it's not usually polite to discuss politics, one family member might find joy in provoking an emotional outburst from Uncle Jim by bringing up a sticky political issue just to see him squirm. If Uncle Jim turns angry, argumentative, or insulting, the person baiting him may feed his emotional fire further just to see where Uncle Jim will go emotionally. If Uncle Jim responds each time in a monotone with, "I don't discuss politics with people I love," the other family member will likely stop baiting him or bringing up such political issues.

Your toddler might be baiting you similarly when he heads for an object that you've told him over and over to stay away from; it could be an electrical outlet, it could be the television, it could be a wood-burning stove. He's fascinated with your response. If your response is the same each time—kneel down to the child's level as you stop her in her tracks, while stating clearly, "I won't allow you to touch the outlet"—most children will get bored and lose interest. If you respond emotionally or erratically, your child may become even more fascinated and compelled to approach any one of these objects, wondering how you'll respond this time and with what level of emotion.

Another reason a young child might keep doing what he's not supposed to do is for the sake of a predictable routine. If your child has discovered that walking toward the wood-burning stove causes a chain of behaviors from you—first an emotional scream, then a yell, and finally a yank as you keep him from burning himself—he'll keep up the behavior because it's a consistent routine that makes life predictable. While such a negative situation is undesirable to the child, he's compelled to keep at it. You, the adult parent in charge, can either build a barricade around the wood-burning stove to keep the toddler safe or be perfectly consistent stopping him each time he begins to approach the hot stove, being firm and kind. Either method keeps the toddler safe, while respecting his curiosity about the stove and the fire within and his newly found fascination with the fact that different people can think and feel differently about the same situation, person, or object. Children need predictable routines; the parent's job is to see that they're positive in nature rather than filled with negative elements (refer back to Chapter 5).

Another important aspect of toddlers' behavior is that they're on the go, highly curious, and have few inner controls. Let's say your toddler is at the sink washing her hands and is about to taste soap, and you tell her, "No! Don't put the soap in your mouth." The likelihood is great that she'll just keep trying to put the soap in her mouth. Remember, she's highly curious and wants to discover what the soap tastes like. Her brain still has little capability for impulse control. Plus she's interested in the fact that you have differing opinions about the soap going in her mouth.

Many parents will wonder why she doesn't stop it. Such situations perplex most parents and anger others. Why won't the child comply? She just can't. She doesn't have the mental flexibility to think of something else to do with the soap, so she just keeps doing more of what she's not supposed to do. Therefore, when parents want to keep their toddler away from a hazardous object, the full burden of doing so lies with the parent, not the child. If you consistently guide the child to use the soap only for washing and not for tasting or eating, the child in time will use it appropriately. The control you provide eventually transfers from you to the child. Keep in mind that, with a child's immature ability to inhibit behavior, she will have a much easier time responding to a request to do something ("Use the soap for washing") rather than to not do something ("Don't eat the soap").

There are many ways to move through this period of development gracefully; some you'll find in this chapter and some in the appendices that follow. While some of the behaviors characterizing this period are challenging, some are heartening. You'll realize that not only is your child aware that you think differently than she, but that you feel differently as well.

Prior to eighteen months, your child was oblivious to the fact that people think differently than he. Now he realizes it and he can't leave the fact alone. Not only is he fascinated with the fact that he's interested in tasting soap and fully aware that you don't want him to put the soap in his mouth, he's intrigued and aware that the two of you can feel differently about the situation. He feels excited about the prospect of tasting the soap; you feel angry that he's attempting to taste it one more time. He notices the difference—it's the beginning of empathy.

Empathy also involves the realization that how you behave and speak affects others. If people didn't acquire empathy, they would just act any way they liked without consideration for others. A person would pick a neighbor's flowers without thinking that the one who planted them and nurtured them might be disgruntled about it. An older sibling in the process of learning empathy might grab a toy from a younger sister, thinking, "I see the toy, I want it, I'm going to get it any way I can." Eventually the older child will realize that grabbing lacks consideration for the sister who is playing with the toy right now. The older sister will learn to wait until the younger sister is finished playing with it. Children begin to develop empathy at about age eighteen months, but it isn't fully in place for years, and some children have a more difficult time than others acquiring it. They need lots of help from parents saying words to the effect of "Look at your sister, she's crying, she didn't like that you grabbed that toy from her."

Empathy is, of course, the ability of one person to step into the mind and emotions of another and imagine what that person is thinking and feeling. Let's say the morning is going well for everyone, then after a phone call from a friend, you're in tears because your friend called with the news that her mother died last night after a battle with breast cancer. Your toddler isn't sad himself, but he realizes that you are and comforts you with a loving pat on the back. While the toddler is copying behavior that you've exhibited when he was sad or hurt, he's also aware that you're feeling sad and he isn't and that he wants to ease your sadness.

You might find yourself weeping from an emotional overload or tearing up because you've cut your finger while chopping carrots. Your toddler, aware that you're feeling sad or hurt, might bring you his blanket or a bandage. What's emerging is your child's sense of empathy. While your child doesn't feel what you're feeling, he understands that you're emotional about the situation and seeks to help you through your emotional moment.

Realizing People Think and Feel Differently

Parents and researchers have wondered what's going on within the child as she begins to realize that others think and feel differently than she does. It must be daunting and sometimes even overwhelming when a child's mental ability advances to the point when she realizes, "I'm thrilled to be smearing applesauce all over the table, but huh, Mommy isn't pleased that I'm doing so. Isn't it interesting that we can feel differently about the same thing?"

Of course, the researchers wondered at what age young children learn that two people can have differences of opinion about certain objects and behaviors. And at what age do children realize that people can feel differently at the same moment in time or even about the same incident? Researchers Betty Repacholi and Alison Gopnik conducted a study to investigate these questions.

The Research

In a laboratory, an experimenter sat on one side of the table, and one fourteen-month-old child after another, accompanied by a parent, sat on the other. After the experimenter and the child got to know each other with a little playtime, a tray was brought out and two bowls were placed on the table, one containing Pepperidge Farm Goldfish crackers, typically a favorite of young children, the other raw broccoli. Almost every fourteen-month-older preferred the Goldfish crackers. With each child, the researcher tasted the two foods, clearly communicating a love for one and disgust for the other, with emotional facial expressions of happiness or disgust, accompanied by corresponding remarks such as "Eww! Crackers! I tasted the crackers! Eww!"

Afterward, with an open hand, palm up, midway between the bowl of crackers and the bowl of broccoli, the researcher asked the toddler, "Can you give me some?" Of the children who responded to the request, the typical child, whether he had witnessed the researcher's demonstration of strong preference for the broccoli or the crackers, offered her the yummy Goldfish crackers—what he himself liked. Why? One possible explanation is that a fourteen-month-old child can't fathom that anyone could desire something different than he.

The same research study was conducted with eighteen-month-old children, which revealed far different results. In this case, when the researcher relished the raw broccoli, and then, with open hand between the broccoli and crackers, asked, "Can you give me some?" usually the cracker-loving eighteen-month-old toddler handed over to the researcher what she had apparently loved—the raw broccoli.

This experiment reveals that by eighteen months, a child's thinking is more advanced, and she realizes that other people can desire one food item while she desires another (Repacholi and Gopnik, 1997).

The Interpretation

The limited thinking of a fourteen-month-old might go something like this, "Even though it seems you prefer the broccoli to the Goldfish crackers, I can't imagine that would be the case. Since I love the Goldfish crackers, you must too." The young toddler lives with the immature notion that everyone in the world thinks and feels as she does and all people's desires are like hers.

An interpretation of the more mature child's thinking might be: "Even though I would never consider eating the broccoli myself, I realize you have a different desire, so here is some more of the broccoli you love."

One experiment with Goldfish crackers and broccoli is not enough for any self-respecting toddler to understand the consistent or inconsistent desires between him and another person. The toddler is fascinated with the fact that he and others are not like-minded and so makes it his mission to discover just where these conflicting desires begin and end. A child in this stage of development will set up situations to see a parent's response. For instance, a child will start to jump on the sofa and look at his parent to see if the parent agrees or disagrees with this activity. The next day when visiting Grandma, he'll test out jumping on Grandma's sofa to see how Mom and Grandma feel about it. He'll color on paper and then take the crayons to the wall and see how Dad feels about coloring on this space. And so it goes with a toddler until he's between two and three years, when he's more aware of parents' standards and is then able to comply with them.

When a child persists doing exactly the opposite of what a parent requests simply to verify the fact that people can think and feel differently about the same situation, parents will often say with exasperation in their voice, "Boy, she's really got a mind of her own." Of course she does, but what's happening really isn't that the child is asserting her own mind; she's always been doing that. Now she realizes that you have a mind different than hers, and she's out to see just exactly what the two of you are in conflict over and what the two of you are like-minded about. If the child could think out loud, he might say, "Oh this is interesting, my dad and I both think coloring on paper is okay, but when it comes to coloring on walls, I like it but my daddy doesn't."

What Should Parents Do?

Parents need to realize that their child will go about setting up situations to test out when she and her parents are in agreement and when they're in conflict. When there's a conflict, sometimes parents will let it pass. If a child is taking pots and pans out of the cupboard, you may not be thrilled with this activity, but you realize that it's harmless, so you go along with your child's interest in engaging in the activity. Other times, you'll find a way to compromise with your toddler. If your child wants to jump on the sofa, and you feel it's inappropriate, you might pull out an old mattress in the basement for him to jump on. And sometimes you'll need to assume control of the situation, particularly when it's dangerous, and not permit the child to proceed with an activity. If your child wants to poke the dog with a broom, you'll say "No!", put the broom away, and put the dog in the garage, even if doing so provokes a temper tantrum from the child.

Reading about Wesley and his parents will further explain what parents should do as their child travels through this interesting and sometimes challenging period of development.

Meet Wesley

A mom and dad were so in love with their little one, Wesley. He was such a delight: adorable, lively, curious, responsive, and smart. More than the apple of their loving eyes, he had won their hearts and minds. But then Wesley reached that interesting age of eighteen months. While, of course, they still loved Wesley, they couldn't understand his behavior. Most of his exasperating behavior centered on the television set.

He'd watch Dad push the buttons on the remote control, fiddle with the cable box, turn the set on and off, or change channels. One minute there would be no picture, the next minute football or sometimes Barney. Wesley saw how powerful, competent, and even magical Dad was and decided to try out the controls for himself. Unfortunately, it was Super Bowl Sunday.

During the game, Wesley toddled over, grabbed the remote control, and pressed the channel changer button. He was amazed how easy it was—touch one button and bingo! Good-bye Super Bowl, hello *Sesame Street*.

Wesley felt powerful because he could control part of his environment, a factor important to everyone. But it wasn't nearly as exciting as watching Dad leap out of his chair, with body rigid and face intense, grab the remote, and yell, "Don't ever touch that remote control again."

Changing the TV channel was a thrill, but it wasn't nearly as thrilling as getting Dad to leap from his chair and yell. At some level Wesley must have thought, "You mean all I have to do is touch one of those buttons and I can get my dad to do that? I'm a powerful person. I can control my dad's emotions. This is exhilarating." Now some children would stop because of the parent's actions, and some might be upset, but not Wesley. He was controlling Dad's emotions and he liked this power, as many children do.

From that event on Super Bowl Sunday, whenever Wesley wanted to stir up a little action around the house, he'd head for the TV.

His parents simply couldn't figure it out. Why didn't Wesley comply with their request and leave that TV alone? The reason was simple: his curiosity about his environment and his need to control it and develop competency in managing it were stronger than his desire to comply with his parents' wishes. Also, at only eighteen months, Wesley did not have the inner controls to back away from the TV that was offering him so much enjoyment. Additionally, he wanted to use the TV as his parents did; he was imitating their behavior. In his eyes it was confusing that they could control this magical box and he couldn't.

After Super Bowl Sunday, when Wesley would go for the TV's buttons, one or both of his parents would yell or scream at him to stop, or they'd threaten a time-out. Nevertheless, Wesley would keep going for those buttons. Then Mom and Dad started wondering, "Just how many times am I going to have to yell at Wesley to get him to listen and behave?"

Wesley's mom and dad didn't understand that Wesley's behavior was normal for an eighteen-month-old. They didn't understand that Wesley needed to explore the house. They didn't understand that he had discovered that his parents had desires different than his and that he was determined to discover what he and his parents were like-minded about and what they were in conflict over. They didn't realize that it was exciting to Wesley that he could control their emotions by touching the TV. No doubt the TV set was one significant source of conflict.

Jennifer and Mark took it all personally; it was them against him. They were enraged at Wesley, but they were baffled, exhausted, and overwhelmed too. What happened to the sweet little baby they once knew? What should these exasperated parents have done?

Two events were occurring here: (1) Wesley's fascination with the cause and effect of punching the TV buttons and seeing various pictures pop on and off the TV screen, and (2) his interest in the fact that he and his parents had a conflict of desire. Wesley wanted to touch the TV to mimic his parents and learn to be competent in doing so, and his parents wanted him to leave it alone.

Wesley's parents asked a friend for advice. She suggested simply putting the TV up out of Wesley's reach, ending the battle without any more fuss. Her suggestion did not satisfy them. They wanted to win. They wanted a way to bring Wesley under their control, for him to comply. They wanted a parenting technique to stop Wesley from touching the TV and other enticing objects around the house.

Day after day the battle continued, until the parents finally realized that not only were they exhausted, but they were not reaching their goal either. Finally, after reading about toddler behavior, they slowly grew receptive to exploring options to defuse the battle of wills. They took time to calm down and cool off. Setting aside their angry stance, they decided to take the time to develop a plan and take on a matter-of-fact attitude.

Rather than trying to stop Wesley from touching the TV, "just because I said so," they asked, "How can I guide Wesley to learn to be successful in his home, which includes the TV, while at the same time maintaining a modicum of control over it and over him so that we are not angry and out of control ourselves?"

They decided to put the TV up out of Wesley's reach. They realized that it was best for Wesley if he didn't have lots of screen time anyway; they didn't want the TV to be the main focus of his day. They now understood that as a toddler Wesley simply didn't have the self-control to stay away from this magical box. When they put it up out of his reach, they didn't need to monitor him every moment, fearful that he'd touch the television set. With the TV up, they ended the negative interactions between them and Wesley over this enticing magical machine.

Because his parents were also aware that Wesley was attempting to learn to be successful and competent in his home environment, they gave him the opportunity to turn the TV on and off once a day. When it was Wesley's designated time to watch *Teletubbies*, they would lift him up to push the TV's on and off button (for full satisfaction, they would allow him to do so several times). When the program was over, they'd lift him up again to turn the TV off. Some days they would offer him the remote control. With this plan in motion, Wesley was getting some of the power and competency he needed as a developing toddler to manage his environment, but in a positive and controlled manner. His parents proudly reestablished peace in their home. Of course, with a child like Wesley, there are many more adventures waiting just around the corner.

Another object of interest was the wood-burning stove. Wesley's parents had to explore a different option to keep Wesley safe, as there was no available compromise; they couldn't move the stove. Therefore, they set up a barricade around it, and when Wesley showed interest in it, either Mom or Dad would bend down next to him and have him feel the heat and say, "Hot."

Wesley was also highly interested in learning to open and shut cupboards and drawers. His parents decided that they would allow him to do so at will. Again, they realized that Wesley was interested in being competent in his home environment. Part of that competency was opening and shutting cupboards and drawers. Of course, they worried that he might slam his fingers in a cupboard or drawer as he shut it. So when Wesley decided to do a little drawer and cupboard opening and shutting, they would be near. They would sit on the floor as he worked to master this skill. If they saw a finger in harm's way, they could quickly intervene.

Another concern was that unsafe objects might be housed in the cupboards or drawers that Wesley was using to refine his skills. To fix this, they rearranged the contents so that only safe items were available to Wesley. They needed to put safety devices on the cupboards and drawers that contained dangerous substances. With this approach, Wesley's parents afforded him the opportunity to master the skills to manage his first and most important environment: his home.

Wesley's parents learned exactly the right amount of their involvement needed in different situations to guide Wesley toward competency. Parents of toddlers (and really parents with children of all ages) can consider these same three options when offering guidance:

1. In dangerous situations (wood-burning stores and the like), keep the object out of the child's reach. The full burden of keeping the child absolutely safe lies with the parent and not the child.

2. In challenging situations (TV sets and the like), offer a compromise that includes teaching the children skills to eventually manage the situation for themselves.

3. In safe situations (cupboards and drawers and the like), with an eye on the child to protect her, allow the child to explore at will to satisfy her curiosity while permitting her the opportunity to develop her competency and master tasks.

*   *   *

As you parent your children, you'll do best by them if you respect the fact that they have minds of their own. While offering that respect, parents also need to guide and influence their children responsibly and in the child's best interest. There will be many times when you'll have conflicts. Your child will want to do one thing and you'll want your child to do another. You and your child will not always be like-minded. Rather than thinking that it's you against your child, each time your child enters a new environment or approaches an unsafe object, ask yourself that same question that Wesley's parents asked themselves, "How can I guide my child to learn to be successful in this environment while keeping him safe and healthy and maintaining at the same time a modicum of control over him so that I am not angry and out of control myself?"

Some of the situations that your child may wish to enter are dangerous. The child can't explore the environment without you right there to see that she will be safe. This fact is true for toddlers and teenagers. In other environments that your child enters, your role will be to guide, offer suggestions, provide options, discuss choices, compromise, and negotiate ideas that will lead the child to be successful and competent. And in some settings, you'll let your child explore freely, knowing that the child has everything necessary to succeed without parental interference.

So as your child enters a situation, ask yourself, "What's my role here? Do I need to be right by my child's side, making sure he's safe and protected physically and emotionally? Do I need to offer some guidance and stay in my child's proximity in order to allow my child the opportunity to learn by trial and error, but also be available if he needs me? In this environment, can I allow my child to experience it on his own?" If the child is fully equipped or even mostly equipped to manage a situation without parental interference, as the child does so he feels competent and in control as he determines on his own how to be successful.

As children grow and develop, their world expands. The first environment they explore and master is home. Then it's the neighborhood. Next it's their child-care center or preschool and then elementary school, middle school, and high school. Other environments include airports and airplanes, restaurants, religious events, shopping malls, parks and playgrounds. Some social events in which children eventually need to succeed are holiday celebrations, birthday parties, playdates, and spending the night with relatives and friends. There are so many. Because of the developmental age of the child, coupled with previous experience, a child's brain is eager to adapt to many and ever-expanding situations.

Sometimes children learn from Mom and Dad to manage themselves in a new environment; other times they learn from peers, teachers, coaches, clergy, scout leaders, the media, or extended family members.

It's scary for some parents to think that their children will eventually be on their own out in the world making decisions and learning to manage themselves without Mom or Dad's influence or guidance. While this fear is valid, it's important to proceed confidently knowing that you'll always be an important force in your child's life and an image in your child's mind. Regardless, it's important to honor and respect your child's mind and thinking ability while guiding your child responsibly as appropriate to your child's age and ability.

REFERENCES

Repacholi, B. M., and A. Gopnik. 1997. Early reasoning about desires: Evidence from 14- and 18-month-olds. *Developmental Psychology* 33: 12–21.

Chapter 12

Looking Ahead

As your child moves into her third year, you'll notice several developmental leaps. The more you know, the better prepared you'll be to enjoy, recognize, and manage this interesting and sometimes perplexing period of development.

Most fascinating for many parents to observe is the emergence of pretend play. With or without you, with or without objects, children at about age two slip into their imaginations and into the world of make believe. A simple tea party with dolls and teddy bears or family members tasting invisible cookies and sipping invisible tea reenacts the social experience and expectations of politeness, conversation, and sharing. A child sets up roadways and train tracks surrounding block buildings; she's laying out a cityscape with traffic patterns right in your living room. Through such imaginative play experiences children come to understand the culture in which they live and their place in it.

Two aspects of two-year-old development may surprise you

and bring you gratification. You'll see glimmers of your child being aware of and adhering to your standards for living in your home environment. Going along with your child's ability to recognize your standards for daily living, you'll see that your child can actually complete tasks from start to finish. While this is exciting, it's important to watch your expectations, as your child is, after all, only two years old. He'll not be setting the table and tidying his room all on his own. He may, however, complete a five-piece puzzle or nest all ten of the stacking cups in order from small to large. These are huge leaps from only three or four months ago, when your child was only interested in dumping objects and toting them from one place to the next.

Most children's behavior becomes more predictable. While they still need constant monitoring, they begin to develop self-control. Six months ago your child may have used a chair to climb onto the dining room table; after all, his body was ready to climb, so he found a convenient place to do so. Now at age two, because he's aware of what you do and what others in the home do, standing on the table no longer crosses his mind. He confines his climbing to the play structures in the backyard and at the park.

While your two-year-old has caught on to not climbing on furniture, other standards yet escape her. Let's say your older daughter (four years) is coloring on paper with marking pens, then little sister (eighteen months) wants to get into the act; she's eager to do what her sister is doing but hasn't yet learned the appropriate place to use marking pens. While you're preparing lunch, little sister uses the marking pens on herself and on the table. These non-standards for behavior continue to occur in surprising fashion with toddlers. Gentle and patient guidance is key to developing self-control in children as they learn how to manage themselves in your home and elsewhere.

Pretending Apparent

There will be a day when you realize that your child is using an object symbolically to represent an entity in the real world. Your toddler may use pretend food to feed a toy animal. He may load up a toy dump truck with make-believe rocks, drive it into another room, and then dump out those imaginary rocks. You realize that your child is using his imagination combined with toy props to reenact real-life episodes.

Another time you may hear your child talking to an imaginary friend, "No, don't eat that cookie, you must eat your dinner first." After a trip to the doctor, you may see your child reenacting the experience with his favorite doll or Elmo.

The Research

In an experiment, researchers enlisted children ages fifteen, eighteen, and twenty-four months. After some warm-up play time, the female experimenter would say to each child, "Now we will play with some toys I have." Next, she presented the child with six test episodes involving pretend play, one episode at a time. For any given episode, the experimenter put out some props and played the first part of the scenario, and then encouraged the child to complete it with a specific request.

Each episode had a simple version and a complex version. For example, in the simple version of one episode, the experimenter, using a toy basin, two dolls, and a towel, pretended to fill the basin with water, wash one doll in the basin, and then put the "wet" doll next to the other doll. Next, she would ask the child, "Can you use the towel to dry the baby who is all wet?" To complete the episode, the child would need to have kept track of what had happened, recall which of the dolls had been bathed and was imaginatively wet, and then complete the imaginary episode by using the towel to pretend to dry the "wet" doll.

In the complex version of this bathing episode there was more than one wet/dry transformation for the child to keep track of. The experimenter pretended to fill the basin with water, "washed" both of the dolls, used the towel to "dry" one of the dolls, put the two dolls side by side, and then asked, "Can you use the towel to dry the baby who is all wet?"

Other episodes involved pretending to eat cereal, dry a wet dish, feed a doll and wipe a spill from the doll's shirt, blow bubbles, and change a doll's diaper. Each child was presented with the simple versions of three of the episodes and the complex versions of the other three.

Most of the fifteen-month-olds were unable to continue the stipulated pretend episode, even the simple versions. If they did respond to the request, they usually chose the wrong prop or just copied what the experimenter had done (perhaps washed the baby again) rather than continue the episode (towel-dry the baby). At eighteen months the toddlers were a bit more proficient than the fifteen-month-olds, yet they were unable to complete the pretend play episodes most of the time. What became apparent, however, was that the eighteen-month-olds showed more evidence of recognizing that the adult experimenter was involved in pretense and of understanding her sequence of actions: Compared to the fifteen-month-olds, they responded more, they were more often correct, and they talked more about what they were pretending to do. The twenty-four-month-olds usually responded correctly in both the simple and complex episodes. They were able to understand the episode and enter into collaborative pretend play with the adult partner, keeping track of and finishing off the episode as requested (Walker-Andrews and Kahana-Kalman, 1999).

The Interpretation

You can see from this research study that by twenty-four months your child has become equipped to carry out real life situations through imaginary play. When children engage in pretend play, they're richly involved in using symbols, which stand for their real life counterparts. With the use of a child's imagination, a block turns into a cell phone, a chair becomes a truck's cab, a table with a blanket thrown over it turns into a cave. As pretend play emerges, simultaneously children learn to speak words, which are symbols for objects and events they see and experience. In time they learn to read words, which is another form of a more complex symbol system.

What Should Parents Do?

Most parents recognize the value of pretend play and respect a child's involvement with it. It fascinates most adults to observe children engrossed in imaginative play as they act out scenarios and reenact experiences making sense and coming to terms with daily occurrences and episodes and thereby incorporating them into their minds, emotions, and social ability.

Children need a parent's support for imaginative play in three important ways:

1. *Uninterrupted time:* Today most families are on the go with schedules to meet and activities to attend. While these realities may be imbedded in a family's lifestyle, from time to time each parent needs to ask if the life they're leading allows enough uninterrupted time for children to play in an unstructured imaginative format dictated only by their imagination. If not, make changes in order for your child to relish

and languor in the benefits of imaginative play. Also, when your child sets up a play scene—whether it's building a block city, creating a doctor's office, setting up a grocery store, or replicating a miniature home environment—allow your child to keep the play scene up for a few hours, days, or weeks. As your child plays, she extends her imagination and thinking skills as she delves deeper and deeper into the topic. And when it's time to leave the house for an outing to the grocery store, rather than just insisting your child get in the car right now, enter yourself into your child's imaginary world by saying, "The shelves in your grocery store need stocking. Let's go shopping and see what we can bring home for your grocery store."

2. *Props*: Tape, blankets, boxes, paper, and scarves. As your child enters into her third year and into the world of make believe, when it comes to toys, less is more. What does that mean? If your child is playing doctor, you don't need to go out and buy a doctor's set. Your child will use various objects around the house and pretend that they are a stethoscope, syringe, and bandage. Children don't need something that replicates the real thing; their imaginations will take them there. Go ahead and offer a few Band-Aids or an Ace bandage to add to your child's play; doing so will likely extend it. More importantly, have a box of materials handy so that your child can create his own props.

3. *A partner*: You, an imaginary friend, a doll, or a similar-aged playmate. Your child may need you to be his patient when he's playing doctor. When you're invited into your child's imaginative world, let your child be in charge and lead the play. Resist trying to take over and dominate the action. Play

the part that your child lays out for you. He's the director; you're the actor in the imaginative play scenario.

When your two-year-old has a friend over to play, realize that the pair probably won't play cooperatively in an imaginary situation, like one being the mommy and the other being the daddy while taking care of their baby doll. It won't be until the preschool years that this form of cooperative play emerges.

Since pretend play promotes cognitive development, communicate to your child by your actions and attitude that you recognize and respect its value. Support it with props to extend its purpose. Show your child that you're interested in whatever it is that she's pretending about.

You can also use imaginative play to your parenting advantage. Here's how: Let's say your toddler puts up a fight when it comes to getting dressed. You don't like wrestling her into her clothes each morning, so a lightbulb goes on over your head telling you to slip a sock on your hand while saying, "Mr. Sox says it's time to get dressed." Lo and behold, your child agrees to the task. When you get bogged down in a difficult situation, call on your child's imagination to reach compliance. If your child seems reluctant to practice using the toilet, call on his teddy bear to demonstrate toileting and create a story about his willingness to try. Don't be surprised when your toddler does a little practicing on his own on the toilet after watching Teddy.

Completing Tasks

As your child moves into his third year, you'll see him involved in more purposeful tasks that require planning and completing goals.

He'll stack blocks and leave them standing, finish a simple puzzle or distribute the napkins around the table for dinner, making sure there is one at every place setting.

The Research

In a study designed to track children's ability to stick with a task and complete it, researchers demonstrated three separate activities: building a tower of three painted blocks to form a figure (e.g., a door, window, and roof to form a house), putting four blocks in place inside a wooden box as if to dress the figure whose body is comprised of the box and blocks, and washing a blackboard. Then they asked the toddlers to perform these tasks.

The researchers were interested in the extent to which the children directed and monitored their own behavior and reached the intended goal. It was also important for the researchers to note whether the children stopped the activity once they completed the desired task. Stopping upon completion indicated that they were fully aware of the goal at hand.

The youngest children in the study, the fifteen- to eighteen-month-olds, rarely completed an activity as demonstrated. They manipulated the materials in appropriate ways, but their actions were not systematic and were rarely outcome-directed. They built with the blocks but typically not in the correct order, sometimes adding in extra blocks that were available and then rearranging them, and they enjoyed banging blocks together. They needed prompting to put blocks in the box. They swiped at the blackboard with the sponge, but not necessarily where it needed cleaning, and they played with the sponge in the water.

The children who were a bit older, nineteen to twenty-two months, did some of the same things as the younger children, but they showed more signs of being outcome-directed. They would build a three-block tower and then stop, the stop indicating they had achieved an outcome, yet the outcome was not correct (maybe their tower had the roof on the bottom and the door on the top or some extra blocks added in). They seemed to be aware that there was a standard, but they were not able to achieve it. At this stage, their focus and self-control was more on *how* to do the actions rather than *what* was produced.

The next older group, the twenty-three- to twenty-eight-month-olds, did start to show signs of focusing on *what* they produced and attempted to match the expected outcome, but only the oldest children, those who approached three years old, consistently demonstrated enough self-control to reach the expected goals and stop once they reached them (Bullock and Lutkenhaus, 1988).

The Interpretation

Younger children busy themselves with various tasks, but then they get distracted with something else or use materials in a way of their own making. As this study shows, it takes maturity, self-control, and cognitive ability to stick to a task and complete it as instructed.

What Should Parents Do?

Watch your expectations. Some two-year-olds will be able to finish a project or complete a task, but many won't do so consistently. If you expect your toddler to put toys away, you may turn frustrated if your child begins the task but then gets distracted by a toy dump truck. Now from this research you know that it's unrealistic to expect two-year-olds to finish such tasks from beginning to end.

If you set out a craft activity for your eighteen-month-old, such as gluing hearts on a Valentine card, your child may put on one or ten, or she may spend her time only spreading the glue around. So be it. If you'd like your twenty-month-old to put groceries on the shelf in the pantry, realize that one day he may put them all where they belong, another day he may attempt to put them on the shelf and end up playing with the grocery bag instead. If you expect your two-year-old to dress herself, again, watch your expectations. Not only is the task difficult with respect to using small and large motor skills, but following through with all the various clothing items—underwear, shirt, pants, socks, and shoes—is challenging; it's difficult for toddlers to stay on task.

Over this third year your child will gradually complete tasks from start to finish, but it doesn't happen overnight. Her agenda simply hasn't met with yours as yet.

The day will come when your toddler stacks five blocks, correctly nests the stacking cups, or dresses a doll. When he's accomplished the task, you'll see a smile of mastery on his face. Not only has he completed the task, but he knows that he's completed it as intended. He's pleased with his accomplishments; let him know that you are too. A simple "Look at you, you finished that puzzle all by yourself" is all it takes.

Awareness of Adult Standards

Toward the end of your child's second year, you'll see her point out a crack in the window while saying, "uh-oh." If a wheel is missing from a toy car, your child may notice it as well. If you have a small sore on your lip, your child may touch it and call it a "boo boo." You may see your child put Elmo down for a nap, making sure his blanket is tucked in just right. If you've misbuttoned your blouse, your child may call attention to that mishap as well. Your toddler is becoming aware of the standards by which you live, how things are supposed to be. In turn your child aspires to live up to these standards, notices them, and plays about them with dolls, toy figurines, and stuffed animals.

The Research

Children, ages fourteen and nineteen months, came individually with their mothers to a playroom. The toddlers were given ten flawed and ten unflawed toys to play with. The flawed toys included a boat with holes, a doll with torn clothes or a dirty face, a handkerchief with a mark on it, and a broken telephone. An observer behind a one-way screen narrated the child's behavior into a recorder.

After a twenty-minute play session, an examiner presented the child with each of the damaged toys, to see if doing so would provoke any additional reaction. The results? Not a single fourteen-month-old gave the flawed toys any particular attention, while more than half of the nineteen-month-olds showed signs of concern with one or more of the defective toys: they pointed at them, brought them to their mother, and said things like, "Fix it," "Broke," and "Yucky." (Kagan, 1981).

The Interpretation

Children begin to realize that there's a standard by which your family lives. They notice when things are dirty, broken, or otherwise not the way they should be, and they bring it to a parent's attention. While they are starting to become aware of standards around nineteen months, they're typically not equipped to meet those standards on their own. For instance, your child knows that coats need to be zipped, but he may not be able to zip the jacket himself. Therefore if your child is trying to zip his jacket, help him get started but allow him the experience of zipping it up on his own.

It's a fine line parents walk: they want to encourage their child's interest in living up to their standards, but on the other hand, they want to resist expecting their child to complete tasks or adhere to standards that are beyond the child's skill level. If you pressure a child beyond her ability, she'll experience frustration rather than develop a sense of accomplishment. Your child will be frustrated with his inability to complete tasks that are beyond his abilities.

What Should Parents Do?

Let's say your child realizes that everyone pours his own milk from a carton. Your child really wants to pour his own milk too. All you need to do is provide a small carton that fits your child's hand, making the task more feasible.

Resist insisting that your child draw a picture of a face, use the toilet independently, or dress herself. At age two these tasks are beyond her, but in the coming months she'll likely acquire these skills all on her own, given the opportunity to practice.

Because your child is able to complete simple toddler-appropriate tasks and is aware of the standards of his home culture, don't fool yourself into thinking that your child should be able to follow adult standards regarding behavior 100 percent of the time. She may be aware of your expectations but unable to control herself in a sophisticated social manner, which includes sharing toys with peers, taking turns, and keeping away from tempting objects.

Realize that your child has limited impulse control, which means that if you tell your child not to touch an electrical outlet, he may not be able keep himself from this curious device. In fact one mom swears that her child right around age two knew exactly how long she took when using the bathroom. Her son would use that time to try out various household devices that were off limits.

One day the mom emerged from the bathroom just as her son

was about to stick a screwdriver into an electrical outlet. The mom took the screwdriver from his hand and then offered a brief reprimand, "No! That's dangerous." The child knew not to use the screwdriver in this manner, but his interest in the outlet prevented him from controlling his impulse, especially when he knew his mom was occupied in the bathroom.

The challenge for parents during this period of development is to remain vigilant when it comes to keeping toddlers safe. Even a bathroom break was more than this mom could afford when it came to her child's safety.

Self-Recognition

It might alarm you when you're at your sister's house for the afternoon and your child, twenty-two months, and your niece, twenty-six months, start wrangling over a pop-up toy. You resolve the issue by distracting them with play dough. Later on, you and your sister are amazed as the two children stand in front of a full-length mirror obviously recognizing themselves. These two developmental issues occur around the same time. A child becomes aware of herself and starts to differentiate herself from other people, which seems to lead to an exaggerated sense of ownership.

Certainly prior to this moment of self-awareness in front of a mirror, children have a sense of their own existence. They feel their breath and heartbeat. They know that they are like you, and so copy you. They feel their body move and know its existence in space, but their actual appearance escapes them until about halfway through the second year.

This ability comes at the same time that they realize that the two of you can have different desires. Remember the Goldfish cracker and broccoli research, relating to conflict of desire, described in Chapter 11? The child realizes fully for the first time that she is a separate person from you, with respect not only to her own desires, but to her looks as well.

Prior to age eighteen months, if you put your child in front of the mirror, it likely seemed that what she was looking at was another person; she didn't realize it was actually her. Then sometime during the second half of your child's second year, you'll notice that your child recognizes herself in the mirror; she's aware of her own physical features.

Around this same time, as evidence of understanding themselves as separate and distinct individuals, children are starting to recognize and correctly use pronouns, words like "me," "you," "my," and "your." If you stop to think about it, you realize how confusing it might be to a little one that, for example, the label "me" can refer to different people, depending on who is saying it. But at some point, children get it. You'll find that you no longer need to refer to yourself in the third person with your child— rather than saying, "*Mommy* will be back soon," you'll say, "*I'll* be back soon," knowing your child understands. One mother used to ask her little boy, "Do you want me to hold you?" The toddler started to say "Hold you" with arms uplifted whenever he wanted to be picked up and held. Then one day the understanding of pronouns dawned on him—when he wanted his mother to pick him up, he raised his arms and said, "Hold me."

In the following study, researchers examined how a child's budding sense of self is related to the claiming of toys and other interactions with peers.

The Research

Researchers assessed the self-definition of boys, ages twenty-two to twenty-eight months, using four tests: (1) mirror self-recognition,

(2) pronoun recognition, (3), perceptual role taking, and (4) pronoun production. Then the boys were paired and their interactions were observed.

In the mirror self-recognition test, under the pretext of wiping his face, a spot of rouge was secretly rubbed onto the child's nose. Next the child's reaction to himself in a mirror was observed. Then he was asked to wipe off the red mark with a cloth, and finally he was directed to the mirror image of himself and asked "Who is that?" The child passed the mirror self-recognition test if he spontaneously touched the red mark on his nose after looking at himself in the mirror, if he wiped his face and not the mirror to remove the red mark, or if he said, "Me," when asked, "Who is that?" These responses showed that the child knew that the image in the mirror was a reflection of himself and not an image of another person.

In the pronoun recognition test, as directed by the researchers, the mother asked the child to do things involving the pronouns "my" and "your." For example, the mother would say, "Tickle *my* toes," "Touch *your* nose," and "Comb *my* hair." The child passed this test if he could perform most of the requested actions correctly.

The perceptual role taking test evaluated the child's understanding of the fact that other people see things from their own perspective, not from the child's perspective, and recognizing what that perspective of the other person is. The child passed this test if he responded mostly correctly when his mother asked him to show her a toy or other objects, as well as when she made more challenging requests such as asking him to show her his back, to show her something that was blocked from her view by a removable piece of cardboard, or to name what she was looking at.

Finally, the child passed the pronoun pronunciation test if he is able to use the words "I" and "me" correctly as reported by his mother and as observed during the study.

Children who passed three or all four of the tests were assigned to the high self-definition group, and those who passed two or fewer were assigned to the low self-definition group. Each child was paired with another child from the same group and each pair was given opportunities to interact in a playroom that had two identical sets of toys.

The children in the high self-definition group initiated their peer interactions by claiming toys as "mine." Next, the children began to interact in positive ways, including coming near each other, playing together with toys, imitating each other, verbally communicating, and smiling at each other. The claiming of toys appeared to be a way in which the children were defining themselves and making sense of the other as a separate individual.

The children in the low self-definition group had a different way of interacting. They claimed toys as "mine" much less often and also less often commented on their peer's behavior or possessions. They offered and showed toys to their peer and engaged in less complex forms of interaction compared to the other group.

In their conclusion, the researchers state, "It seems quite important for parents and teachers to appreciate that a child's increased interest in claiming toys may not be a negative sign of selfishness but a positive sign of increased self-awareness. Adults may be more successful in promoting positive peer interaction and social interest if they help children at this age to express possessiveness and then negotiate and compromise rather than simply insisting on sharing." (Levine, 1983)

The Interpretation

Once children realize who they are and that they are their own person separate from others, it's as if they need to go overboard to prove it, and that's when an exaggerated period of possessiveness occurs. You'll hear toddlers claiming objects to be theirs by saying "Mine!" Not to worry, this period doesn't last forever. Remember that the claiming of toys is not a sign of selfishness; rather it is an important developmental step.

What Should Parents Do?

Although it's alarming to see your toddler grab an object, hold onto it, and scream "Mine!", there's no need to panic. This period of possessiveness is only temporary; it will pass. When such moments are tense, use your resourcefulness to resolve these not sharing but grabbing moments.

Here's an example. One day two granddaughters were grabbing and trying to hold onto several items that came in a toy beauty parlor set. The grandma didn't know what to do. She didn't want to put the toys away, for fear of provoking tears and tantrums. She tried to have them take turns with the various items, but it didn't work; both girls wanted all the items. Then the grandma said, "Will you please fix my hair?" The girls thought this was a grand idea, and both proceeded to pretend to cut, curl, and spray Grandma's hair. It's that kind of resourcefulness that's required of nurturing parents, grandparents, and caregivers.

Sense of Self Leads to Cooperation

While this period of possessiveness is challenging when toddlers are placed in social situations, there's a positive side to this strong sense of self that children display. A child who develops a firm sense of self by being possessive when a toddler, is equipped as he gets older to be cooperative with others, eventually learning to resolve disputes over objects when playing games and when solving simple problems, as is shown in this next piece of research.

The Research

At first, a baby sees herself as the universal agent; she is the center of the world and she is the cause of all that happens around her. As she develops, she becomes increasingly able to differentiate herself from others and starts to recognize that others cause their own behavior. In this research study, children ages twelve to thirty-three months were tested to determine their level of development in self-other differentiation as follows. The experimenter modeled several pretense scenarios and after each one said to the child, "Now it's your turn. Can you show me what I did?" The scenarios involved eating, bedtime, going to the doctor, fixing a "boo boo," and grooming, and there were multiple levels for each representing increasing levels of advancement in recognizing others as independent actors. For example, in the eating scenario the levels were the following:

- Level 1: Pretending to feed self with a spoon
- Level 2: Pretending to feed a doll with a spoon
- Level 3: Putting the spoon in the hand of the doll and pretending to make the doll feed herself
- Level 4: Putting the spoon in the hand of the doll and pretending to make the doll feed another doll

Most of the younger children (twelve to twenty-one months) imitated only at Level 1 or 2. The older children (twenty-four to thirty-three months) could imitate at Level 3 or 4. Each child was assigned a score based on the number of times he imitated at each level, a higher score indicating more advanced self-other differentiation.

Next, each child was paired with an unfamiliar other child of the same sex and same age group and presented with a problem that required cooperation to solve. The two children were told that there were some toy animals in a cup and that they could play with them if they could get them out. The cup was part of an apparatus, and solving the problem required that one child operate a spring-loaded handle while the other retrieved the animals. If the children were able to get the animals, after they played with them briefly, the animals were put back into the cup and the children were allowed to solve the problem again.

The youngest children (twelve to fifteen months) did not solve the problem. The next older group (eighteen to twenty-one months) occasionally solved it, but couldn't repeat it. The oldest children (twenty-four to thirty-three months) were able to solve it quickly and repeatedly.

Moreover, the results showed that children with higher scores on the self-other differentiation test were more able to cooperate to solve problems. Also, in order for pairs of children to solve the problem more than once, which suggests they were purposefully and intentionally cooperating to do so, at least one child in the pair had to be able to imitate at Level 3, that is, able to represent another person as acting independently (Brownell and Carriger, 1990).

What Should Parents Do?

Since you know that your child will go through a period of possessiveness, do what you can to manage gracefully such situations without punishing the child when she displays this developmental inclination. Therefore, when your child won't share a toy, honor her need not to do so. Say something to the other child like, "Sarah has the toy; when she's finished with it, then you can have a turn." Find another toy for the other child. Distract the children by drawing their attention to a neutral activity such as play dough, book reading, or going outside to play. Also, guide children to trade and take turns, or set a timer (one child has a toy for three minutes, then the other child gets a turn). Work with a toddler's need to possess objects. This period will pass and will benefit the child in the long run.

Compliance and Self-control

If you're walking down the sidewalk with your fifteen-month-old, you know that you need to stay right by his side, holding his hand or, at least, not being beyond his reach. Why? Because his self-control is uncertain at this age; he does not adhere consistently to the cultural standard that people walk on sidewalks and cars go on streets.

Furthermore, he's unlikely to comply if, as he heads for the street, you say, "Get back on the sidewalk!" He'll most likely pay your demand little notice; he'll keep heading in the direction of the street. You know that the full burden of keeping him safe lies with you and not him, and so you'll need to rush over and gently take his hand and lead him back to the sidewalk.

Children begin to behave in a self-controlled fashion at about the same time that they begin to recognize themselves as separate, autonomous beings who direct their own actions and also inhibit them. As well, their ability to store and recall memories must be developed to the point where they can remember a parent or caregiver's directive and inhibit their own actions.

The first glimmerings of self-control appear in the form of compliance between twelve and eighteen months. While toddlers show an awareness of parents' wishes and expectations, they're only able to obey simple requests and commands. A child's ability to exhibit self-control and comply with parents' wishes is sporadic at best and, therefore, depends heavily on caregiver support, which means that if a parent doesn't want his child to climb on a table or touch a wood-burning stove, he must be near, monitoring the child and being gentle yet consistent.

Toddlers who experience parental warmth and gentle encouragement are more likely to be cooperative, stay away from forbidden objects, and comply with other parental requests.

The Research

In one study, mother and toddler pairs were observed during free play and then in a cleanup task in which the mother asked her child to help pick up toys. The results showed that the more emotionally available the mother was to her child, as observed during the free play time, the more likely the child was to comply with the mother's request to help with cleanup.

The researchers rated each mother's emotional availability based on several factors:

- The degree to which the mother recognized and demonstrated her ability to be responsive to her child

- How in tune the mother was with respect to timing of her interactions with her child

- If there was a natural rhythm as she interacted with her child and traveled through transitions with him

- How attentive she was to her child when her child was distressed

- How genuinely pleased she was to share in activities with her child

- How effectively she negotiated when a conflict occurred

- If her emotional expression toward her child was mostly and appropriately positive

- How well she structured her child's play by inviting interaction, following her child's lead by letting her direct the play activity and elaborating on her child's play themes while keeping the play sessions interesting and stimulating (Lehman, Steier, Guidash, and Wanna, 2002).

As a child's self-control improves, parents catch on to their child's ability to manage himself and then gradually increase the number of rules they expect their toddler to follow, including rules that pertain to safety and respect for property and people. In time, children are also willing and able to follow family routines, display basic manners, and complete simple chores.

In a longitudinal study that focused on rules and compliance, researchers showed that mothers' rules tend to be in sync with the developmental advances of their children. This means that early rules, at about thirteen months, are fewer and are mostly about safety. Later, as cognitive and language skills improve and children begin to develop a sense of self as distinct from others, mothers expand the range of rules to include mealtime routines, manners, self-care, and simple chores such as putting toys away. By age three-and-a-half, rules are more elaborate and pertain to social conventions. Around the same time children are socializing more and are better able to understand reasons for rules. Based on reports by mothers, as the children got older, they were more likely to conform to family rules. Over the course of the study, the children showed signs of gradual development of self-control, needing fewer reminders from parents to follow rules (Gralinski and Kopp, 1993).

The Interpretation

Most parents establish rules for their children starting with rules for safety at about the time when they're fully mobile. Once parents realize that their baby is catching on to certain rules, they add more rules to the child's repertoire. Gradually, parents no longer need to remind children of rules, as children monitor their own behavior internally, exercising self-control.

As children catch on to rules, it's important for parents to be available emotionally and to be sensitive to the child's developing ability to comply and complete various tasks. Also, a semblance of structure is important, which means that it's best to develop consistent routines for compliance regarding rules.

What Should Parents Do?

Establish a few simple rules, tune in to the child's emotions as you enforce a rule, and proceed, being calm and consistent. Let's say you don't want your child to carry snack foods into the living room. You want food items in your kitchen. To enforce this rule, every time your child walks with food to the kitchen door's threshold, repeat the rule, "Food stays in the kitchen." If your child doesn't comply, walk toward the child and gently remove the food while repeating the rule. In time, with consistency, your child will stay in the kitchen when eating cookies and crackers and other snack finger foods.

It's also important to establish only a couple of rules at a time. Once your child catches on to these, and they become a natural part of your child's life, then add a couple more.

Also realize that when you establish a rule and enforce it, sometimes your child may erupt with a temper tantrum. In a situation like the previous example, when the child was walking into the living room with a cracker in hand and the parent reminded the child of the rule while removing it from her hand, it's important to say, "I know you really want to take the cracker into the living room, but I can't allow it." Even though you're being emotionally responsive, however, your child may still erupt with a temper tantrum.

Temper Tantrums

An older infant will react with anger if he's holding an interesting object and someone removes it; if he's participating in an activity and someone takes him away from it; if someone restrains his arms; if a parent leaves for a brief period; or if he expects something from a past experience to occur and now it no longer does. Also, if children are thwarted from doing something that they're capable of doing, they turn angry. For any of these reasons, a child may display a tizzy fit or a full-blown temper tantrum.

Researchers are interested in learning about what causes frustration in young children, how they express it, what helps children learn how to handle potentially frustrating situations, supporting their healthy emotional development, and what factors predict disruptive and destructive behavior later in life. To this end, experiments are conducted that expose children briefly to frustrating situations while the behavior of child and parent is observed.

The Research

In one research study, babies ages four to five months, with a ribbon tied to one arm, learned that moving that arm caused the appearance of a colored image of a happy baby, accompanied by pleasant music, and that the interesting event only occurred with the movement of the beribboned arm (much as the babies in Chapter 5 learned to make a mobile move). The babies discovered that they could make something interesting happen.

After several minutes, the experimenters changed the relationship between the child's arm movements and the interesting event, violating in three different ways for three groups of babies the expectation that the babies had formed.

For one group of babies, the experimenters stopped the interesting event from occurring. The babies kept moving their arms, expecting to make the event occur, but it no longer did, and they didn't know why. They moved their arms faster, trying harder to make that happy baby face appear, but to no avail, and they became frustrated.

For a second group of babies, the experimenters made it so that now the happy baby and music event occurred only once for every third arm movement. To these babies, the significance was that they could still cause the interesting event to occur, but not as much as before. They moved their arms faster and showed signs of frustration.

For the third group of babies, the experimenters made it so that now the event occurred independent of the babies' arm movements. These babies experienced that the interesting event was still occurring, but not in response to their actions. They quickly perceived that they had lost control of it, stopped moving their arms, and became frustrated.

All three of these situations were frustrating to the babies, provoking many to anger. After two minutes' exposure to one of these frustrating situations, the experimenters returned the control to the babies as at the beginning, so that once again they could move their arms and make the happy baby face with music appear (Sullivan and Lewis, 2003).

In another experiment, researchers asked mothers of fifteen-month-olds to gently restrain their child's arms for thirty seconds, preventing the child from playing with an interesting toy. The children struggled, showed angry facial expressions, and vocally protested, cried, or screamed. When the arm restraint was applied a second time, the children got angry more quickly and their anger was more intense (Potegal, Robison, Anderson, Jordan, and Shapiro, 2007).

In another study, two-year-olds were put into a potentially frustrating situation for two minutes. The children were asked if they wanted a snack or to play with an interesting toy. If the child wanted a snack, the experimenter put a cookie in a clear plastic container for two minutes before giving it to the child. The child could see the cookie and touch the container but not open it and get the cookie. If the child wanted to play with the toy, he was allowed to play with it for one minute. Then the toy was put into the clear container for two minutes before it was given back to the child. The mother was with the child, and her behavior along with the behavior of the child was observed. The child's heart rate was also measured, as a way of determining how well the child was able to regulate himself. At another time, the children and mothers were observed in a second potentially frustrating situation. Each child was placed in a high chair without any toys or snacks for five minutes. Typical responses to these two frustrating situations included whining, pouting, fussing, crying, screaming, and throwing tantrums. Some children were more reactive to frustration than others. Each child was rated on a scale of frustration reactivity.

The mothers were also observed during other situations with their child, including free play, helping their child solve a challenging puzzle, and cleanup. The researchers rated the mothers' behavior according to how strict or punitive the mothers were and how often the mothers' statements pertained to their own goals as opposed to facilitating the child's activities. These two factors were combined into one rating that was considered a measure of how controlling the mothers were.

These children were followed through early childhood and those who tended to exhibit high levels of disruptive behavior throughout that period, including aggression, defiance, and temper tantrums typically fit one of two profiles at age two: (1) children who had highly controlling mothers and also were highly reactive to frustrating situations, and (2) children with low maternal control who also lacked skill at self-regulation (Degnan, Calkins, Keane, and Hill-Soderlund, 2008).

The Interpretation

The results of this last study illustrate the sensitivity and adaptability that is called for from parents to help their children learn to deal with life and all its challenges. It's a fine line the parent walks; on the one hand, parents want to strive to not be overly controlling or authoritarian, as their children may turn highly reactive, acting out in destructive ways. On the other hand, because children have not yet learned to regulate themselves, parents need to provide enough structure and support until their children can manage themselves. Since there is no set formula, parents do best for their children by being emotionally available while tuning in to and responding to each child's needs as much as possible.

Let's say one day your toddler takes the broom from the closet into the living room to use the handle to retrieve a ball that's rolled underneath the sofa. You don't like this idea, as you worry that she'll bang something with the broom's handle, so you take it from her. Your daughter throws a temper tantrum when you take the broom from her hand.

This is a perfect example of a child intentionally taking charge of a situation and then responding with a temper tantrum when a parent stops her from carrying out her plan.

You're likely not that different. If you have a vision at work as to how to proceed with a project and your boss thwarts you from proceeding, you'll likely turn frustrated. You probably won't throw a temper tantrum, but you'll feel angry, and then once your anger subsides, you'll decide how to proceed.

The child in the broom situation is left only to feel angry unless the parent, employing patience, decides to guide her successfully and safely to use the broom to retrieve the ball under the sofa.

What Should Parents Do?

When your child is intent on managing a situation for himself, ask yourself if there's a way that he can do it or a way that you can guide him to complete the task. If you don't, not only will your child have temper tantrums, but your child will also see you as someone who frequently pulls in the parenting reins, keeping him from developing his capabilities, and power struggles may follow. Children are much more capable than parents sometimes think. If your child sees you as a conduit to self-reliance and independence, and as a person who warmly and lovingly supports his cognitive development, you'll fare better in your relationship with your child and your child will likely thrive and reach his potential.

* * *

All parents want well-behaved children who exhibit self-control. Some parents strive for quick disciplinary fixes. While some approaches are effective in reaching the goal of a better-behaved child, it's critical that in order for any disciplinary approach to be effective, it needs to be administered by a nurturing parent. What's a nurturing parent?

A nurturing parent is affectionate and friendly.
Parents prove their love and friendliness in the following ways:

- By saying, "I love you."
You do love your child, so be sure to communicate it with words anytime during the day: when zipping a coat, when diapering, when tucking your child into bed at night, and when leaving for the day.

- By offering gentle touch.
Gentle touch communicates love without saying a word. Every time you pull your child on your lap, gently pat, or embrace your child, you're expressing affection.

- By conveying love and limits simultaneously.
When you need to keep your child from doing something that you feel is unsafe or inappropriate, be sure to communicate that you're doing so out of love. You do this with your body language, tone of voice, and the way you handle your child. If your child is approaching a hot stove, say firmly and lovingly, while moving between the stove and your child, "No! That's hot." You can even go on to say, "I won't let you hurt yourself; it's only because I love you so much."

- By spending time with your child in activities of particular interest to your child.

When you spend time with your child on her terms and let your child lead the activity, you're expressing love. The child feels powerful, competent, and loved by you. Plus, there's an added bonus ... if after such a play session, it's time for bed, your child will likely be willing to comply with your requests for a bath, pajamas, and a story. Why? Since he's had the chance to be in charge, it's easy for him then to go along with your agenda.

A nurturing parent considers a child's feelings, desires, and needs.

Parents prove to their children that they are considerate of their feelings, desires, and needs in the following ways:

- By expressing interest in their child's opinions and ideas.

Children offer all kinds of opinions and ideas, some reasonable, some outrageous, and some fanciful. While you won't always agree with their opinions or go along with their ideas, you can always express interest in them and validate them. This approach does not mean that you need to help carry out those ideas, although you can if it's appropriate, but that out of respect for the child, you show interest in her thoughts.

- By reiterating your child's point of view

When your child expresses a position, all you need to do is restate it. "So you'd like a playdate this afternoon?" By doing so, you're not necessarily going along with the idea, you're simply letting the child know that you've received his communication. If you agree, fine; if not, at least you've proved by your reiteration that you've heard the request.

- By validating a child's wishes

When your child says, "I really want to go to the playground," you can always respond by saying, "You wish that you could go to the playground. You wish that you could swing on the swing and slide down the slide. I wish that we could do that too, but it's time for dinner, and besides it's raining." By hearing you describe his wishes your child imagines them coming true, almost as if experiencing them firsthand. This approach makes it easier then for a child to accept reality when his wish is not coming true. Sometimes, of course, parents grant those wishes by saying, "Sure, let's stop by the playground on the way home. Great idea!"

- By acknowledging emotions, but limiting accompanying negative behavior

Children experience all sorts of emotions: happiness, sadness, disappointment, regret, anger, fear, excitement, jealousy, and pleasure, to name only a few. Whatever emotion your child feels, acknowledge it. "You're jealous of your sister, I understand that. It's hard to share time with Mommy. It's okay to feel jealous, but I can't allow you to poke the baby." Feelings that go unnamed confuse children. When a parent names an emotion, the child then begins to understand the emotion, thus reducing subsequent confusion when the emotion arises again. Plus, when a parent or other loving caregiver identifies an emotion, usually it magically dissolves.

A nurturing parent is interested in a child's daily activities.

Parents prove to their children that they are interested in their activities by proceeding in the following ways:

- By completing the cycle of a conversation

When your child comes home from preschool and says, "My teacher's cat had kittens," do you say, "How many?" If so, you're completing the cycle of the conversation. By asking a question, you're communicating, "I heard what you said, I'm interested, and I want to know more."

■ By offering props to support your children's play or hobby

If your child is doctoring her dolls, you can easily support her imaginative play by providing a few bandages. If your child is involved in pretend play that includes various construction vehicles, backhoes, tractors, cranes, and the like, you can take your child to a construction site to see the equipment firsthand. If your child collects baseball cards when he's older, you can help him look for a special one. If your child is interested in archaeology, you can travel to various digs to view sights, so that she can see them up close for herself.

■ By attending your children's activities

Whether a ballet recital, soccer game, or theatrical performance, you'll willingly attend, smiling, clapping, showing interest, and supporting your child's efforts and abilities.

■ By noticing when your child comes and goes

You likely greet your child lovingly when he wakes in the morning, and offer a kiss and hug when leaving him at child care. These gestures communicate that his presence and absence makes a difference to you and that you care about where he is and what he's doing. Most likely this comes naturally to most parents but think about a child whose parents never notice when she's coming or going, how sad that would be for the child.

■ By mentoring your child to succeed

Children take on many challenges but often need guidance to complete a task. Your job is to give them just enough assistance so that they feel as if they've completed the project for themselves, without being left completely to their own devices.

**A nurturing parent expresses
pride in a child's accomplishments.**
Parents prove pride for children's accomplishments in the following ways:

- By noticing small steps toward competency

Children are working to master many skills. Each one takes many steps until the child reaches mastery. Your child needs recognition for attempts as she practices each skill. The first time your child writes her name, any approximation deserves a posting on the refrigerator. With time and practice, your child's efforts will improve.

- By cheering children on as they learn various skills

Learning to ride a tricycle, kick a ball, bat a ball, and swim are only some of the skills children learn. As they do, cheer them on from the sidelines, saying, "Way to go!", "Good for you!", "I'm so proud of you. I bet you're proud of yourself." Another approach is to say, "When I saw you up on the stage dancing, I was so proud to be your parent."

- By saying, "I like it when . . ." and "I appreciate it when . . ."

When your child first carries his plate from the table to the counter, say, "I really appreciate that you carried your plate from the table to the counter." When your child thanks Grandma for a birthday gift, say, "I really like that you thanked Grandma for the birthday gift."

- By challenging children to work toward mastery

Let's say your child is becoming proficient at writing her name, but you notice that she doesn't know to dot the i's in her name, Emilia. You've ignored it up until now, as she's been working so hard at writing all the letters, but now since she's proficient at the others, you point out that lower case i's have a dot above them.

She willingly adds the dots above the i's, happy to be writing her name correctly.

- By limiting criticism

Here's where parenting gets tricky. In the previous example, if you had pointed out the undotted i's at first, it would have been a criticism. Why? Because the child is working so hard to form all the letters of her name that dotting the i's really isn't that important at first. By waiting and limiting your criticism, you're allowing your child to practice the task and accomplish it in her own way and time. When you wait until the right moment, your child is open to your information. It's the teachable moment you're waiting for. If you had insisted on dotted i's at first, it would have been criticism; because you waited, it's teaching.

- By observing children's achievements

When your child walks for the first time, you likely stop what you're doing and just watch. Taking your time to observe a child as he learns to stack blocks, work a button into its hole, pedal a tricycle, and eventually write his name, communicates pride without saying a word. All you need to say is "You know how to write your name? Show me, I'll watch you."

- By describing a child's accomplishments

While you can say, "I'm so proud that you can draw a picture of a face, I hope you're proud of yourself," you can also, instead, describe a child's accomplishments, which is another way to communicate the pride you feel: "I see that you drew a picture of a face. Look, you drew eyes, a mouth, and a nose. Good for you." Because you've precisely described what your child has accomplished, you've reinforced the behavior and your child senses your pride in what she's achieved. Such careful descriptions often mean more to a child than a simple "I'm proud of you."

A nurturing parent offers support and encouragement during stressful times.

When children face adverse situations, parents prove their support and encouragement in the following ways:

▪ By offering empathy and understanding

Parents' natural inclination is to protect children from adversity. Yet no matter how they try, children, even young children, face stressful situations such as the birth of a sibling, the death of an animal, or the loss of a beloved blanket or doll. When they do, parents do best by their children when they offer empathy and understanding. "I know you feel sad that you lost your dolly. I'm sad too."

▪ By expressing faith that the stressful situation will improve

While you don't want to diminish the sadness that your child feels, you do want your child to know that in time she won't always feel so sad. "I know that you're so sad that your kitty died. With time you won't feel quite so sad; your sadness will slowly go away."

▪ By encouraging your child to play about the adverse situation

Play helps children work through difficult experiences. One child, after the death of the family's dog, whom they buried in the backyard, then pretended to bury the dog over and over. As disturbing as this play session was for the parents to observe, they realized that it was therapeutic for their son. Once he was finished playing about the dog's death and burial, the child emerged content and settled. As children age, they use hobbies as a source of solace when faced with an adverse situation, be it the loss of a friend, the breakup of their parents' marriage, or not making the basketball team. Hobbies provide children with a feeling of control and competency when external events make them feel out of control and incompetent.

- By encouraging the child to come up with ideas to solve a problem

If the family dog dies and your child is sad about it, ask your child what she could do so she wouldn't feel quite so sad. Often parents jump in to solve such problems for the child, bringing home a new puppy or a least promising one soon. Instead ask, "What can I do to help?" A child may say, "I'd like a picture of Goldie next to my bed." Or "I'd like a stuffed animal that looks like Goldie." So much better for children to tackle such problems on their own rather than always relying on the parent to manage the situation. Children have good minds and can often solve problems for themselves, if only given the chance.

- By asking the child what you can do to help

If a child is sad because his neighborhood friend moved away, validate the loss and then ask, "What can I do so that you won't miss him so much?" The child might not be able to come up with an answer, but at least you've communicated that you care and that you're willing to help out when he's feeling distressed.

- By asking yourself, "Who can help my child face this difficult situation?"

There will be times in your parenting career when you alone can't help your child through an adverse situation. Maybe you're going through a divorce and troubled yourself, so therefore you don't have the wherewithal to support your child. This is when you call on a loving aunt, friend, or counselor to offer your child guidance.

Maybe your child feels challenged to construct a project for a school science fair. You're a writer and have no talent in this area, and your spouse is an attorney who can't offer assistance either, so you call Uncle John, who is a scientist and willing to provide the guidance your child needs. A friend or family member can step in to help relieve your stress and your child's about the science fair project.

- By being available to talk about the stressful situation

You might like to talk about the dog's death in the early morning when you're relaxed and rested, but your child isn't interested or willing. Then she brings it up as you're rushing out the door for work. Sometimes you can set aside your agenda to focus on the child's concerns; other times you'll need to put your child off. When you do, be sure to get back to your child as soon as possible. Just know that when you make yourself available to talk about a stressful situation in your child's time frame and on your child's terms, you're doing the best by your child.

A nurturing parent works to stay present with a child.
Parents prove that they're present for their child in the following ways:

- By not allowing peripheral feelings, thoughts, and issues to interfere in parenting

This is an extremely difficult challenge for parents today. Life is complex. Parents have much to manage: work, household chores, finances, extended family situations, volunteer tasks, to name only a few. It's difficult to manage them all while peacefully tending to children's needs. It's worth a parent's time to learn how to set aside all those other demands to be present for his or her children.

■ By cutting out activities that interfere with your parenting

Let's say you have the opportunity to take a job that will require you to travel. You may decide to forgo this opportunity because you know that it will take away from valued time with your children.

■ By eliminating difficult people who sap your energy

You may have a friend or family member who is demanding of your time. If so, you may need to remove this person from your life so that this relationship no longer takes away time and emotional energy required for your children.

■ By checking in on yourself before managing a challenging parenting issue

Whether temper tantrums, incidents of noncompliance, or other annoying behaviors are coming from your child, before addressing the issue or blaming the child, take a few deep breaths and ask yourself how you might be contributing to the situation. Are your expectations realistic? Are you feeling resentment or anger toward your child? Are you trying to control something that you can't control in regards to your child's behavior? Are you being impatient? Are you distracted? If so, shed your own agenda and focus positively on the child. When parents are present for the child's sake and at peace themselves, it's amazing how the child in turn becomes well behaved and peaceful too, and both will roll with things that come along with fewer problems.

These approaches to being a nurturing parent are effective all the years you parent your children.

REFERENCES

Brownell, C. A., and M. S. Carriger. 1990. Changes in cooperation and self-other differentiation during the second year. *Child Development* 61: 1164–74.

Bullock, M., and P. Lutkenhaus. 1988. The development of volitional behavior in the toddler years. *Child Development* 59: 664–74.

Degnan, K. A., S. D. Calkins, S. P. Keane, and A. L. Hill-Soderlund. 2008. Profiles of disruptive behavior across early childhood: Contributions of frustration reactivity, physiological regulation, and maternal behavior. *Child Development* 79: 1357–76.

Gralinski, J. H., and C. B. Kopp. 1993. Everyday rules for behavior: Mothers' requests to young children. *Developmental Psychology* 29: 573–84.

Kagan, Jerome. 1981. *The Second Year: The Emergence of Self-Awareness.* Cambridge, Massachusetts, and London, England: Harvard University Press.

Lehman, E. B., A. J. Steier, K. M. Guidash, and S. Y. Wanna. 2002. Predictors of compliance in toddlers: Child temperament, maternal personality, and emotional availability. *Early Child Development and Care* 172: 301–10.

Levine, L. E. 1983. Mine: Self-definition in 2-year-old boys. *Developmental Psychology* 19: 544–49.

Potegal, M., S. Robison, F. Anderson, C. Jordan, and E. Shapiro. 2007. Sequence and priming in 15-month-olds' reactions to brief arm restraint: Evidence for a hierarchy of anger responses. *Aggressive Behavior* 33: 508–18.

Sullivan, M. W., and M. Lewis. 2003. Contextual determinants of anger and other negative expressions in young infants. *Developmental Psychology* 39: 693–705.

Walker-Andrews, A., and R. Kahana-Kalman. 1999. The understanding of pretence across the second year of life. *British Journal of Developmental Psychology* 17: 523–36.

Appendix 1

Temper Tantrums

No matter how wonderful a parent you are, your toddler is likely to exhibit temper tantrums from time to time. When your child shifts into high gear with a tantrum, take a few deep breaths yourself, shift yourself into low emotional gear, and move toward your child. Usually within only a few minutes this approach is all it takes for your child's tantrum to end. Many toddlers have three to five tantrums a day, some only tizzy fits, others full-blown tantrums. Here are a few additional suggestions for how to proceed when your child throws a temper tantrum:

**Gently stop your child from hitting you
(or anyone else) or destroying property.**
Resist manhandling your child. Simply keep him from striking you or damaging objects. It's not okay for a child to hit others or destroy property; it's up to parents to keep children from either of these destructive actions.

Put your child's anger into words.

If your child pitches a fit because you won't allow her to play with food containers in the refrigerator, close the refrigerator door while saying, "You want to play with containers in the refrigerator. You're mad because I won't allow it." Putting your child's anger into words serves two purposes: (1) you communicate that you understand what the child is thinking and feeling; (2) your child hears words to describe what he's thinking and feeling so in time he'll be able to communicate his anger with words rather than an emotional outburst.

Stay near your child.

Being out of control with anger is scary to a child. It's overwhelming. By staying near, you provide emotional protection, helping absorb and, therefore, dissolve your child's angry emotions.

Resist trying to talk your child out of her anger.

Too often parents try to explain anger away. For instance, if a child demands one more cookie, the parent might say, "No," provoking a tempter tantrum. Then a parent might try to explain as the child is throwing her tantrum, "You had one cookie this morning and you just ate another. You'll have two more tomorrow." The parent hopes that the child will understand his reasoning and quickly stop her emotional outburst. Usually this doesn't happen. In fact, often such explanations make the situation worse because the child is out to prove that she really wants another cookie right now despite the fact that she's already had two today and will have more tomorrow. Besides, when children—and adults too—are emotional they have trouble understanding intellectual reasoning, logic, and explanations.

Don't spank your child.

Most parents today don't spank their children. Parents have discovered alternatives to spanking as a means for effective guidance and discipline. In most cases, the parents who do spank their children do so because it's how their parents raised them and so they use this method for punishing children even though research tells us that other approaches are more beneficial. Without pondering the issue of should you or shouldn't you, if you do spank your child, it's critical not to do it when he is having a temper tantrum. It will only make the situation worse. Your child will likely fly into a rage, prolonging his anger and frustration. You need to provide emotional protection during emotional outbursts, to help your child to eventually manage his anger while diminishing the length and frequency of the temper tantrums.

Give the child permission to be angry.

It's important to separate out the feeling of anger from the accompanying negative behavior. Most people—and this includes children—will feel angry from time to time. That feeling is not going away. It's the negative behavior—hitting, destroying property, and verbal tirades—that parents hope to eliminate. Say something to the effect of "I know that you're very angry. It's okay to feel angry, but I can't allow you to hit me or break your toys."

Don't give in.

Once you tell your child that she can't have another cookie and she has a tizzy fit over the matter, try your hardest not to change your mind. You don't want temper tantrums to work for the child. If they do, your child will learn that bouts of anger bring desired results. The child receives the message "All I need to do is throw a temper tantrum and I get what I want." This message is not going to help a child on the road to competency. Therefore be careful what you say no to and make sure that you'll be willing to hold to your no.

Try to distract your tantruming toddler.

Some toddlers have from three to five tantrums or tizzy fits a day. If you can distract your child as one is taking hold by reading his favorite book or by alerting your child to look at a fire engine that's going by, do so. It will prevent lots of emotional turmoil for yourself and your child. Once your child reaches the preschool years, resist trying to distract your child with TV, food, or the promise of a new toy. Allow your child to ride out her anger, getting to the other side of it. Doing so will build your child's character while helping her to learn to manage her angry feelings.

Allow the child time to return to his emotional equilibrium.

Anger is physiological. The heart beats faster and adrenaline pumps, as your child prepares for fight or flight. It will take time for your child calm down. Don't expect your child to instantly put on a happy face; she needs time (usually from three to thirty minutes) to return to her emotional equilibrium.

Explain the situation.

Too often parents try to explain a child's anger away. They talk too much during a temper tantrum, trying to reason with the child using logic or even shifting into a problem-solving mode. When your child (or anyone for that matter) is angry, he can't think clearly. It's best to wait until the temper tantrum is over before explaining, reasoning, or problem-solving with your child.

Appendix 2

Managing Behavior

Below are twenty parenting skills for guiding young children toward positive social behavior. Keep in mind that toddlers need constant monitoring until their behavior becomes somewhat predictable, which generally doesn't occur until between three and five years old.

1. Use your attention wisely.
Children need attention—particularly from parents. When your child is behaving in ways that are appropriate, reinforce the behavior by looking at your child. Doing so reinforces that behavior. When your child is exhibiting a behavior that you hope will disappear, don't establish eye contact. Just remember, children continue to behave in ways for which they receive attention. Let's say your child finished her meal, and then starts dropping food from her high chair tray to the floor. It's best to simply wipe the child's face and hands

and then clean up the floor, and get her down without establishing eye contract. You can say, "Please don't drop food on the floor," but resist making a big deal about it, as too much attention reinforces the behavior. In time, your child will stop dropping food on the floor.

2. Describe what your child does that is right.

It's important to give children credit for what they do that's appropriate before making your next request. For instance, when your child insists on walking from the parking lot to the grocery store, for safety's sake you must hold hands. Rather then simply grabbing your child's hand, say, "Look at you, you climbed out of your car seat all by yourself. Good for you. Now please hold my hand in the parking lot." Because you took time to notice a positive behavior (climbing out of the car seat by himself), the likelihood is great that he'll be willing to hold your hand when walking in the parking lot.

3. Use proximity control.

You can't guide children effectively while sitting in an armchair or when standing across the room. When your child is beginning to get disruptive or out of control, quietly and gently move close to your child. Often your calm presence is enough to settle your child. With this approach the child's behavior often improves without you saying or doing anything more than being near him.

4. Redirect your child.

If your child is touching something she's not supposed to touch, show your child what she *can* touch. For example, when at Grandma's your child touches a precious bowl sitting on the coffee table, remove the bowl and bring out plastic ones for her to play with. If your child is jumping on the sofa, show her where she can jump.

5. Remove an object.

If your child is coloring on the wall, remove the crayons and say, "No coloring on the wall." Later, demonstrate how and where to use crayons appropriately. If your child is misusing a toy by throwing it or banging it on the wall, floor, or window, remove the toy and put it away for a while. Later, demonstrate the proper use of the toy.

6. Lay out two realistic expectations.

Before going to a cousin's birthday party, give two realistic expectations regarding your child's behavior. "Remember, when we visit Aunt Carla's house, there's no standing on her furniture, and running is for outside only." You'll still need to monitor your toddler, providing proximity control when necessary. If you don't lay out your expectations prior to attending a new event, how will your child know how to behave? Use this technique as your child enters new, ever-expanding environments, whether it's traveling on an airplane or attending an anniversary party for Grandma and Grandpa. It's easy for children to focus on two age-appropriate expectations when you lay them out.

7. Stay away from difficult situations.

If going to the grocery store has become a problem for you and your child, go when your spouse or neighbor can watch your child. A respite of a month or so from taking your child to the grocery store is often enough to give you and your child the opportunity to start up a new grocery store routine. When you return with your child to the grocery store after a month, your child's behavior will likely improve, particularly if you develop a new grocery store plan and lay out two new expectations.

8. Avoid lots of change at once.

Don't move into a new house, fly to Disneyland, and buy a new puppy all in the same month. Most young children do not have the coping skills to adjust gracefully to all that change. Often families find it necessary to move when they're about to bring a second child into the family. When this is the case, realize that the firstborn will need more time and positive attention from Mom and Dad. Children need emotional support during such periods of transition.

9. Remove your out-of-control child.

When your child becomes disruptive—particularly in a public place—take him from the scene of the misbehavior. Take your child for a walk, retreat to another room, or go outside to play. Be sure to stay calm yourself and remain with your child until he regains control of himself.

10. Provide the control your child lacks.

If your toddler climbs on the dining room table, say, "I can't allow you to stand on the table. Do you want to get down by yourself or do you want me to get you down?" While it's courteous to offer a choice, most toddlers are unresponsive to them; you'll likely need to get your child down from the table. If you say, "Get down right now," your child will probably continue to stand on the table. She needs your help. Therefore, provide the control your toddler lacks by getting her down. In time, control transfers from you to your child; your child will be able to manage herself without you needing to step in and take control of the situation.

11. Give clear commands and demonstrate.

Rather than saying, "Put the toys away," it's better to be specific: "Put the trucks in this box. The dolls go in this basket. The books go on the shelf. I'll put this truck away; I bet you can put one away too. I'll watch you." Remember, children are copycats, so they'll do what you do. They like your attention, so be sure to watch them as they complete desired tasks. Additionally, they're learning language, so if you describe the task with words, in time they'll catch on to the broader concept of "putting toys away."

12. Look to the next event.

Children live in the moment. It's often difficult to move a child from one activity to the next or one place to the next. Such transitions come easier when you describe what your child is doing right now and then explain what's coming up next. "You're having fun riding your tricycle with Jaime. In five minutes we're going to get in the car, drive by the fire station, and go to the grocery store." Looking ahead helps children leave one situation and move on to the next.

13. Offer a choice in a "no choice" situation.

"You must sit in your car seat. Do you want to look at a book or hold your blanket?" While offering choices is an effective approach that parents can use in many situations all the years they parent their children, it often isn't effective with toddlers. Toddlers may not agree to sitting in the car seat and want both the blanket and the book. They don't understand "this or that." In such a situation it's up to the parent to simply strap the child in the car seat, being firm but kind, ignoring any protests, and then hand the child either the book or the blanket, or both.

14. Establish rules.

Work to establish one or two reasonable rules at a time and refer to them. Children as young as two can learn a couple of rules at a time. For example, "We eat food only in the kitchen," and then, "What's the rule about food?" If a child starts to walk out of kitchen with a cracker in her hand, remove the cracker while restating or referring to the rule. The key is to be consistent by enforcing each rule and living by the rules yourself.

15. Describe your child's wishes.

Children have wonderful imaginations. When your child wants something and you're saying no to it, you can do so effectively by describing his wishes. "You wish you could eat the whole plate of cookies. You wish you could eat as many as you like, anytime you like. I understand that, but I can't allow it." When you describe a child's wishes, he imagines eating all the cookies. Imagining the experience is almost as good as experiencing it for real.

16. Ease transitions.

Help your child make a transition from one activity or situation to another by singing a song or reciting a poem that you make up that pertains to the situation. You can create a song or poem for getting to the dinner table, leaving the house, or going to bed. The song or rhyme triggers the child's memory of the event to come and the routine involved, which makes the transition smoother for both you and your child.

17. Surrender to tense moments.

When a situation with your child seems unmanageable or when your child is overwhelmed and out of control with tears and tantrums, sit on the floor near your child and take a few deep breaths. Be with your child. Let the tense moment pass. Don't feel you always need a perfect solution to a difficult or unpleasant situation. Sometimes it's better to let it pass by not doing or saying anything except being near your child.

18. Let your child be in charge.

Children need the opportunity to be the boss. When the two of you are playing doctor, building with blocks, or playing with play dough, allow your child to be in charge of the task, directing the activity. Copy what your child is doing. Resist taking over; instead follow the child's lead. The child feels competent and in control when you allow her to direct the agenda. The bonus for you: putting a child in charge of certain situations increases the likelihood he will comply with your next request.

19. Engage your child's imagination.

Let's say you have trouble getting your child dressed each morning before heading out the door to work and child care. Play into your child's imaginative world by slipping a sock on your hand and saying, "Mr. Sock says it's time to put your shirt on." See what happens. Most likely your child will do as Mr. Sock suggests. If potty training becomes a power struggle, back off for a while but find a doll or teddy bear who imaginatively uses the toilet. A doll who demonstrates the task inspires the child to practice and eventually perform on the potty.

20. Use the lines "When . . . " and "Then . . ."

Let's say several dolls are scattered about the room. You ask your child to put them in the doll bed. Your child refuses. Then when your child asks you to read her a book, your response is "When you put your dolls in the stroller, then I will read you a story." When your child wants to walk to the neighborhood park but refuses to put her shoes on, your line is "When you put your shoes on, then we will walk to the park."

Appendix 3

Using Time-Out

Time-out is today's buzzword for what to do when a child misbehaves. Time-out can be overused and misused until it's ineffective for changing or improving a child's behavior.

Time-out means the child is taken away from the person, place, or thing that is contributing to his misbehavior. If two children are not getting along, separate them; have them take a time-out from each other. If your child is being disruptive at a family holiday gathering, have her take a time-out from the place; go with her into another room or take her outside for a few minutes to walk or play. If a child is misusing a toy, remove it; have him take a time-out from the toy. Remember, the goal is for your child to learn to play well with another child, behave at family events, and use toys appropriately. While brief time-outs are sometimes necessary for stopping negative behavior, it's important to teach and demonstrate how to get along with another person, behave in large groups of people, and play appropriately with toys. Because it often makes the situation worse, time-out does not necessarily involve isolating the child.

A Procedure for Time-Out

Let's say your child kicks you when he's angry. Inform him during a peaceful time that when he kicks, you'll place him in a spot you've designated for time-out.

When kicking occurs, here's how to proceed:

1. Identify the misbehavior.
"That's kicking; kicking is not allowed. In our home we do not kick people." Use a stern—not angry—voice.

2. Remove the child.
Take the child to the designated time-out area, where she should stay for a few minutes. This place could be a chair to sit on, a room where she is away from others, or it could involve a brisk walk outside. The child does not have to be isolated. By removing the child and staying with him, the parent says, "I'm not going to allow you to kick people, but I'm not deserting you." Isolation in a bedroom or confinement on a chair often makes children angrier. Keep the goal—to stop the kicking—in mind.

3. Use empathy.
Affirm the child's emotional state. "I know you're angry; you want all the ice cream to yourself and you don't want to share it. We are going to share this ice cream and I won't allow kicking." This step is important because you are letting your child know that you

understand her feelings and point of view. Additionally, by describing the situation at hand you are modeling the use of words.

4. Stay near.
When the child is in time-out, stay near to monitor his behavior. Being with the child let's him know you are not rejecting him, only his negative behavior. Your presence helps the child regain control. Parents need to keep their own emotions in check.

5. Allow the child to return to the scene of the misbehavior.
Once the child gains control, talk briefly about why she was in time-out. Demonstrate or coach her in more acceptable behavior or a solution to the problem. Finally, spend some positive time with the child.

Various Forms of Time-Out

- **Toy Time-Out**
If your child misuses a toy, give the toy a time-out.

- **Friend or Sibling Time-Out**
When children are not getting along, they need to take a time-out from each other.

- **Holding Time-Out**
Hold your child to end misbehavior or to help him regain control. Then assist your child to reenter the group or situation.

- **Talking Time-Out**
Take your child away from the scene of the misbehavior. When the child is calm, talk about alternatives for better behavior.

■ **Walking Time-Out**

Take your disruptive or angry child outside to walk or run around for a few minutes. Any form of exercise—swinging or riding a rocking horse—can help an out-of-control child gain composure.

■ **Family Time-Out**

If the day is not going well, change the tenor by going to the park, getting out play dough or coloring, or putting on some lively music and dancing.

■ **Adult Time-Out**

Take a time-out when you're feeling overwhelmed. Give yourself a parenting break for a few minutes or, if possible, a few hours.

■ **Resting Time-Out**

If you sense your child is beginning to get antsy and out of control, escort her to a quiet spot, read her a story, and then have her look at a few books on her own until she is calm.

JAN FAULL, M.Ed., has taught parent education, child development, and behavior guidance for more than twenty-five years. She is the author of the *Your Brilliant Baby* and *Your Clever Toddler* series at Babyzone.com. She has written for *Ladies' Home Journal*, *Healthy Kids*, *American Baby*, and *Better Homes and Gardens'* online service, as well as Disney's online service for parents. She also wrote a weekly parenting column for the *Seattle Times* for ten years.

JENNIFER McLEAN OLIVER, Ph.D., is a National Science and Engineering Graduate Fellow, earned a master's of science degree in applied mathematics and a doctorate in cognitive psychology at the University of Washington in Seattle, where she conducted research and mathematical modeling in attention, memory, and perception. At the Talaris Research Institute in Seattle, Dr. Oliver focused on early learning research and compiled findings for translation into tools for parents and caregivers. As an independent consultant and contractor, she provides research and analysis in the areas of cognitive development and learning, as well as usability, user experience, human-automation interaction, social networking, and social media. She also holds a bachelor of science degree, summa cum laude, in applied mathematics from the University of Colorado Engineering School in Boulder and started her career as a member of the technical staff at NASA's Jet Propulsion Laboratory in Spacecraft Navigation Systems. She resides in Seattle with her husband and son. Visit her blog at JenniferMcLeanOliverPhD.blogspot.com.